AF505974

Core Executive and Europeanization in Central Europe

Previous Publications by Dr. Radoslaw Zubek

Refereed Journal Articles

"Core in Check: The Transformation of the Core Executive in Poland," *Journal of European Public Policy* 8, no. 6 (2001): 911–932.

"Complying with Transposition Commitments in Poland: Collective Dilemmas, Core Executive and Legislative Outcomes," *West European Politics* 28 no. 3 (2005): 592–619.

"Government, Parliament and Lawmaking in Poland," *Journal of Legislative Studies* 13, no. 4 (2007) (with K.H. Goetz).

Book Chapters

"Czech Republic: A Core Neglected." In *Governing after Communism: Institutions and Policy*-Making, edited by V. Dimitrov, K. H. Goetz, and H. Wollmann, with R. Zubek and M. Brusis. Lanham, MD: Rowman and Littlefield, 2006 (with V. Dimitrov).

"Poland: A Core Ascendant?" In *Governing after Communism: Institutions and Policy-Making,* edited by V. Dimitrov, K. H. Goetz, and H. Wollmann, with R. Zubek and M. Brusis. Lanham, MD: Rowman and Littlefield, 2006.

"Poland: Unbalanced Domestic Leadership in Negotiating Fit." In *Enlarging the Euro-Zone: The Euro and the Transformation of East Central Europe,* edited by Kenneth Dyson. Oxford: Oxford University Press, 2006.

"Regulatory Impact Assessments in Poland 2001–2005." (in Polish) In *System oceny skutków regulacji - doświadczenia i perspektywy,* edited by W. Szpringer and W. Rogowski. Warsaw: C. H. Beck, 2007.

"Poland: From Pacesette, to Semi-Permanent Outsider?" In *European States and the Euro: The First Decade,* edited by K. Dyson. 2nd ed. Oxford: Oxford University Press, forthcoming 2009.

Core Executive and Europeanization in Central Europe

Radoslaw Zubek

CORE EXECUTIVE AND EUROPEANIZATION IN CENTRAL EUROPE
Copyright © Radoslaw Zubek, 2008.

First published in 2008 by
PALGRAVE MACMILLAN™
175 Fifth Avenue, New York, N.Y. 10010 and
Houndmills, Basingstoke, Hampshire, England RG21 6XS.
Companies and representatives throughout the world.

PALGRAVE MACMILLAN is the global academic imprint of the Palgrave Macmillan division of St. Martin's Press, LLC and of Palgrave Macmillan Ltd. Macmillan® is a registered trademark in the United States, United Kingdom and other countries. Palgrave is a registered trademark in the European Union and other countries.

ISBN-13: 978-0-230-60265-6
ISBN-10: 0-230-60265-7

Library of Congress Cataloging-in-Publication Data
Zubek, Radoslaw.
   Core executive and Europeanization in Central Europe / Radoslaw Zubek.
      p. cm.
   Includes bibliographical references and index.
ISBN 0-230-60265-7
1. International and municipal law—Europe, Central. 2. European Union—Europe, Central. 3. European Union countries—Relations—Europe, Central. 4. Europe—Economic integration. I. Title.
   KJC5057.Z83 2008
   341.242'2—dc22

                                                                2007035491

A catalogue record for this book is available from the British Library.

Design by Macmillan India Ltd.

First edition: April 2008

10 9 8 7 6 5 4 3 2 1

Printed in the United States of America.

For Anna

Contents

Figures

Tables

Acknowledgments

This book started life as my doctoral thesis, which I completed at the London School of Economics and Political Science (LSE) in 2005. I am greatly indebted to my thesis supervisors at the LSE—Klaus Goetz, Ed Page, and Howard Machin—for inspiring me and providing invaluable guidance. I would also like to thank all the people who took the time to offer helpful comments on the manuscript or its parts, including Vesselin Dimitrov, Antoaneta Dimitrova, Sebastian Balfour, Martin Brusis, Kevin Featherstone, Bob Hancke, Simon Hix, Abby Innes, Brigid Laffan, Jan-Hinrik Meyer Sahling, Frank Schimmelfennig, Gwen Sasse, Uli Sedelmeier, and Hellmut Wollmann.

I am thankful to the many politicians and civil servants who agreed to be interviewed in Warsaw, Budapest, Prague, and Brussels. I am particularly grateful to the officials at the UKIE in Warsaw, the Prime Minister's Office in Budapest, and the Government Office in Prague who introduced me to the inner workings of their national "European" core executives. I would also like to thank Krisztina Jáger and Vlastimil Nečas for research assistance in Hungary and the Czech Republic.

I would like to acknowledge the support of the Volkswagen Foundation, the LSE Research Studentship Scheme, and the Ernst & Young Better Government Programme.

Last but not least, I would like to thank my parents for their interest in my research and my wife, Anna, for her loving support, patience, and encouragement.

CHAPTER 1

Introduction: Understanding Europeanization in Central Europe

This book examines the process of Europeanization in Central Europe. In doing so, it focuses on how Central European states adopted European Union (EU) rules prior to becoming members of the EU. During the accession process—which lasted from 1998 to 2004—all the prospective members were required to implement EU laws (the so-called *acquis communautaire*), except for a small subset of policies for which they were able to obtain temporary exemptions. The legal alignment involved the transposition of a few thousand EU directives spanning almost the entire policy spectrum. Besides the directives, there were also many decisions and regulations that had to be rendered into domestic law to create conditions for the direct applicability of such EU measures after accession. The adoption of EU rules was an explicit condition for membership, and full compliance had to be achieved before accession.

At its heart, this analysis is concerned with an empirical puzzle— evidence of variation in the patterns of EU rule adoption both between countries and across time. Even a cursory look at the European Commission's regular reports that mapped the progress of legal alignment in the accession states shows major differences in transposition and implementation records. The largest Central European state—Poland—complied with its EU rule adoption commitments only to a limited extent in the first two years of the accession negotiations, but its responsiveness improved markedly since 2000. Some other countries, notably Hungary, carried out their legislative reforms at a steady pace throughout the preaccession period. The Central European states also reached the finish line of membership with widely varying rule adoption records. According to the July 2004 Internal Market Scoreboard, the Czech Republic was the worst transposition laggard among the new member states, while Hungary and Poland came top of the league (European Commission 2004a).

This book aims to explain such cross-temporal and cross-country variation in EU rule adoption. The analysis relies on a combination of a longitudinal case study of Poland's compliance during the crucial stages of the preaccession process and a cross-sectional comparative analysis of Hungary and the Czech Republic. In contrast to the existing research on Europeanization in Central Europe, in analyzing these questions, the book links variation in rule adoption to differences in the configuration of domestic executive institutions. It focuses, in particular, on institutional mechanisms that cabinets and prime ministers have at their disposal for mobilizing and monitoring ministerial compliance. The impact of the core executive is contextualized by controlling for the influence of external incentives, party constellations, and ministerial resources. This new approach makes it possible to capture the real-life complexity of Europeanization and to identify processes that are likely to shape postaccession compliance.

This introductory chapter first presents conditionality-centered explanations that have so far dominated research on EU rule adoption in Central Europe and identifies their shortcomings. Second, it introduces a core executive model in which the importance of executive configurations is explicitly modelled. Third, it discusses the research design and the methods of data collection. Fourth, the chapter shows how this research contributes to wider debates on EU compliance and core executive. Fifth, it concludes by previewing individual chapters.

Explaining Rule Adoption through EU Conditionality

Research on EU rule adoption in Central Europe has been dominated by accounts that identify conditionality as the key mechanism that shaped adaptation of domestic laws in Central Europe (Schimmelfennig, Engert, et al. 2003; Schimmelfennig and Sedelmeier 2005; Grabbe 2006; Vachudova 2005). The conditionality involved the offering of material and nonmaterial rewards in return for achieving regulatory alignment. The theoretical case for the impact of EU conditionality is built on two principal assumptions. The first assumption is that legal adaptation during preaccession was a bargaining game in which the EU enjoyed a supreme advantage over the accession states. The EU's high bargaining power stemmed from asymmetries in the distribution of information and benefits, and was further reinforced by institutional levers such as monitoring reports and country streaming that the union acquired during the negotiation process (Schimmelfennig and Sedelmeier 2005). The other assumption is that the weak institutionalization of policy environments in Central Europe enhanced the effectiveness of conditionality by making domestic accommodation relatively less complicated than in the highly institutionalized systems of the old EU member states. Moreover, the exigencies of modernization and democratization that ran in parallel to Europeanization are claimed to have made the postcommunist elites highly receptive to EU policy templates (cf. Grabbe 2003; Schimmelfennig and Sedelmeier 2005).

Conditionality-centered explanations have found that the timing and success of rule adoption depended on the determinacy of EU conditions, size and speed of rewards, and the credibility of threats and promises (Schimmelfennig and Sedelmeier 2005, pp. 12–17). Of such contextualizing variables, the credibility of the promise of membership is judged to have been the most important factor. Schimmelfennig and Sedelmeier write that once accession negotiations started, "the massive benefits of EU membership being within close reach, the fulfilment of EU *acquis* conditions became the highest priority in CEEC [Central and Eastern European countries] policy-making, crowding out alternative pathways and domestic obstacles" (2004, p. 671). They find that adaptation costs and veto players did not play a decisive role and can, at best, explain some of the variation in the pace of rule adaptation. But the domestic factors "do not lead to systematic variation in the success of EU rule transfer" (Schimmelfennig and Sedelmeier 2004, p. 672). More nuanced renditions of the conditionality argument link the success or failure of rule adoption to the interaction of EU pressures and domestic factors. Grabbe writes, "The scope of the Europeanization effects in would-be members is determined by two conditions: the precision and certitude of EU demands [. . .] [and] the degree of political will and institutional capacity to implement a given policy in CEE" (2006, p. 206; see also Grabbe 2001, 2002, 2003; Dimitrova 2004).

But the conditionality-centered models of EU rule adoption in Central Europe suffer from two fundamental problems. The first problem is that, by focusing on the top-down hierarchical mechanism of Europeanization in Central Europe, they prejudge the importance of the EU as the primary causal variable driving policy change at the domestic level. It is thus biased against considering the potential impact of non-EU-related external and domestic variables. In particular, the model tends to treat legal adaptation to EU legislation prior to enlargement as a process that is largely separate from the modernization of Central European states (but see Mattli and Plümper 2004 and Hughes, Sasse, et al. 2004 for notable exceptions). Further, the model does not allow for the role of domestic rule entrepreneurs and the impact of their actions on the patterns of legal change. The reluctance to consider such explanations sets the conditionality argument apart from research on rule compliance in the old member states that devotes increasing attention to "inside-out" perspectives on Europeanization (see Goetz and Hix 2000; Börzel 2001; Goetz 2003; Featherstone and Radaelli 2003). By failing to consider such alternatives, it may oversimplify the modalities of domestic change and, thus, fail to capture the actual dynamics of Europeanization of public policy in Central Europe.

The second and related problem is a limited understanding of the domestic processes of rule adoption. Even if relevant hypotheses are introduced, this is rarely done with systematic reference to insights from comparative politics. Inadequate attention is thus paid to factors such as legislative technique employed in EU rule adoption and the need for interministerial coordination or implementation across levels of government. Yet, as the available data demonstrate, both old and new EU member states clearly differ in the way in which they organize the process of rule adoption internally, not least because of disparate legal systems and administrative traditions (Page 1998; Heinrich 1999; Bovens and Yesilkagit 2004). There is also evidence of extensive socio-economic entanglements within which domestic legislators operate in Central Europe (Górniak and Jerschina 1995; Stark and Bruszt 1998; Staniszkis 1999). This relative neglect of domestic variables stands in stark contrast to findings from research on rule compliance in the old EU member states (see Ibanez 1999; Caporaso, Cowles, et al. 2001; Héritier et al. 2001; Knill 2001; Falkner, Hartlapp, et al. 2004; Mastenbroek 2005; Falkner, Treib, et al. 2005; Steunenberg 2007).

Core Executive Model

This book adopts an explicitly "inside-out" perspective on Europeanization in Central Europe. It first defines the problem by arguing that EU rule adoption before accession is likely to have been perceived by domestic cabinets as a reform project that brought mainly nonexclusive collective benefits and required extensive cooperation from many departments. This assertion is based on three observations. First, given the high uncertainty surrounding rule adoption, ministers in Central European cabinets could hope to reap the collective benefits of EU accession even when minimizing their real contribution to legal alignment. Moreover, while the uncertainty about requirements may have declined over time, EU rule adoption continued to carry a high opportunity cost for Central European executives. Lacking the experience of policy formulation, ministers and departments were unsure about individual benefits and offset adaptation costs only against the collective benefits of policy modernization and EU accession. The final observation is that rule adoption in Central Europe required joint legislative action from most, if not all, cabinet ministries. Many of the EU measures dealt with horizontal, crosscutting policy problems, and full alignment required the collaboration of many different agencies.

Reform projects that bring nonexclusive collective benefits and require extensive cooperation are notoriously difficult to implement in cabinet settings. At least three collective dilemmas impinge on policy development in such cases. First, if ministers believe they cannot be excluded from enjoying the collective benefits, irrespective of whether they contribute to these benefits being produced, they will have strong incentives to free ride on the efforts of their cabinet colleagues. Second, high opportunity costs of collective action tend to encourage ministers and departments to commit resources to other uses that offer more favourable individual cost-benefit ratios. Third, the need for coordination provides a further bias against engaging in collective action because ministers are likely to delay their contributions until it is clear that others also contribute or that enough contributions have been made to ensure the success of the policy reform. These theoretical insights are applied here to understand the dynamics of EU rule adoption in Central Europe.

In developing its hypotheses, the book focuses on the role of the domestic core executive (see Dunleavy and Rhodes 1990; Rhodes and Dunleavy 1995). The central argument is that the core executive represents a unique institutional response to collective dilemmas in the production of the legal rules that bring diffuse benefits to many voters and require interministerial cooperation. Hence, in the present context, the probability that governments improve their EU rule adoption record is hypothesized to be positively related to the institutionalization of selective incentives and monitoring that are extended to line ministers by the domestic core executive. More specifically, that probability is highest in two situations. First, this is the case where the prime minister or some other nonsectoral minister acts as a central authority in the area of EU rule adoption within the executive. Under this hierarchical solution, the prime minister or a nonsectoral minister has—by virtue of his or her institutional position—individual incentives to sanction and/or reward ministers, act as a competitive agenda setter and monitor ministerial action. Second, the probability of EU rule adoption within the executive is highest where institutional rules exist that require ministers to manage the transposition record as a group. Under this collectivity-based arrangement, collective action problems are solved by core executive institutions that mobilize ministers to constrain each other's agenda-setting powers and to monitor compliance with collective decisions.

Although the primary focus is on the role of domestic executive institutions in shaping EU rule adoption, the impact of institutional rules originating outside the executive must not be overlooked. Three contextualizing variables are employed: (i) institutional opportunities generated by the European Union, (ii) institutional rules within party organizations and governing coalitions, and (iii) institutional incentives provided by domestic nonexecutive actors. All the three types of rules may be employed—in the language of the collective action theory—to extend selective incentives and monitoring to ministers and departments in Central European cabinets. As such, they can directly contribute to solving the collective action problems that hinder EU rule adoption. The European Commission may act as the central authority inducing and monitoring domestic ministers and departments. EU-induced selective incentives and monitoring may also originate within the collectivity-based arrangements such as the association council/committee, expert meetings, or negotiation sessions. Central European ministers and departments may also be subject to party-based incentives that originate within their own party or the governing coalition. The incentives may also be extended by parliament or within the context of linkage institutions that channel social and business interests.

Research Design and Sources

This books combines within-case analysis and cross-case comparison. Its core is a longitudinal study of EU rule adoption in Poland. The case study uses the congruence method and process tracing (George and

Bennett 2004). It first employs deductive theory to predict the value of the dependent variable for a given value of the independent variable. The theoretical expectations are then checked against empirical data on rule adoption paths. In a second step, if the data confirms the prediction, the study employs process tracing to identify causal mechanisms (or causal chains) that link the explanatory variable with the observed effect. The book complements the case study of Poland with a cross-country analysis of Hungary and the Czech Republic. This is to check whether variation in core executive configurations can explain the key differences in the rule adoption records at the time of EU accession. The research design in this section is that of a controlled cross-sectional comparison.

The dependent variable is EU rule adoption. In the Polish case study, the rule adoption record is operationalized as the extent to which departments comply with self-imposed commitments to transpose EU laws. It is measured using quantitative indicators of domestic legislative activity. This operationalization differs from that employed in the EU compliance literature, a choice that is necessitated by the lack of systematic data on EU-imposed legislative deadlines. At the same time, it enables the analysis to focus on the executive institutions and to control for the impact of the legislative process in the national parliaments. The cross-country comparison operationalizes the rule adoption record as the extent to which the Central European states had notified the transposition of EU directives to the European Commission by the end of the accession process. It is measured as the number of nonnotified directives. This operationalization makes it possible to move beyond the world of self-imposed deadlines and test the usefulness of the core executive model for explaining cross-country variation in complying with EU-imposed transposition deadlines.

The data on rule adoption for Poland comes from an original examination of National Programmes for the Adoption of the Acquis (NPAAs) and transposition plans adopted by the Polish cabinet and its European Integration Committee (KIE). Besides the transposition programmes, the book also draws on unpublished records maintained by the Cabinet Agenda Department at the Prime Minister's Chancellery (KPRM) in Warsaw and the TAIEX (Technical Assistance and Information Exchange Office) Progress database developed and maintained by the TAIEX in Brussels. The data on the rule adoption records of Hungary and the Czech Republic come from two sources. First, the book makes use of the data regularly published by the Secretariat General of the European

Commission on the progress in the notification of national measures implementing all EU directives. The second source of information is the Single Market Scoreboards published biannually by the European Commission's DG Internal Market.

The independent variable is the core executive. It is operationalized as the existence of specific core executive rules that can be used to mobilize and monitor line ministries in the area of EU rule adoption. Three types of rules are of special importance: position, authority, and information rules. If such rules exist, they can be sustained by hierarchy, collectivity, or a mixture of the two organizational arrangements. In searching for changes in institutional configurations, the book adopts a regulative definition of institutions that are taken to denote the formal and informal rules of the game that shape human behaviour (North 1990; Scott 2001).

Two methods of data collection have been employed to map cross-temporal patterns of institutional change. First, documentary analysis was conducted covering primary and secondary sources. In Poland, the author was granted permission to access internal documents and correspondence maintained in the public archives of the Prime Minister's Office (PMO) and the Office of the Committee for European Integration (UKIE). The research was based on a final selection of 82 internal UKIE and PMO documents and 195 pieces of official correspondence (internal memos, letters, and faxes). In Hungary and the Czech Republic, the author reviewed the academic and nonacademic literature as well as the official documentation available in English, Czech, and Hungarian. The second method of data collection was semistructured interviews. Between June 2001 and March 2007 the author undertook numerous field trips to Warsaw, Prague, Budapest, and Brussels, during which 89 interviews were made with 84 interviewees. The interviews were taped and transcripted, unless the interviewee did not agree to having the conversation recorded. In that latter case, detailed notes were taken during the interview. The interviewees included high- and middle-ranking officials (60 per cent), ministers (34 per cent), and advisors (6 per cent) (see Annex 1). The interviews were conducted on a nonattributable basis.

Wider Relevance

This volume has relevance beyond its focus on Europeanization in Central Europe. It contributes to at least three broader theoretical debates in political science. The first contribution is to the literature on differential patterns of national compliance with the EU legislation at the national level (for recent overviews, see Sverdrup 2004; Falkner, Treib, et al. 2005; Mastenbroek 2005). The book represents one of the first attempts to undertake a systematic investigation into how executive institutions affect the extent to which a country complies with EU law. EU compliance—both in preaccession states and in member states—has generally been considered to be driven mainly by the executive branch of government (see Siedentopf and Ziller 1988; Page 1998; Lippert, Umbach, et al. 2001; Fabbrini and Dona 2002). It thus seems natural to expect that the internal life of the executive will have a significant impact on legislative outcomes. Yet, the EU compliance literature has so far paid limited attention to institutional configurations at the center of government. This neglect stands in stark contrast to a sustained interest in the way central governments have adapted to European Union membership that informs parallel streams of Europeanization research both in its Western and in its Eastern variants (see Laffan 1981; Guyomarch 1993; Metcalfe 1994; Meny, Müller, et al. 1996; Wright 1996; Rupp 1999; Kassim, Peters, et al. 2000; Bulmer and Burch 2001; Lippert, Umbach, et al. 2001; Laffan 2003; Nowak-Far 2004). Although implicitly assuming an important role of the "European" core executives, this literature has stopped short of examining causal linkages between institutional configurations and policy outcomes. This book connects that latter research with the study of EU compliance.

It further contributes to research on national core executives in Europe (see for example Rhodes and Dunleavy 1995; Weller, Bakvis, et al. 1997; Peters, Rhodes, et al. 2000; Rhodes 2000; Goetz and Wollmann 2001; Hayward and Wright 2002; Dimitrov, Goetz and Wollmann 2006). This literature is based on a realization that growing sectoralization, budgetary pressures, and crosscutting nature of the policy agenda have, over the last decade, underscored the importance of effective centers of government. Responding to Rhodes and Dunleavy's appeal for more theory-guided research on core executives (Rhodes 1995, p. 27), this study develops a conceptual approach on the basis of collective action theory. In doing so, it argues that the core executive represents a unique institutional response to collective dilemmas that impinge on the production of legal rules (or policies, more broadly) that bring diffuse benefits to many voter constituencies and that entail high coordination costs. This conceptualization links up with those functional definitions of central agencies that emphasize their role in ensuring democratic control and accountability within government (see for example Daintith and Page 1998).

Finally, research on core executives has so far employed institutional configurations at the center of government as a dependent variable. More recently, attempts have been made to explore the effect of core executive configurations on policy volatility (Manning, Barma, et al. 1999; Evans and Manning 2000; Blondel and Manning 2002) and fiscal discipline (Brusis and Dimitrov 2001; Von Hagen 2003; Hallerberg 2004b; Dimitrov, Goetz, and Wollman 2006). This book contributes to that new stream of core executive studies by focusing on how intraexecutive relations between the center and ministerial departments may affect the government's capacity to implement policy decisions that are integrative and welfare maximizing. In doing so, it informs a broader debate about institutions and institutional effects within the rational choice institutionalism (North 1990; Scharpf 1997; Weingast 1998). Defining institutions as constraints on opportunistic behaviour, this tradition has spawned a rich literature exploring the role of political institutions in leading individual actors to optimal political, economic, and social outcomes (see for example Shepsle and Weingast 1994; Döring 1995; Lane and Ersson 2000; Scarpetta and Tressel 2002; Plümper and Martin 2003; Döring and Hallerberg 2004).

Plan of the Book

The book comprises seven chapters including this Introduction. Chapter 2 sets out the theoretical framework for examining EU rule adoption in Central Europe. It starts by arguing that preaccession legal alignment is likely to have been perceived by Central European cabinets as a reform project that brought nonexclusive collective benefits and required cooperation by numerous departments. It shows that, in such conditions, individual ministers and departments will have had limited incentives to engage in rule adoption. The chapter hypothesizes that the probability of rule adoption is positively related to the institutionalization of specific position, authority, and information rules that the domestic core executive could use to extend incentives and monitoring to line ministries. It further identifies other variables that are likely to have contextualized the impact of core executive rules, in particular, EU constraints and accession dynamic, party controls and inter-party cooperation, and domestic extraexecutive constraints.

Chapters 3, 4, and 5 present the longitudinal study of EU rule adoption in Poland. Chapter 3 measures the extent to which Polish ministries complied with EU-related legislative commitments in the run-up to the accession. Three quantitative indicators are used. The first indicator is the proportion of transposing measures envisaged for adoption in a given year that were actually adopted that year. The second indicator is the nominal number of transposing bills adopted by the cabinet over time. The third indicator is the proportion of Polish domestic laws that are fully compatible with the European Community law. The chapter finds that the compliance record varied significantly over time. In 1997–1999 the Polish cabinet complied with its transposition commitments only to a limited degree. The situation changed in 2000, when a marked upward shift in compliance occurred. Compliance deteriorated slightly in 2001 but was back to a high level in 2002. The chapter closes by showing that, although policy type, actors preferences, and ministerial resources are likely to have had some impact, the effect of those factors is not sufficient to account for the variation in compliance patterns.

Chapter 4 maps cross-temporal variation in position, authority, and information rules that the Polish core executive employed in order to extend selective incentives and monitoring to cabinet ministers and departments. It finds that over the first two years of the Buzek government, the core provided limited mobilization for ministries to comply with EU rule adoption commitments. The dearth of institutional incentives was most evident with regard to authority rules that denied a key cabinet EU committee the power to manage the compliance process. The situation looked hardly any better regarding information rules that provided for only lightweight monitoring of line ministries. The chapter finds that in mid-1999, the extent to which the core executive mobilized line ministers and their departments increased, in particular at the level of position and information rules. It then documents the emergence and consolidation of a strong "European" core within the Polish executive under the Buzek and Miller cabinets. The chapter describes the changes to position, authority, and information rules and explains institutional developments with reference to prime-ministerial entrepreneurship, the role of the accession crisis, and internal coalition dynamic.

Chapter 5 brings together the data on core executive institutions and compliance in Poland, checking for congruence with theoretical predictions. It finds that the variation in core executive rules has been over time consistent with changes in the compliance record. To further substantiate such congruence, the chapter provides process-tracing evidence of causal mechanisms that link the two variables. Toward the end, the chapter assesses the impact of incentives and opportunity structures originating outside the executive, in particular EU incentives and party configurations.

Chapter 6 contains a cross-country analysis. The chapter selects two countries that vary on the core executive variable—Hungary and the Czech Republic—and checks if the outcomes of rule adoption in these countries are consistent with the expectations of the core executive model. It first maps the emergence of core executive institutions in Hungary and the Czech Republic to show major differences in the institutionalization of authority and information rules. It then presents evidence on transposition records of Central European countries at the time of the EU accession. The data show significant variation in the success of EU rule adoption among the accession states. The chapter argues that the strong Hungarian core executive contributed to a good transposition record, while the relative weakness of the Czech "European" core led to relatively poor rule adoption. The chapter closes by assessing the importance of other possible explanations such as EU conditionality, party configurations, and parliamentary dominance.

Chapter 7 teases out wider implications from the Polish case study and the comparative analysis of Hungary and the Czech Republic. This is done under three principal headings. The first heading is that of EU rule adoption in Central Europe. The chapter shows how the book contributes to painting a more fine-grained picture of Europeanization in this region. The second heading is that of compliance with EU law in Europe. The chapter demonstrates that the book's findings resonate well with the literature on EU compliance in the old member states. It finds that the core executive argument is compatible with—and may be used to improve the predictive power of—theoretical models employed in that research. The third heading covers the theme of executive solutions to collective dilemmas in producing public good policies. The chapter argues that the saga of EU rule adoption in Central Europe can inform our understanding of how governments can organize to implement policies that deliver general benefits but impose group or sectoral costs.

CHAPTER 2

A Core Executive Model

This chapter argues that EU rule adoption was likely to have been perceived by Central European cabinets as a project that brought mainly nonexclusive collective benefits and required cooperation by many departments. It shows that, in such conditions, cabinet ministers and their staff will have had limited incentives to engage in rule adoption. The chapter hypothesizes that such collective dilemmas may be solved by incentives and monitoring extended by domestic core executives to individual ministers and departments.

The Problem

Collective Dilemmas in Cabinet Settings

The approach adopted in this book relies on theoretical insights from public choice theory of policy change (cf. Downs 1957; Buchanan and Tullock 1962; Mueller 2003). As such, it is based on three private interest assumptions. First, ministers use policies to maximize electoral support for their personal reelection. The most natural source of such support is the socioeconomic clientele within their own policy jurisdiction. This is because the public tends to judge a minister's success in office according to how effectively he or she advances the interests of such private stakeholders. The party leadership may further bind ministers to cater to selected electoral constituencies. Second, ministers use public policy to further the position and interests of their own department. In doing so, they wish to secure the loyalty of ministerial bureaucrats who are generally assumed to adopt bureau-shaping and budget-maximizing attitudes (Dunleavy 1991). The cooperation of civil servants is important because it determines a minister's ability to achieve goals as the head of department. Third, both ministers and their staff are rational utility maximizers who seek to derive the highest possible benefits from public policy at the lowest costs. As government resources such as legislative time, finance, and personnel are limited, opportunity costs must always be taken into account.

Given these interest assumptions, it may be predicted that, absent any constraints, a policy reform should be more likely if the benefits it brings to ministers and their staff are exclusive and concentrated and if the policy production involves a small number of ministerial departments (cf. Von Hagen and Harden 1994; Hallerberg 2004b). This is because political and civil service careers depend on catering to special departmental interests. The utility-maximizing attitude further predisposes ministers and their staff to minimize cooperation with other departments because the more departments become involved, the higher the costs of coordination and the higher the uncertainty as to the final outcome of policy change. Arguing a contrario, one can predict that, where a policy reform brings benefits that are mainly collective and diffuse over many electoral constituencies and where the reform requires many departments to be involved, ministers and their staff will have limited incentives to contribute to policy change (Olson 1965; Frohlich, Oppenheimer, et al. 1971; Cox and McCubbins 1993).

Three collective action problems impinge on policy development in such latter cases. The first problem is a *free-rider problem* that arises if ministers and departments believe that they cannot be excluded from enjoying the collective benefit regardless of whether they contribute to producing the benefit. In effect, individual ministers may have strong incentives to maximize net individual utility by not engaging in the development of such legislation and by free riding on the efforts of their cabinet colleagues. This strategy is the best choice no matter if other ministers choose to comply or not. This theoretical insight lies at the heart of the public goods theory (Olson 1965; Hardin 1982). Free riding may complicate, for example, cabinet attempts to improve fiscal discipline. It is not uncommon for the implementation of such projects to be stymied by ministerial unreliability, as cabinet members who collectively support the policy would rather see other departments take the main brunt of spending cuts.

Standard free riding is not possible if all ministers and departments believe that their contribution is critical to the production of the collective benefits (cf. Hardin 1982, pp. 50–66). But, in such cases, collective action is still complicated by the *problem of high opportunity costs.* If it is impossible, or at least difficult, for ministers and departments to take credit for providing benefits vis-à-vis their own sectoral constituencies, they will have limited incentives to engage in the development of a policy. If resources are limited (as they usually are) and ministers have opportunities to commit them to policies that yield more favorable individual cost-benefit ratio (as they usually have), then a strategy of not contributing to collective action may be expected to dominate. This is particularly true since collective benefits tend to take longer to be generated. If benefits are not only collective but also remote, while costs are incurred in the short term, ministers and departments may discount them, concluding that their present value is insufficient to compensate for legislative or political costs.

The final problem is that of *coordination.* The logic here is that, if all must contribute for a policy to yield benefits, any minister is better off by complying if others also comply, but is better off by not complying if others choose not to comply (cf. Runge 1984; Ostrom 2003a, p. 246). The temptation not to contribute arises if one thinks that others will not comply. This uncertainty is likely to lead ministers and departments to minimize risks by withholding or delaying inputs to collective action. The strategy of withholding cooperation may be expected in particular if inputs must be supplied simultaneously. If contributions are made sequentially, ministers are more likely to adopt a delaying tactic, waiting until it is clear that enough contributions have been made to ensure the implementation of the policy. The coordination problem may be expected to impinge typically on the production of legal measures that span multiple policy jurisdictions and that may be produced only if two or more ministers coordinate their lawmaking actions.

Cabinet Dilemmas and EU Rule Adoption

The above insights are applied here to the study of EU rule adoption in Central Europe. The key argument is that Central European cabinets are likely to have perceived preaccession legal alignment as a reform project that brought nonexclusive collective benefits and required cooperation by many departments. This assertion is based on three main observations. The first observation is that, given the high uncertainty surrounding the rule adoption, ministers in Central European cabinets could hope to reap the collective benefits of EU accession even if minimizing their real contribution to legal alignment. This is chiefly because what was regarded as compliance was subject to bargaining between national governments and their counterparts on the EU side. It was not clear how much rule adoption had to be achieved to produce the benefit of EU membership. Many national decision makers believed that the decision on membership would be a political one, and ministers hoped that the EU would treat some rules as more important than others. The governments were unsure about the timing and precise standards to be achieved as well as the political salience of individual policy areas (cf. Grabbe 2001).

The second observation is that, although the uncertainty regarding the minimum legal requirements may have declined over time, EU rule adoption carried a high opportunity cost for Central European executives. Lacking the experience of policy formulation, ministers and departments were unsure about what individual benefits to expect and so were able to offset adaptation costs only against the collective benefits of policy modernization and EU accession. Even when they were able to identify concentrated benefits, they expected such benefits to materialize only after enlargement. This was because the largest financial and political benefits were to become visible after accession, while most adaptation costs had to be incurred before they joined the EU. Although the discount rates applied to such individual benefits are certain to have fallen the closer the country moved to membership, it is important to note that the date of accession had not been preagreed and depended on progress in rule adoption.

The third observation is that rule adoption in Central Europe required joint legislative action by numerous governmental agencies. At a most general level, the collective rule adoption was necessary because the Community's acquis contained several thousand legal measures that spanned almost the entire policy spectrum. The ministries in Central European executives had to transpose more than 2,000 directives covering various policy fields. For example, in Poland, the adoption of 666 EU measures identified in the European Commission's 1997 Single Market White Paper required action by 19 ministries and central agencies. More importantly, at a level of individual laws, many of the Community measures dealt with horizontal, crosscutting policy problems that required the collaboration of many different ministries for full transposition. The misfit between the scope of EU measures and national portfolios is common in the old EU member states (Page 1998; Bovens and Yesilkagit 2004) and was also pronounced in a preaccession country. For example, in Poland, more than 60 percent of the White Paper's measures required legislative inputs from two or more agencies for full transposition (UKIE 1997).

In sum, having been perceived as a reform project bringing nonexclusive collective benefits and requiring intensive cooperation, EU rule adoption in Central Europe was likely to have been complicated by collective cabinet dilemmas. The uncertainty regarding minimum requirements would create strong incentives for ministers to free ride on the rule adoption effort of their cabinet colleagues. The high opportunity costs of rule adoption would encourage ministers and departments to commit resources to other, most likely domestic, legislative uses that could bring more favorable cost-benefit ratios. The extensive need for interministerial cooperation was likely to provide a further bias against rule adoption as ministers and their staff would prefer to focus on legislation that may be adopted through individual decision. In practice, such collective action problems would result in Central European executives finding it difficult to initiate and adopt EU-related legislation.

Explanatory Hypotheses

Generic Solutions

The literature on collective action provides four broad types of explanations on what facilitates or impedes the resolution of collective action problems. These are: (i) change in the nature of the policy program to be adopted, (ii) change in actor preferences, (iii) change in action resources appurtenant to actors, and (iv) change in institutional incentives and opportunity structures. Naturally, these explanations are not mutually exclusive. Indeed, attempts have been made to incorporate all four into a single analytical framework (see Ostrom 1990, pp. 182–216). The first approach focuses on the extent to which a policy program offers actors the opportunity to obtain exclusive individual benefits in addition to the collective benefit. If such private incentives exist, the rational self-interest may lead individuals to contribute to the collective action. In the present context, if a minister and his staff could use EU-related legislation to produce exclusive individual benefits for their own clients, stakeholders, and departments, then the probability of improving the collective rule adoption record would be increased.

Although this approach is certain to provide interesting insights, its usefulness for the study of a preaccession state is reduced because Central European governmental actors will have operated under incomplete information. As argued earlier in this chapter, ministers and their departmental staff were likely to be uncertain about the precise consequences of transposition for their electoral constituencies besides the collective benefit of an improved transposition record. Insufficient knowledge of the acquis communautaire may have also prevented ministries from using transposition strategically to produce individual benefits. There was also a general perception among political decision makers that the largest financial and political benefits from rule adoption would become visible only after a country joined the EU.

The second approach links the likelihood of cooperation to actor preferences. It is often pointed out that actors may not always be guided by rational self-interest whose maximization is responsible for producing collective action problems. Specific extrarational motivations such as morality, the desire for self-development through participation, ignorance, and misunderstanding may have an important impact on individual incentives and help resolve collective action problems (cf. Hardin 1982, pp. 101–124; Ostrom 1998). In the present context, this would mean that some ministers may be more inclined to contribute to the collective rule adoption record than others because, for example, they may have a personal desire to be seen as strong champions of European integration or because rule adoption was perceived as a patriotic duty. Without rejecting such arguments, it must be noted, however, that ministers and their departmental staff in Central European cabinets had limited time and opportunities to develop strong internal motivations that could lead them to favour the collective EU transposition record more than individual interest benefits.

A third argument holds that a change in resource endowment may help actors resolve collective action dilemmas by changing their cost-benefit calculations. In the present context, this would imply that different levels of resources such as personnel, finance, or time may influence the priority that ministers and their staff may give to contributing to the production of transposing legislation. The logic would further imply that larger amounts of action resources would increase the likelihood that actors contribute to the collective action. This said, this argument is not without its problems. For one thing, although more action resources may indeed increase a pool of resources that any individual sets aside for donations to the collective action, this effect is likely to be small since actors will have strong incentives to use the additional resources to further their individual rather than group interests.

The fourth approach—pursued in this book—centers on changes in institutional incentives and opportunity structures (Olson 1965; Frohlich and Oppenheimer 1970; Frohlich, Oppenheimer, et al. 1971; Ostrom 1990). The theory holds that collective action problems are most acute where institutional rules exist that encourage actors to "go it alone" or pursue their narrow self-interest. Conversely, the probability that actors resolve collective action problems is highest where there are rules that mobilize them to adopt coordinated strategies. Such latter conditions are posited to obtain in two institutional contexts. First, the likelihood of cooperation is positively related to the existence of rules that provide actors with *selective (private) inducements* to contribute to the collective good. Such incentives may take various forms such as rewards and facilitation, or constraints on agenda-setting powers, sanctions, and exclusion. Their principal function is to transform dominating defection strategies into contingent strategies of cooperation.

Second, the selective incentives must be accompanied by institutional rules that make *information* available about the behavior of individual actors. These rules may take the form of, among others, oversight procedures, reporting requirements, or disclosure mandates. Their task is to ensure the credibility of selective incentives by eliminating opportunities for shirking. Perhaps, more importantly, information serves to reduce the level of uncertainty associated with any group action. This is crucial because members of a group are likely to behave strategically by making their contribution to the collective good contingent on the actual choices of others in a group (cf. Frohlich, Oppenheimer, et al. 1971; Runge 1984; Ostrom 2003a). The key task of information-enhancing rules is thus to transform such contingent behavior into dominant strategies of cooperation.

The selective incentives and monitoring may be sustained within two organizational configurations: (i) hierarchy and (ii) collectivity (cf. Frohlich, Oppenheimer, et al. 1971; Fiorina and Shepsle 1989; Cox and McCubbins 1993; Andeweg 2000). The *hierarchical* relationship posits the existence of a central authority. This role has three institutional features: (i) the central authority has at its disposal selective incentives with which to reward or sanction members of the group, (ii) it incurs the cost of monitoring the behavior of individual members, and (iii) it is rewarded for its role in solving the collective problems through a compensation mechanism that links its personal interests with the extent of the collective behavior (Cox and McCubbins 1993, pp. 90–94). The central authority's role is essentially that of an enforcer and monitor. It provides selective incentives to change the payoff structure in a way that makes coordinated behavior desirable and supplies information to dispel uncertainty about strategy choices. The authority may contribute to the resolution of collective dilemmas by fulfilling two other functions. It may act as an arbiter of conflicts that arise between members of a group and thus lower the costs of achieving collective interests (Cox and McCubbins 1993, p. 94). It may also function as a competitive agenda setter (Fiorina and Shepsle 1989). In this latter role the central authority mobilizes other members of a group toward the achievement of collective interests by constraining their agenda-setting powers.

Under the *collectivity* relationship, there is no central authority and the group is self-governing (cf. Ostrom 1990, pp. 15–18). Institutional rules exist that (i) enable all individuals in a group to extend to one another selective incentives such as sanctions, rewards, or exclusion, (ii) make it possible for individual members to share the costs of monitoring, and (iii) establish an allocation mechanism through which the personal interests of the group members are linked to the extent of cooperation. Most commonly, such institutional rules provide for a committee-type mechanism or similar collective constraints on the individual autonomy of sequence, contingency, and frequency of action. It is interesting to note that collectivity-administered selective incentives and monitoring are frequently untenable without some recourse to hierarchy. For example, absent an external monitor or enforcer, large groups may suffer from inherent problems of unobservability, while small groups will find it difficult to "group punish" noncompliant members in such a way as to allow for further cooperation. Thus, it is a frequent practice for self-governing groups to hire an external agent to help them with internal policing (cf. Ostrom 1990, pp. 15–18).

In analyzing the impact of such institutional rules on the resolution of collective action problems, this book adopts a regulative definition of institution (Scott 2001, pp. 71–89). Institutions are thus taken to denote rules of the game that shape human behavior (cf. North 1990). Such rules may be less or more formal depending on the carrier or repository in which they are embedded. The formal rules will include laws, protocols, routines, or standard operating procedures that have been formalized in legal texts. Informal rules will include such behavioral characteristics of a group as norms, conventions, and social capital (cf. Blondel and

Manning 2002). For present purposes, three categories of rules are of special importance (Hood 1983; Scharpf 2000; Ostrom 2003b):

- position rules—create institutional positions that may be occupied by individual or multiple actors; in the present context, these rules mandate the existence of hierarchical or collective institutional configurations.
- authority rules—identify actions that actors in a particular position may or must take in specific situations; in the present context, these rules specify the powers to reward, sanction, exclude, or facilitate, or otherwise affect, the behavior of individuals in a group.
- information rules—mandate information flows among actors; in the present context, these rules specify how the actions of actors are planned and monitored.

While focusing primarily on the role of institutions in the resolution of collective dilemmas, this study recognizes that there are limits to what can be explained through an institutionalist lens. The operation of institutional rules is influenced by other variables, notably those mentioned at the start of this section. Thus, accepting the significance of such other factors, the present study qualifies its institutionalist account with references to their effect, particularly when institutions alone are not sufficient to tell the full story.

Core Executive as Solution to Collective Dilemmas

In searching for solutions to collective dilemmas, this book focuses on the role of the domestic core executive (cf. Dunleavy and Rhodes 1990; Rhodes and Dunleavy 1995). The core executive is typically taken to comprise the prime minister, finance minister, and nonsectoral ministers as well as "the complex web of institutions, network, and practices surrounding the prime minister, cabinet, cabinet committees, and their official counterparts" (Rhodes 1995, p. 12). The key argument is that the core executive represents a unique institutional response to collective dilemmas in the execution of policies that bring collective benefits and require interministerial cooperation. Hence, in the present context, the probability that ministers and departments engage in EU rule adoption is hypothesized to be positively related to the institutionalization of incentives and monitoring that are extended to line ministers by the domestic core executive. More specifically, that probability is highest under two institutional configurations: (i) where the prime minister or some other nonsectoral minister acts as a central authority in the area of EU rule adoption and (ii) where rules exist that require ministers to manage rule adoption as a group. These solutions point to hierarchy and collectivity as two strategies for delivering incentives and monitoring within the executive (cf. Andeweg 2000; Hallerberg 2000, 2004b).

Under the hierarchical solution the prime minister or a nonsectoral minister has—by virtue of his institutional position—personal incentives to act as monitor, arbiter, and competitive agenda setter with a view to ensuring that other ministers adopt cooperative strategies. His or her ability to mobilize individual ministers toward a collective interest crucially depends on the configuration of three types of institutional rules: (i) position rules that link the personal interests of the prime minister or nonsectoral minister to the achievement of collective interests, (ii) authority rules that specify his or her powers to sanction and reward ministers and to act as agenda setter and/or arbiter, and (iii) information rules that determine his or her position within an information network. More specifically, it is hypothesized that the ability of the prime minister or nonsectoral minister to resolve collective action problems in the improvement of the collective transposition record depends on the existence of the rules identified in table 2.1 (cf. Weller 1985, 1991; Müller, Philipp, et al. 1993; Aucoin 1994).

To use such powers effectively in furthering the collective interests of the government, the prime minister or minister for transposition needs to possess appropriate resources such as organization, personnel, and finance. These resources are typically concentrated in central agencies such as the PMO and other specialized secretariats at the center of government (see, for example, Weller 1991; Müller-Rommel 1993; Peters, Rhodes, et al. 2000). These agencies are responsible chiefly for analyzing information from sectoral ministries, generating specialized advice, and providing secretarial and administrative support. The resource capacity of such units will determine the prime minister's and the minister for transposition's ability to act as a central authority.

Under the collectivity-based arrangement, collective action problems are solved through the introduction of institutional rules that require ministers to manage EU rule adoption as a group (cf. Andeweg 2000). Such rules will facilitate the improvements of the collective transposition record by, inter alia, encouraging ministers to act as monitors or competitive agenda

Table 2.1 Rules facilitating the resolution of collective action problems through hierarchy

Position rules	*Authority rules*	*Information rules*
• There is a minister responsible for transposition (MfT) • MfT reports to prime minister (PM)	• PM may appoint/dismiss or otherwise reward/sanction ministers • MfT may alert the PM if ministers do not contribute to transposition • PM/MfT may require amendment to draft legislation and may arbitrate conflicts • PM may reject/accept bids for resources such as finance and legislative time • PM may decide which priorities are allocated resources	• PM/MfT may impose transposition agenda and timetable • Ministers are required to report to PM/MfT about legislative actions in transposition • PM/MfT may require information on transposition • PM/MfT has information on transposition and nontransposition demands on resources • PM/MfT has information on the availability of resources

setters for one another and to consider the full effect of individual legislative actions for their collective interest. The efficacy of this solution depends on the configuration of three types of rules: (i) position rules providing for the requirement to manage rule adoption as a group, (ii) authority rules that specify the powers of individual ministers to intervene in other ministers' legislative actions, and that determine what action should be taken if noncompliance is detected, (iii) information rules that specify how ministers learn about one another's actions. More specifically, the possibility that collectivity will solve the collective action problems in the improvement of the collective transposition record depends on the existence of the rules identified in table 2.2 (cf. Aucoin 1986; Baylis 1989; Thiebault 1993; Andeweg 1997).

For such institutional rules to bring ministers round to more cooperative strategies, they must be backed by organizational resources available to ministers as a group. Such resources are typically housed in the Cabinet Office or other committee secretariats (see Campbell 1988; Barker and Peters 1993; Peters and Barker 1993; Bakvis 1997; Savoie 1999). These units produce assessments of legislative proposals that are independent from departmental views and are informed by the collective interest

Table 2.2 Rules facilitating the resolution of collective action problems through collectivity

Position rules	Authority rules	Information rules
• The full cabinet is involved in managing the transposition record • There exists a permanent cabinet committee for transposition (CfT) • The CfT consists of cabinet or junior ministers	• The cabinet/CfT works on transposition legislation and has selective incentives for rewarding and sanctioning • Conflicts are resolved in cabinet/CfT • The cabinet/CfT requests amendments to draft legislation • The cabinet/CfT rejects/ accepts bids for resources • The cabinet/CfT decides which priorities are allocated resources	• The cabinet/CfT determines transposition agenda and timetable • Ministers are required to report in cabinet/CfT about legislative actions in transposition • The cabinet/CfT reviews progress in improving transposition record regularly • The individual record of ministers is clearly visible to all cabinet/CfT members

of the government. They also ensure that legislative drafts are routed according to preagreed operational rules and that all the cabinet or cabinet committees have enough information to monitor the behavior of individual ministers and enforce mutual commitments.

Hierarchy and collectivity as organizational vehicles for administering incentives and monitoring are not mutually exclusive. It is true that they point to different logics of executive organization. Prime ministerial governments tend to resort chiefly to the former, while cabinet governments would rely on the latter. But, in practice, the choice between hierarchy and collectivity is at best a question of degrees (cf. Rhodes 1995; Andeweg 1997; Elgie 1997). Even the most extreme types of prime ministerial governments allow some collective decision making, and the most collegial cabinets delegate some powers to the premier. In functional terms, both organizational choices entail similar effects for power relations inside the executive. They postulate the institutionalization of rules at the center of government that can constrain ministerial agenda-setting autonomy in the policy-making process. Both can be contrasted with the conditions of a ministerial-type government under which the center of government has only limited institutional mechanisms for mobilizing ministerial departments who enjoy far-reaching autonomy in making legislative decisions.

The Emergence of Selective Incentives and Monitoring

Although this study is chiefly interested in exploring the effect that intraexecutive rules have on the resolution of collective action problems, it is necessary to have some theoretical insight into how such rules emerge over time. The first thing to note here is that the supply of institutional rules to solve collective dilemmas is itself a second-order collective action problem (Ostrom 1990). As it is difficult to exclude others from benefiting from such rules once they are supplied, individual actors will prefer to free ride on the efforts of others. A similar dominating strategy of noncooperation may also derive from high opportunity and coordination costs. Hence, to a large extent, the preconditions for institutional change within the executive mirror those for the resolution of the first-order problem in the improvement of the transposition record.

Two principal approaches may thus be discerned with regard to the mechanics of institutional change. First, institutional innovations may originate as a result of a collective commitment by all actors to provide for new rules that would govern their mutual interactions (Ostrom 1990, pp. 15–18). In the present context, the transformation of core executive institutions would thus be possible if the cabinet or a cabinet committee adopted new rules that enhance the hierarchy or collectivity of decision making in the area of EU rule adoption. Second, institutional rules may be supplied by entrepreneurs who find it personally profitable to organize a group for the provision of a collective good. Such individuals will find this role attractive only when the total benefits they receive exceed their total costs (Frohlich, Oppenheimer, et al. 1971, pp. 6–7). In the present context, the reinforcement of the core executive would be possible if some central actor, most likely the prime minister, senior cabinet member, or party leader, acted as an entrepreneur for EU rule adoption and incurred the cost of organizing the cabinet for that purpose. It must be noted that an entrepreneur-inspired institutional change need not lead to a hierarchical configuration of selective incentives and monitoring. The prime minister or other actor may just as well provide for collectivity-enhancing rules.

The likelihood that institutional change occurs is related to three institutional factors that affect the support that a leader or group members may have for change to the status quo rules. First, there are international opportunity structures imposed by external regimes. Such institutional incentives create opportunities for profits to be earned through group organization. In this context, it is possible that the EU may encourage the prime minister or the cabinet to supply institutional rules that address the collective action problem in the improvement of the transposition record. Second, similar incentives may be provided by domestic extraexecutive institutions. For present purposes, it is important to note the opportunity structures extended by the electoral system, socioeconomic interests, and nonexecutive state actors such as parliament or courts. Third, the support for change to the status quo rules—and hence to solve or preserve a collective action problem—is expected to be shaped by the characteristics of the party composition of the cabinet (cf. Hallerberg 2004a, 2004b; Dimitrov, Goetz and Wollmann 2006). The likelihood of institutional change is thus related to factors such as the internal cohesiveness of coalition parties, the ideological distance between them, and the expectation of whether they will run together or against each other in the next elections. More robust core executives are thus likely to emerge in single-party governments or coalition governments in which parties are internally cohesive and close in ideological terms and expect to run together in the next elections.

Last, one needs to consider the dynamic of institutional change. At a most general level, change at each decision point in time may be expected to be relatively minor if ministers and departments are able to adapt incrementally the status quo rules. In such situations, change will proceed in multiple steps as the prime minister or ministers test different institutional solutions in response to the collective action problem (see, for example, Argyris and Schön 1996). The assumption here is that actors will be able to respond flexibly to changes in external opportunity structures and the results of their own experiential learning. If, however, for systemic, informational, or other reasons, such incremental adaptation is not possible, one may expect internal and external pressures to accumulate over time and, at some point, create a "critical juncture" or a "window of opportunity" at which radical institutional change may occur. This latter case would be associated with the emergence of a crisis situation involving the perceived failure of the existing rules.

Contextualizing Variables

Although the primary focus of the study is on core executive and its contribution to the solution of collective problems in EU rule adoption, the impact that institutional rules embodied in nonexecutive organizational carriers may have on individual behavior must also be taken into consideration. Three types of such institutional rules will be analyzed in the present context: (i) institutional opportunities generated by the European Union, (ii) institutional incentives provided by political parties and governing coalitions, and (iii) institutional incentives extended by domestic nonexecutive organizations. In the language of the collective action theory, all these rules may be used to extend selective incentives and monitoring to ministers and departments. As such, they may directly contribute to solving the collective action problems that impinge on EU rule adoption.

The European Commission may act as the central authority inducing and monitoring domestic ministers and departments. The tools it may use are positive and negative inducements, otherwise known as "conditionalities." Such conditionalities involve the offering of material and nonmaterial rewards in return for supplying improvements to the transposition record. Material rewards may include financial assistance. The Commission may for instance make the disbursement of the Phare and other preaccession funds conditional on the transposition of specific EU measures. Nonmaterial rewards and sanctions would take the form of various mechanisms that shape the international and domestic image of the government (cf. Schimmelfennig and Sedelmeier 2005). The chief objective of conditionality is to increase the individual cost of noncompliance (or the individual benefit of EU rule adoption) for domestic ministers. Besides conditionality, the Commission may also act as monitor. In doing so, it may impose comprehensive informational requirements on national administrations and feed the information back to the domestic arena through public or nonpublic channels. EU-induced selective incentives and monitoring may also originate within collectivity-based arrangements such as the association council/committee, expert meetings, or negotiation sessions. The collective pressure may also originate from rules that increase natural competition among accession states in improving their individual transposition records.

Political parties contribute to the resolution of collective action problems because their organizations provide party leaders with institutional levers for mobilizing their members toward collective goals and for monitoring their behavior. Selective incentives that party leaders may offer to their members include career advancement within the party hierarchy, membership of prestigious parliamentary committees, or senior government positions. In the present context, such incentives may be used by party leaders to mobilize ministers to engage in EU rule adoption. The significance of political parties as a solution to collective dilemmas is most evident in two-party systems, in which parties appeal to the broad electorate and tend to form single-party governments. The situation is more complex in multiparty systems, in which parties represent narrower socioeconomic interests and are likely to form coalition governments. Yet, even in that latter case, collective dilemmas may be solved through party-based mechanisms if coalition parties cooperate and develop institutions that enable them to implement joint policies (see Blondel and Cotta 1996; Blondel and Cotta 2000; Müller and Strøm 2000; Thies 2001). These party-based institutions may take the form of coalition summits, overlapping jurisdictions between ministries or the shadowing role of junior ministers. These institutional levers could be used by coalition leaders to ensure that ministers contribute to the EU rule adoption.

Finally, Central European cabinets may be subject to incentives and monitoring extended by nonexecutive domestic organizations. Two sources of such nonexecutive incentives are crucial here. First and foremost, ministers and high-ranking government officials are exposed to close scrutiny by parliament. Their preferences in this regard may be shaped in bilateral contacts with parliamentary leaders or within collective frameworks of parliamentary committees. Second, the incentives and information may be supplied within the context of linkage institutions that channel social and business interests. These may include in particular bilateral contacts with lobby groups or collective mechanisms such as tripartite commissions or similar roundtables.

Conclusion

This chapter has presented the theoretical framework for examining EU rule adoption in Central Europe. It has argued that legal alignment before accession presented major collective action problems for cabinet governments in the region. *The probability of rule adoption is hypothesized to have been positively related to the institutionalization of specific position, authority, and information rules that the domestic core executive can use to extend incentives and monitoring to line ministries.* The chapter has also identified three other variables that are likely to have contextualized the impact of core executive rules: EU constraints and accession dynamic; party controls and interparty cooperation; and domestic extraexecutive constraints.

CHAPTER 3

EU Rule Adoption in Poland

This chapter examines the dynamics of EU rule adoption in Poland between 1997 and 2002. It finds that, during this period, the dynamics of legal alignment was subject to significant variation. In 1997–1999, the Polish cabinet had a low transposition record. From 2000, that record had improved and remained at a high level until 2001 when it deteriorated to a medium level. The year 2002 brought a return to a high level of transposition. The chapter closes by concluding that, although policy type, actor preferences, and ministerial resources were likely to have some impact on the variation in EU rule adoption, the effect of those variables is not sufficient to fully account for the variation and leaves ample room for other explanations.

Transposition before EU Accession

In the EU member states, transposition is typically taken to denote the incorporation of Community directives into national legal systems through the passage of appropriate domestic measures (Ramsey 1996; Samuels 1998). Such an incorporation is necessary because, unlike regulations and decisions, directives are binding as to the result to be achieved but leave the choice of form and methods to the member states (cf. Craig and De Burca 1998, pp. 108–109). National governments must thus adopt domestic legislation to realize the objectives set out in directives (Nicolaides 1999, 2002). Transposition in a preaccession state is similar in technical-legal terms but may have a slightly different scope. It may be often required for measures that are not normally subject to it. This is necessary because domestic institutions need to be prepared in advance for the direct applicability of

Community regulations and decisions. The relevant domestic measures are, of course, transitory and are repealed when a country gains full membership (cf. Herrnfeld 1996, p. 102).

In Poland, transposing measures could take the form of an act of parliament (*ustawa*) or an executive regulation (*rozporzadzenie*) adopted by the prime minister, the council of ministers, or an individual minister (UKIE 2003b). A rough estimate put the number of directives that had to be transposed through parliamentary legislation in Poland at 300 out of a total of 980 (EuroPap 2001). The remaining 680 directives had to be transposed through secondary law. It must be noted, however, that parliamentary legislation is central to transposition since, in a closed system of sources of law such as Poland's, no secondary legislation may be adopted without an earlier express delegation of implementing powers in an act of parliament. Thus, transposition frequently had to start with parliamentary legislation, while secondary legislation could follow only later.

Transposition, as defined here, began in Poland only in the second half of the 1990s. Until then, domestic adaptation to the Community law had been dominated by the logic of modernization and had largely proceeded through a mimetic transplantation of selected EU and/or member states' policy models into the Polish legal system. This had been the time when Polish economic legislation was undergoing a process of rapid transformation and national legislators looked to the Community legislation and the national laws of the EU member states for policy blueprints. Indeed, the "pick and choose" method of legal adaptation had been strongly advocated by leading law professors and practitioners (Rada Legislacyjna 1994; Sołtysinski 1996).

Besides creative transplants, legal adaptation had also focused on passive screening of all new Polish legislation for compliance with the acquis. This process was initiated as early as 1991 and was gradually extended to cover all government legislative drafts (Wojciechowski 1996, 1998; Jaskiernia 1999). Transposition in the strict sense was largely absent, and where it was attempted, it rarely succeeded at the adoption stage. A Polish commentator noted that "the major problem with [early adaptation plans] was the absence of any reference to specific provisions of the Community law that the planned measures sought to implement" (Górka 1997, p. 14). The closest the Polish government came to active transposition of the Community legislation was in conceptual preparatory work, but its real impact was rather limited (Drabczyk 1998, pp. 13–14).

The first EU transposition commitments were made by the Polish cabinet when, in mid-1995, it resolved to incorporate into national law 666 directives listed in the European Commission's Single Market White Paper. Ministers and departments were required to draw up a list of Polish legislation in areas covered by the White Paper directives, examine their compatibility with the Community acquis, and specify what legislative actions had to be taken to achieve full compatibility. In a second step, legal adaptation was reoriented toward transposition with the onset of preaccession alignment in 1997–1998. In response to the 1997 Accession Partnership in which the European Commission set out priority areas for Poland's legal adaptation, the Polish cabinet prepared an NPAA. The first such program was prepared in June 1998 and was subsequently revised on an annual basis (1999, 2000, and 2001). The NPAA consisted of 32 chapters, each devoted to a separate policy sector. The chapters identified action to be undertaken, the ministry or agency responsible, the timetable for implementation, and the financial resources available. The first two versions of the NPAA were accompanied by detailed annexes listing all legislative tasks assigned to individual ministries, with deadlines for their adoption.

This chapter measures the extent to which Polish ministers complied with self-imposed deadlines for transposition written into the NPAA transposition plans. In doing so, it relies on one principal and two subsidiary quantitative indicators. The principal indicator of compliance is the proportion of Polish transposing measures envisaged for adoption in a given year (or shorter period) that are actually adopted that year (or within such a shorter period). Two other indicators are used to cross-check evidence from the principal indicator. These are (i) the nominal number of transposing bills adopted by the cabinet over time and (ii) the proportion of Polish domestic laws that are fully compatible with the Community law (see table 3.1). In mapping the values of such indicators over time, attention is paid to two principal aspects of the dynamic of the transposition record (cf. Monge 1995). The first one is the magnitude of change. Magnitude refers to how much the amount of a variable changes from one point in time to another. Over time, magnitude may change slightly or significantly or remain constant. The second aspect is the rate of change that denotes how fast the magnitude changes over time. Magnitude can change rapidly or it can increase or decrease over a longer period of time.

Table 3.1 Compliance indicators

Indicator Type	Indicators
Primary indicator	The proportion of Polish transposing measures envisaged for adoption in a given year (or shorter period) that are actually adopted that year (or within such a shorter period).
Secondary indicators	The number of transposing measures adopted by the cabinet over time.
	The proportion of Polish domestic measures that are fully compatible with the Community law.

Source: Own compilation.

Evidence

Compliance with NPAA Plans

The first indicator is the proportion of Polish transposing measures envisaged for adoption in a given year (or shorter period) that were actually adopted that year (or within such a shorter period). To develop a dataset for this indicator, one needs to find reliable deadlines against which deviation from schedule could be captured. In addressing the issue, this book uses the data on transposition deadlines contained in the four consecutive national programs for the adoption of the acquis (1998, 1999, 2000, and 2001). Admittedly, this choice is not without problems. Besides the credibility problems mentioned at the end of the previous section, the precision of the transposition deadlines as well as the quality of the information on what transposing measures would be adopted varied both across policy areas and across programs. The problem was addressed by limiting the focus of the analysis only to bills to be submitted to parliament and by selecting measures that were clearly identified by name and deadline. Excluded from the selection were (i) measures with no deadlines, (ii) measures that had been passed before the date of the program, and (iii) measures with deadlines dependent on an external event (e.g., economic situation). Also, only deadlines for cabinet adoption were used.

Another problem with the data arose because, as a rule, the NPAA programs were adopted in midyear and, though planned transposition for the following one-and-a-half years, were updated in yearly cycles. As a result, there was an overlap of around six months, and deadlines for many measures were provided simultaneously in two consecutive programs. The problem was solved by selecting only the transposing measures that were scheduled for adoption during the half-year period until the end of the year in which the program was adopted. So, for example, the score for 1999 is based on the sample of measures to be adopted between mid-1999 and the end of that year. Besides the yearly NPAAs the analysis also uses data on deadlines derived from short-range planning instruments. Those took the form of internal transposition agendas adopted by the cabinet or the KIE committee for periods ranging from five to twelve months. Four such plans were used (January–May 2000, May–September 2000, January–September 2000, and January–December 2002).

Having selected transposing measures scheduled for adoption in a given year (or a shorter period), their individual transposition record was traced using data from three principal sources. First, the parliament's online database was searched, and where two or more acts with similar names were adopted, reference was made to the explanatory notes. Second, the transposition statistics were cross-checked with the information contained in the official annual reports on the implementation of the transposition programs. Finally, reference was made to the dataset developed for the second indicator presented in figure 3.3 given later in this chapter.

The data demonstrate that the extent of compliance changed very considerably over time (see figure 3.1). Between 1998 and 1999, the proportion of the domestic measures scheduled for adoption that were indeed passed by the cabinet remained at a relatively low level.

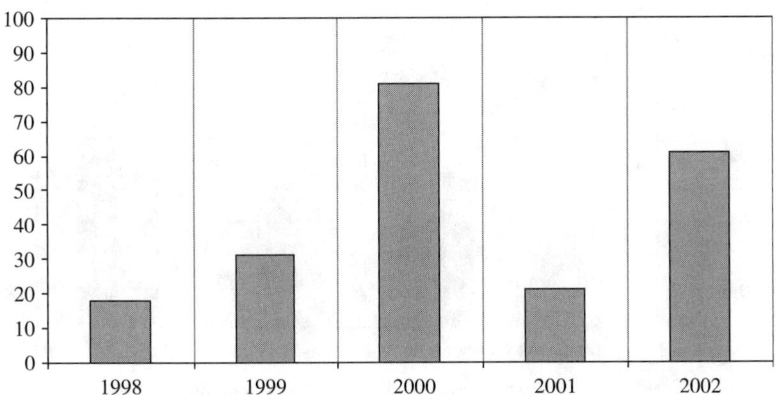

Source: Own compilation ([†]2nd half of each year except 2002 where data for the whole year was used).

Figure 3.1 Compliance with transposition commitments (percentage of adopted drafts) based on data from the NPAAs

The scores were 16 and 31 percent, respectively. In 1998, only four measures were adopted out of the scheduled twenty-four. The score improved in the following year as 14 out of 45 measures were adopted within deadline. The most significant change in the value of the timeliness indicator occurred in the year 2000. Out of the 63 drafts scheduled for cabinet adoption in 2000, 51 were submitted to parliament. In effect, the percentage score rose to 81. As compared with the earlier shift between 1998–1999, the magnitude of change in 1999–2000 was slightly higher—the percentage score in 2000 was two-and-a-half times higher than that in 1999 relative to a twofold increase in 1998–1999. Significantly, timeliness took a major dip in 2001. The percentage of measures adopted within the deadline declined to a low level of 21. This change is, however, likely to have been due to the parliamentary elections in September 2001 that disrupted the flow of the government's business in the second half of that year. The score was back to a high level in the year 2002. As many as eight out of the thirteen parliamentary measures scheduled for adoption were passed by the cabinet. As a result, the percentage score rose to 61.

The results for 2000–2002 are confirmed by the data derived from the short-range planning instruments (see figure 3.2). The first thing to

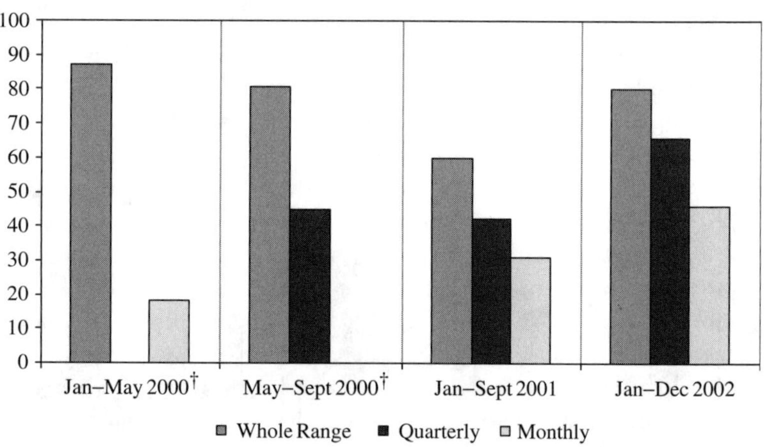

Source: Own compilation based on data obtained from the UKIE ([†]quarterly values are missing for January–May 2000; monthly values are missing for May–September 2000).

Figure 3.2 Compliance with short-range transposition commitments (percentage of adopted drafts)

note is that all four plans were implemented to a high degree. The whole-range score varied between 60 and 87 percent. Between January and May 2000, 33 out of 38 scheduled transposing measures were adopted by the cabinet during the five-month period. The May–September plan contained 38 measures out of which 31 were adopted on time. In January–September 2001, 29 out of 48 measured were adopted, while in 2002 the score was 51 out of 63 measures.

The second observation is that the quarterly and monthly deadlines were more likely not to have been complied with. The score for the former remained within the range of 45–66 percent, while that for the latter was between 18–46 percent. This said, it is possible to discern an upward tendency in such short-range timeliness. The monthly and quarterly scores rose from a low level in 2000–2001 to a much higher level in 2002. Finally, it is important to notice a relative decline in the values of the indicator for the first three quarters of 2001. This seems to indicate that the drop identified in figure 3.1 for the implementation of the 2001 NPAA was part of a more general downward trend that started already in the first half of 2001.

Transposing Measures Over Time

The second indicator is the nominal number of transposing measures adopted by the cabinet between 1997 and 2002. To compile the dataset for this indicator, one had to first single out EU-related drafts from among all legislation submitted to the cabinet. This was rather difficult since, in the period under examination, the Polish government did not operate a reliable flagging system that would have facilitated such a selection. This is particularly true for secondary transposing legislation that incorporated the EU legislation almost without any indication that the legislative action was undertaken for transposition purposes. Although such information may have been disclosed in the explanatory notes, those documents are not publicly available for all secondary legislation. The situation looked better for parliamentary bills. Since early 2000, the government had formally declared to parliament whether a draft law it submitted was a transposing or domestic legislation. This said, that system was started rather late and did not systematically cover the years 1997–1999, though the parliamentary and government services made some efforts to catalog such early transposing measures (see, for example, UKIE 2000).

Besides limited coverage, it must also be noted that the decision to flag a law as a transposing measure was political rather than technical in character. This means that, due to strategic calculations, drafts could be submitted to parliament as EU-related measures, though, in fact, they did not contain transposing provisions, and vice versa (interview 25, pp. 17–18).

Given the scarcity of reliable and comprehensive public data, the decision was made here to review all draft acts of parliament submitted by the cabinet to parliament between 1997 and 2002 and to select those measures whose explanatory notes made explicit reference to the Community legislation. In effect, 265 drafts were identified as transposing measures out of a total of 840 draft parliamentary laws submitted to parliament. Out of the 265 drafts, 216 had a formal government declaration of transposition status, while the remaining 49 were included based on the information in the explanatory notes.

The data demonstrate that between October 1997 and December 2002 transposition proceeded unevenly (see figure 3.3). In 1997 (fourth quarter) and 1998 the Polish cabinet adopted a total of 14 transposing bills. There was almost no change quarter-on-quarter as

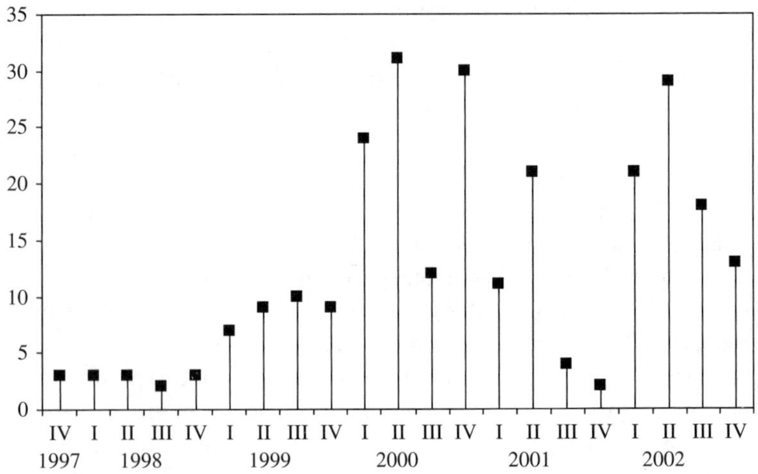

Source: Own compilation based on the data available on www.sejm.gov.pl.

Figure 3.3 Nominal number of EU transposition drafts adopted by the cabinet (quarterly)

the cabinet adopted two or three drafts every three-month period. Some increased legislative activity was registered in 1999. Between the first and the fourth quarter of that year the cabinet adopted 35 EU-related parliamentary bills—more than twice as many as in the previous five quarters. The change was of medium magnitude and its rate was rather incremental (increase from three through seven to ten), but the year 1999 marked a clear, though minor, departure from the previous pattern. The most significant change in the nominal number of transposing drafts came in the year 2000. Between the first and the fourth quarter of that year the cabinet adopted 97 draft laws—three times as many as the year before. What is striking is the magnitude of change. The score for the first quarter of 2000 stood at twenty-four drafts up from only nine the quarter before. Also, the change occurred at a fairly rapid rate. Whereas in 1998–1999 it took four quarters for the number of transposing drafts to treble from three to ten, the jump from nine to twenty-four occurred over only two quarters.

The new transposition dynamic was sustained in the first two quarters of 2001, though the peak value in the second quarter was lower than the analogous values in 2000. The cabinet adopted a total of 32 drafts, twice as many as in the equivalent period in 1999. The transposition almost halted in the third and the fourth quarter in 2001, but this was largely due to the parliamentary elections in September 2001 and the changeover from the Solidarity Electoral Action (AWS) to SLD-PSL-UP (Democratic Left Alliance, Polish Peasant Party, and Labour Union) government. In 2002, the transposition pattern was back to the high of the year 2000. Between the first and the fourth quarter, the cabinet adopted 81 bills, with the quarterly score ranging between 13 and 29 drafts.

The overall picture that emerges from this data is that of rather limited legal adaptation in the years 1997–1999, perhaps with a minor acceleration in 1999, and rapid transposition in the years 2000–2002, with a slight slowdown in the second half of 2001 due to the parliamentary elections. Finally, one needs to notice the prominent periodicity of transposition during the years 2000–2002. The peaks in the number of transposing legislation seem to alternate every other quarter, and the highest yearly scores occurred in the second quarter of the year 2000, 2001, and 2002. Interestingly, such periodicity is not found in the data for the years 1997–1999.

Substantive Compatibility

The final indicator is the proportion of domestic measures that are fully compatible with the Community law. To develop a dataset for this indicator, one would need to find a way, first, to select domestic measures that cover a policy area regulated by the Community legislation and, second, to measure substantive compatibility of such measures over time. For the latter, special attention would need to be paid to domestic legislation that catches an area covered by more than one Community measure. In such cases, one must allow for the possibility that a domestic law is compatible with one Community measure but not compatible with another. Such information could hardly be drawn from generalized assessments of EU compatibility contained in domestic studies or the Commission's regular progress reports (cf. URM 1995a; UKIE 1998).

Accordingly, with permission from the Office of the Committee for European Integration in Warsaw, access was gained by the author to the data stored in the European Commission's Progress Database. The database was originally developed in 1997 by the TAIEX in Brussels to monitor the adoption of Polish domestic legislation implementing the European Commission's Single Market White Paper. The Progress Database was later extended to cover the entire acquis communautaire as well as the screening process. The database was updated every two to three months based on inputs from the Polish ministries. The information contained in the database was well suited for the present purposes. For one thing it listed all Polish legislation that operated in substantive areas covered by Community measures. The database also contained information on how compatible domestic measures were with the corresponding Community acts. Four degrees of compatibility were used: full, partial, none, or unknown.

The precision of the data stored in the database must be approached with caution. The information on compatibility was updated on the basis of assessments provided by the Polish government, and the quality of these inputs may have varied over time as the Polish staff developed their expertise in Community law. In some instances, the data may have also reflected strategic games behind the adaptation process. Finally, the database does not determine the precise time at which measurements were taken because there may have been a lag between the compilation of data by the Polish authorities and the uploading of the database. Nevertheless, the potential for such bias aside, the Progress Database provided the best available source for assessing the way in which substantive adaptation changed over time in aggregate terms.

This analysis used Microsoft Word tables generated from nine updates of the Progress Database to arrive at comparable information on cross-temporal changes in substantive adaptation. A domestic measure was defined as a group of legal provisions corresponding to a single Community law rather than as a self-contained piece of domestic legislation. In this way, it has been possible to control for cases where a domestic law contained provisions corresponding to many different Community measures. The analysis was performed on a sample consisting of Polish measures corresponding to the Community legislation listed in the European Commission's 1997 White Paper. It was necessary to use a sample because the earlier versions of the database did not contain information on the entire acquis.

The analyzed data demonstrate that, between May 1998 and February 2002, the level of substantive adaptation varied significantly (see figure 3.4). Between May 1998 and December 1999, the percentage of fully compatible measures declined as a proportion of all domestic

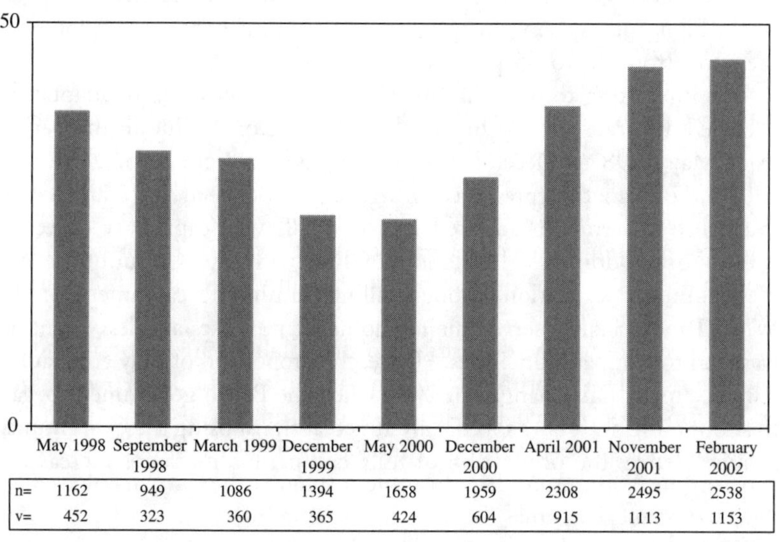

	May 1998	September 1998	March 1999	December 1999	May 2000	December 2000	April 2001	November 2001	February 2002
n=	1162	949	1086	1394	1658	1959	2308	2495	2538
v=	452	323	360	365	424	604	915	1113	1153

Source: Own compilation (v = nominal number of fully compatible measures).

Figure 3.4 Percentage of fully compatible domestic measures (White Paper sample) based on data from Progress Database

measures corresponding to the White Paper's acquis. The drop was from 39 to 26 percent over the one-and-a-half year period. As is clear from the data in figure 3.4, the decline in percentage values occurred against the backdrop of a rising nominal number of all domestic measures within the catchment of the Community laws. After an initial decline, their total number increased from 1,162 in May 1998 to 1,658 in May 2000.

The new legislative measures were, however, partially compatible or noncompatible, which resulted in the lower percentage values of the compatibility indicator. Although, after an initial drop, the nominal number of fully compatible measures rose too, from 323 to 424, the rate of change was not high enough to compensate for the rapid increase in the overall legislative activity. This trend was reversed from May 2000. Although the Polish government continued to add substantially to the total number of domestic measures corresponding with the White Paper's acquis, the legislative measures adopted between May 2000 and February 2002 had a higher compatibility with the Community acquis on average. The total number of domestic measures increased by nearly half from 1,658 to 2,538, but the nominal number of fully compatible measures also rose sharply from 424 to 1,153. This resulted in a relatively high increase in the proportion of fully compatible domestic measures from 26 to 45 percent.

It is interesting to note that the change to higher levels of adaptation occurred at a rate slightly higher than the rate of decline in the period from May 1998 to December 1999. These data seem to be consistent with the information presented in figure 3.3. Between 1997 and 1999, the Polish government adopted very few bills whose primary objective was to bring domestic legislation in line with the Community law. New domestic legislation, though falling within the catchment of the White Paper's acquis, served mainly domestic purposes and less attention was paid to compatibility issues. Hence, the proportion of fully compatible laws declined. This changed in 2000 when the Polish government began to adopt more draft laws specifically aimed at transposing the Community acquis. Hence, the proportion of fully compatible measures increased.

Overall Assessment

The picture that emerges from the above data demonstrates that the period between 1998 and 2002 may be divided into four consecutive stages each characterized by a distinct pattern of EU rule adoption

Table 3.2 A summary of variation in the dependent variable

Period	Principal indicator	Secondary indicator	Secondary indicator	Overall assessment
	Compliance with NPAAs	Number of measures	Compatibility	
1998	Low	Low		Low
1999	Low	Low to medium	Declining level of substantive adaptation	Low
2000	High	High		High
2001	Medium	Medium to high	Increasing level of substantive adaptation	Medium
2002	High	High		High

Source: Own compilation.

(see table 3.2). First, in 1998 and 1999, the Polish government had a low transposition record. All indicators registered low scores for the whole period. Although one secondary indicator (nominal number of transposing measures) had a slightly improved score for 1999, this does not provide sufficient evidence for a major upgrading in the overall assessment. Second, the year 2000 was characterized by a high transposition record. Two indicators registered a high score. The compatibility indicator showed a negative score until May 2000 as the compatibility of domestic legislation with the White Paper acquis continued to decline but the score improved for the rest of that year. Third, in the year 2001, the Polish government had a medium compliance record. Two indicators had a medium score and one had a medium to high score. Fourth and finally, the year 2002 was characterized by a high compliance record. All the indicators showed a highly positive score.

The Effects of Policy Type, Actor Preferences, and Ministerial Resources

This section explores the effect of variables that do not constitute the main focus of the study but nevertheless have been identified in Chapter 2 as having potential impact on the resolution of the collective dilemmas that impinged on EU rule adoption.

Policy Type

The first such variable is the cost of planned transposition. It is logical to expect that ministerial responsiveness is influenced by how costly a legislative commitment is for a given ministry. To check for the impact of adaptation costliness, one would need to find a way to measure cross-temporal variation in the extent to which legislation entailed adaptation costs. A quantitative assessment of costliness over many cases is difficult for the lack of reliable data, and so a decision has been made to use a much simpler indicator by exploring the ministry distribution of planned transposing measures (see table 3.3). The obtained data show the association between costliness and compliance to be at best limited. In 1998–2002, the bulk of transposition commitments were invariably made in areas in which the acquis entailed high adaptation costs (transport and telecoms, finance, economics, and agriculture) (Rada Ministrów 2000; UKIE 2003a). Although the proportion of commitments made in areas in which transposition was less cost-intensive increased gradually

Table 3.3 Ministry distribution of transposition commitments (by planned bills)

Ministry	1998	1999	2000	2001	2002
Transport and Communications	12	10	5	2	11
Finance	5	6	12	5	8
Economics	3	2	10	8	7
Agriculture	3	8	14	11	12
Labour	0	0	4	4	3
Environment	0	1	2	1	3
Health	0	0	6	4	5
Competitions Office	0	10	2	0	2
Justice	0	6	3	6	4
Home Affairs	0	0	3	2	4
Culture	1	2	0	1	3
Education	0	0	2	1	1
Foreign Affairs	0	0	0	1	0
State Treasury	0	0	0	3	0
Total	24	45	63	49	63

Source: Own compilation based on the NPAA programs (1998, 1999, and 2000) and short-term plans (2001 and 2002). The score for the Economics Ministry covers measures allocated to the Public Procurement Office, Measures Office, Exchange Commission, Standardization Office, and Regional Ministry. The score for the Justice Ministry covers measures assigned to Personal Data Protection Office.

(justice, home, culture, and education), it is important to note that in 2000, the year in which compliance improved substantially, the share of such measures in the transposition program actually declined.

Actor Preferences

The second variable is actor preferences. The theoretical prediction here is that the likelihood that ministers and their staff complied with commitments may have been related to their individual preferences and capabilities. For example, some ministers may have had a higher personal desire to be seen as strong champions of European integration or wanted to be perceived as team players complying with collective decisions. Similarly, some ministers may have had better management skills than others. To check for the impact of such idiosyncratic factors, one would need to identify all personal qualities that are likely to have affected transposition, measure the incidence of such qualities in the population of Polish ministries over time, and then cross-tabulate it with evidence of the transposition record. For present purposes, a simpler test is employed by checking whether any of the cross-temporal changes has been associated with a prior major cabinet reshuffle. Admittedly, this a rather crude measure, but, nevertheless, it gives us some idea regarding the potential impact of individual preferences.

The data on ministerial replacements (figure 3.5) indicate that in 1997–2002 there were four major cabinet reshuffles. The first one occurred in early 1999 when four ministers were changed. The second shake-up came in the second quarter of 2000 when the Freedom Union (UW) withdrew six ministers. Interestingly, the fourth round of changes took place in the third quarter of 2001, when Jerzy Buzek replaced four ministers only months before parliamentary elections. The last major reshuffle occurred in the third quarter of 2002 when Prime Minister Leszek Miller replaced three ministers. This data tentatively suggest that ministerial replacements may have had some impact on the compliance dynamic. For example, the cumulative effect of cabinet changes in 1999 may have altered the constellation of actor preferences within the cabinet. The change of UW ministers may also have added a further boost to transposition in mid-2000. This said, the cabinet reshuffles either in late 2001 or in 2002 do not seem to have coincided with changes in the transposition record. All in all, although actors preferences may have had some effect, their impact seems at best limited.

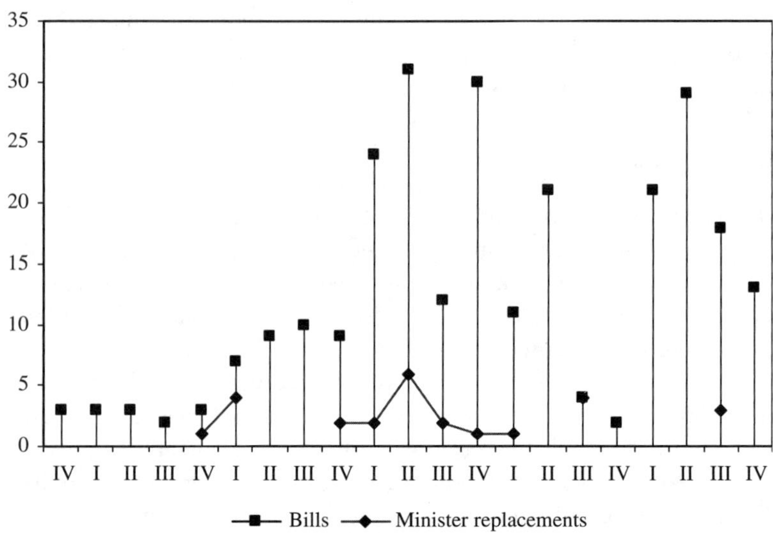

Source: Own compilation based on data from Prime Minister's Chancellery.

Figure 3.5 Cabinet reshuffles and adoption of parliamentary bills by the cabinet

Ministerial Resources

The third variable is resource endowment. The theoretical assumption is that the more resources a minister has at his or her disposal, the higher the likelihood that he or she makes voluntary donations to collective action. The resource that is likely to have a significant effect on the transposition record is the number of staff who deal with EU-related legislation in line ministries. These officials played a crucial role in supporting line departments in transposition, and it seems logical to expect that their resource endowment should affect the transposition record. To create a dataset for this indicator, all Polish ministries were approached for information on cross-temporal changes in the semiannual staff figures for EU divisions. Nine out of the fourteen ministries provided the data: ministries for economics, labour, home affairs, transport, communications, justice, agriculture, health, and education. Three ministries (economics, labour, and agriculture) provided only annual figures for periods ending December each year. In those latter cases, a decision was taken to retain the semiannual periodicity and use the annual figure for both half-year periods. Staff levels have been measured in full-time equivalents rather than in head count, with the exception of the Home Affairs Ministry. To control for the impact of resource endowment of departments other than the EU departments, the data on the total number of staff in ministries were obtained. Finally, the data on staff changes have been compared over time with variation in the transposition record.

The data demonstrate that there is some positive association between transposition record and staff levels in European integration departments (see table 3.4). The first observation is that the two upward shifts in the transposition record did coincide with increases in the level of EU-related staffing. In the first half of 2000, the full-time staff increased to 244 from 227 in the previous half-year period, and the high level persisted in the following six months. In the first half of 2002, the staff level rose to 270 from 231 in the second half of 2001 and increased further in the following six months. The other observation is that a decline in the transposition record in 2001 is associated with a reduction in staffing. The number of staff declined in the first half of 2001 to 233 from 244 in the previous half-year period. The finding is confirmed by the data on total ministerial staff levels. The largest growth in all staff occurred in the first half of 2000, when the number of personnel increased by 246, and in the first half of 2002, when it increased by more than 180 staff. The data for 2001 are, however, ambiguous with the total staff increasing in the first half of 2001 but falling in the second half.

This said, there are four major problems with treating these observations as evidence of a causal relationship. First, the transposition record remained unchanged despite fairly high staff increases in EU departments in mid-1997 and mid-1998 (9, 5, and 10 percent, respectively). It was only from the year 2000 that staff variation started to be associated with changes in the transposition pattern. This would suggest that there was some other factor that activated the personnel variable. Second, personnel changes have had asymmetric effects. A staff increase by 10 percent led to a major change from low to high transposition record, while the change from medium to high record was accompanied by a 17 percent rise in staff numbers. Third, none of the changes in the EU-related staff levels marked a major departure from the overall growth trend and amounted, at best, to an average increase of two to four full-time equivalents per ministry. As such, these changes in staff levels were unlikely to make a substantial contribution to the resolution of the collective action problem. Fourth and finally, the lack of time lag between the movements in staff numbers and the changes in the

Table 3.4 Ministerial staff[†] and compliance record

Ministry	I-1997	II-1997	I-1998	II-1998	I-1999	II-1999	I-2000	II-2000	I-2001	II-2001	I-2002	II-2002
Economics	33.67*	33.67	35.5*	35.5	38.67*	38.67	41*	41	44*	44	43*	43
Labour	26.88*	26.88	29*	29	25*	25	26*	26	21*	21	45*	45
Home Affairs	14*	14	20	23	26	25	28	30	31	32	35	44
Transport	14.5	17.05	18.75	25.75	25.75	21.75	21.75	18.75	21.75	27.75	28.75	27.75
Communications	15.5	17.5	20	21	18.5	16	19	18	13			
Justice	25.5	25.5	25	31	33	35.5	36.5	37.5	37	41	42.5	47.5
Agriculture	37*	37	21*	21	27*	27	32*	32	26.5*	26.5	34.8*	34.8
Health	0	12	11	15	13	12	13	13	15	14	16	16
Education	28	30	31	31	23	26	27	26	24	25	25	28
Total EU departments	195.05	213.6	211.25	232.25	229.92	226.92	244.25	242.25	233.25	231.25	270.05	286.05
All staff	4084.98	4155.53	4239.14	4396.16	4404.91	4429.47	4675.91	4577.15	4730.89	4610.1	4792.82	4833.62
Rule adoption record	Low	Low	Low	Low	Low	Low	High	High	Medium	Medium	High	High

[†] Full-time post equivalents.

* Annual figures are used to fill in semiannual gaps.

Note: Shaded area: In autumn 2001 the Communications Ministry was merged with Transport to form the Infrastructure Ministry.

Source: Own compilation based on the data obtained from individual ministries under the Freedom of Information Act.

transposition record casts some doubts on the direction of the causality. Though staff increases may have led to higher compliance record, it is just as probable that higher transposition record necessitated staff growth. In that latter case, some external variable may have been responsible for the transposition effect, while ministries may have used the sustainability of transposition to justify new recruitment. All in all, the result is inconclusive and, as such, invites further research.

Besides changes in absolute terms, resource endowment may also vary over time in relative terms. In the present context, this means that resources available to transposition would be the higher the less non-EU-related demands are placed on the total government resources. To check for the effect of relative changes in resource endowment, one may examine cross-temporal changes in the proportion of legislative output devoted to transposition. The theoretical prediction is that improvements in the compliance record would be associated with major increases in the relative resources committed to transposition. In developing a dataset for this indicator, the data used for figure 3.3 were supplemented with information about all non-EU related bills adopted by the Polish cabinet between 1997 and 2002.

The data confirm that changes in relative resource endowment are indeed associated with variation in the transposition record (see figure 3.6). The upward shift from low to high transposition record in

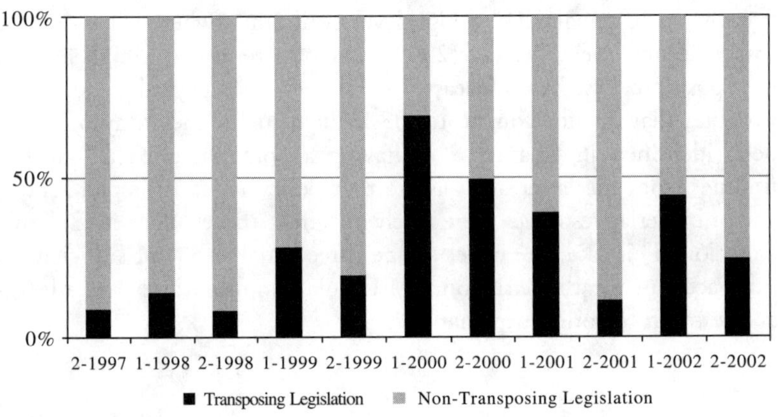

Source: Own compilation based on data from www.sejm.gov.pl.

Figure 3.6 Transposing laws as a percentage of the cabinet's total legislative output of draft parliamentary laws

the year 2000 occurred against the backdrop of a major reallocation of government resources to transposition. Almost 70 percent of the cabinet's total legislative output in parliamentary drafts was devoted to the transposition of the Community legislation. Similarly, the shift from medium to high record in 2002 was, in part, due to a relative increase in resources committed to transposition. The proportion of transposing laws rose from 11 percent in the second half of 2001 to 44 percent in the first six months of 2002. Conversely, a decline in the relative share of government resources devoted to transposition coincided with a downward shift in the transposition record that started already in the second half of 2000. Yet, as already indicated above, although changes in relative resource endowment may have led to higher transposition record, it is just as probable that higher transposition record necessitated shifts in resources. In that latter case, some external variable may have been responsible for inducing ministers to assign relatively more resources to transposition.

Conclusion

This chapter has mapped cross-temporal variation in the dynamics of EU rule adoption in Poland. The chapter shows that, in the period under investigation, the transposition record varied significantly. In 1997–1999, the Polish cabinet had a low record. From 2000, it had improved and remained at a high level until 2001, when it deteriorated to a medium level. The year 2002 brought a return to a high level of transposition. Last but not least, the chapter has analyzed the effect of variables that do not constitute the main focus of the study but have been identified in Chapter 2 as having a potential impact. The key findings from the latter analysis are that policy type, actor preferences, and ministerial resources were likely to affect the changes in EU rule adoption. This said, the effect of the three variables is not sufficient to fully account for the variation in EU rule adoption, and hence leaves ample room for other explanations.

CHAPTER 4

Core Executive Institutions in Poland

This chapter maps cross-temporal variation in position, authority, and information rules that the Polish core executive employed in order to extend selective incentives and monitoring to cabinet ministers and departments. It finds that over the first two years of the Buzek government, the core provided limited mobilization for ministries to comply with EU legislative commitments. In mid-1999, there was increased mobilization of lines ministries and their departments by the core executive. The chapter documents the emergence and consolidation of a strong "European" core under the Buzek and Miller cabinets.

Early Adaptation of the Core Executive

Internal and External Pressures for Institutional Change

In the mid-1990s the Polish "European" core executive came under increasing adaptation pressures. The need for institutional change was, first and foremost, due to a new integration dynamic that emerged after the EU reformulated its policy vis-à-vis the Central and Eastern European states. Having agreed to work toward enlargement at the 1993 Copenhagen summit, the EU became more actively involved in guiding adaptation processes in Poland, putting pressure on domestic actors to respond to the new integration challenges. In the area of legal alignment the European Commission published a Single Market White Paper that identified the core of the acquis communautaire to be adopted during the first stage of the preaccession.

At the same time, the Polish government became increasingly aware that the existing domestic institutions did not guarantee effective response to the new challenges (cf. NIK 1996). Since 1991, EU affairs had been coordinated inside the executive by a cabinet plenipotentiary, who had a noncabinet rank of undersecretary of state and was placed within the Office of the Council of Ministers (URM). The chief problem was that the plenipotentiary had too low a rank to redirect ministerial attention to EU adaptation (interview 13, p. 3; URM 1995b, p. 33). He was not a member of the cabinet, and his interlocutors in line ministries typically had the rank of director or undersecretary of state, which limited his coordination role to an administrative level.

The plenipotentiary's predicament was thus summarized by the parliamentary Europe Agreement Committee, writing in 1994 to Prime Minister Pawlak,

> The present organizational structure does not ensure sufficient degree of' adaptation, in particular due to lacuna in inter-ministerial coordination; the plenipotentiary for European integration and foreign assistance does not hold [sufficient] powers to perform [his] functions [. . .] which means that he is not able to secure and control the implementation of adjustment processes by appropriate ministries.
>
> (Komisja ds Układu Europejskiego 1994)

Unsurprisingly, when the Oleksy government resolved in November 1995 to prepare a comprehensive program for the transposition of the White Paper directives into the Polish legal system, the plenipotentiary met with serious problems in coordinating this process. Most significantly, he found it difficult to arbitrate competence conflicts where EU legislation cut through a number of ministerial portfolios. A close observer noted,

> The plenipotentiary did not have any powers [. . .] he ran into serious problems because he could not arbitrate conflicts. [. . .] It was simply not possible to solve a majority of conflicts without the involvement of the political level in the decision-making process. This is why a change was necessary.
>
> (interview 15, p. 4)

These internal and external pressures found their window of opportunity when the Oleksy government launched a comprehensive center of government reform in 1995. Plans for a systematic overhaul of the core executive had been developed already in early 1990s, following the breakdown of a change-team model of government characteristic for the Balcerowicz reforms (Zubek 2006). In 1995, the SLD-PSL cabinet returned to the reform idea, after the coalition had met with acute problems when implementing its "Strategy for Poland" (URM 1995b; Rydlewski 2002, pp. 87–88). Accompanied by a rhetoric of anticipatory adaptation to the EU, the center of government reform aimed to improve central coordination of government policies by reinforcing the powers of the prime minister, establishing new central agencies, and reorganizing line ministries (cf. Zubek 2001; Rydlewski 2002). The domestic management of EU-related affairs constituted a key focus of the center of government reform. The convergence of Europeanization pressures with a broader internal thrust for more effective governance thus paved the way to institutional change within the core executive.

New Position Rules: A Mixture of Hierarchy and Collectivity

In October 1996, the central agencies responsible for EU coordination went through a major reconfiguration. At the political level, the KIE was established as a collective supreme organ of state administration with a status corresponding to that of an individual minister.[1] It comprised eight cabinet ministers and had competence to coordinate Polish EU policy. The government intended the KIE to operate as an inner cabinet that would be much more powerful than traditional cabinet committees. Speaking in parliament the center of government reform minister said,

> The institution we are talking about here resembles, in some sense, a small cabinet for European integration. [. . .] Within [. . .] [its] competence and if no objection has been raised, its decision has binding force for [. . .] [its] members and the government administration. Let me emphasize that this institution has the power to make decisions.
>
> (Pol 1996a, 1996b)

The government maintained that, if an advisory committee were to be established, "all its decisions of strategic nature would need to be submitted to the full cabinet. This would lengthen the decision-making process, whereas adaptation to the EU must proceed smoothly" (Pol 1996c). This position was in line with a more general tendency within the center of government reform to reinforce central coordinating units. The government may also have been influenced by the experience of intense intercoalition conflicts that troubled the SLD-PSL cabinets (cf. Rydlewski 2000). It thus wanted to create a small forum in which the prime minister and the KIE secretary would be able to push through decisions without the involvement of the full cabinet. By arguing for a committee with wide decision-making powers, the government was also guided by more immediate political calculations. It planned to constrain the competences of the foreign minister in EU affairs, not least because, under the 1992 Small Constitution, the latter was one of three presidential ministers over whom the cabinet and the prime minister had hitherto limited influence (interview 20, p. 4; Nowina-Konopka 1996). The KIE's organizational format was modelled on domestic administrative blueprints, including the Committee for Scientific Research and other similar committee-type supreme organs (Pol 1996a). It also had some functional resemblance to the Presidium of the Council of Ministers, an inner cabinet that was abolished in the early 1990s.

The 1996 decision to establish the KIE committee and its permanent secretariat (UKIE) institutionalized new position rules, providing an organizational vehicle for administering selective incentives and monitoring in the area of EU transposition. The rules mandated the emergence of both collective and hierarchical relationships. The collective relationship arose through binding selected cabinet ministers to make decisions on EU matters as a group. The KIE committee thus emerged as a primary collectivity-enhancing mechanism. The hierarchical relationship was introduced through the creation of the KIE chair and the KIE secretary. The KIE chair had a formal mandate to manage the internal and external business of the committee. The KIE secretary—a position activated whenever the prime minister chaired the KIE committee—may be viewed as an agent retained by the KIE committee to assist the KIE chair in the day-to-day management of the committee. Another hierarchical relationship existed between the committee and the non-KIE members of the cabinet. The KIE enjoyed the status of an inner cabinet with powers to make binding decisions in lieu of the full council of ministers in matters related to EU integration. This arrangement was predicated on the prime ministerial chairmanship of the KIE.

The Limited Development of Authority and Information Rules

Despite its broad coordination mandate, the KIE had rather weakly institutionalized powers in EU transposition (interview 13, p. 3; interview 14, p. 3). As a UKIE official said, "The parliamentary act establishing the KIE [. . .] provides for compatibility screening and refers generally to coordination and monitoring [but] this is a very soft mandate" (interview 26, p. 4). The vagueness of the KIE's brief was, in large part, a result of deliberate design. In its desire to pool ministerial competences in a committee with decision-making powers, the government was constrained by the constitutional principle of ministerial autonomy. If it had specified the KIE's powers and those of its chairman in too much detail, the entire construct would have been liable to strong opposition from cabinet ministers and, possibly, a legal challenge before the constitutional court. Hence, the KIE's position was reinforced through a supreme organ status, but the government stopped short of furnishing it with specific coordination and control powers.

In 1996–1997 the indeterminacy of the KIE's formal mandate did not become evident, not least because the principal responsibility for facilitating, monitoring, and enforcing collective commitments made by Polish ministers within the KIE rested with Prime Minister Włodzimierz Cimoszewicz, who became the first chair of the KIE. He had both formal and informal authority to direct the work of the KIE committee and to represent it in relations with other ministers. The KIE chairman received operational support from the KIE secretary, Danuta Hübner, who headed the UKIE. The prime minister could rely on his strong political and institutional position to provide the necessary leadership for the KIE. Thanks to his involvement, the KIE was able to review transposing legislation, adopt an adaptation program, and attempt to resolve conflicts among ministers (cf. Internal Memo KIE 26/03/1997 1997; KIE Protocol 4/1997 1997; KIE Protocol 5/1997 1997; Official Communication SekrMinDH/533/97/DK-jp 1997).

Yet, given the approaching parliamentary elections, the KIE secretary and her secretariat had little time to institutionalize their powers vis-à-vis other ministers. In effect, when Hübner was leaving in October 1997, no regular monitoring was in place to control transposition work at ministry level. Ministers were required to report progress in the implementation of the new transposition program only every six months (cf. KIE Protocol 3/1997 1997). The first such reporting exercise was scheduled for December 1997. Neither did the KIE secretary provide routine transposition guidance. The only instrument in this regard was provided by a largely reactive EU compatibility assessment carried out for all government-initiated legislative drafts. However, a proposal to redesign the compatibility screening procedure in such a way as to authorize the KIE secretary and the UKIE to issue legislative guidelines was not implemented (Official Communication SEkrMinDH/174/97/DHP 1997; UKIE Internal Document March 1997 1997; interview 13, pp. 3–4; interview 21, pp. 6–7). Finally, the KIE secretary developed limited enforcement powers independent of the prime minister and frequently had to rely on the latter's personal intervention in case of ministerial noncompliance (interview 14, pp. 3–4; interview 15, p. 3).

To summarize, between autumn 1996 and autumn 1997, the position rules creating the KIE committee and the KIE chair/secretary operated with limited related authority and information rules. The latter had to be developed through separate institution-building processes that would require time and resources. Hence, in the meantime, selective incentives and monitoring were extended primarily by invoking the established authority and information rules attached to the position of the prime minister, who acted as the KIE chair. The prospect of sanctions or rewards from the prime minister provided a central incentive for ministers and departments to make contributions to EU rule adoption. Of course, given the overloaded schedule of any prime minister, such mobilizations were likely to be erratic and limited to specific issues. In any case, given the availability of alternative rules and the prospect of the oncoming parliamentary elections, only a few authority and information rules emerged in the period that were directly attached to the position of the KIE committee and the KIE chair/KIE secretary. Three such rules stand out. First, ministers agreed to implement a joint transposition program and to review progress twice yearly within the KIE, while the KIE secretary was asked to act as the monitor. Second, the KIE committee also started to acquire competence to consider transposing legislation, though mainly in emergency situations. Third, the KIE secretary retained the power to screen legislation for EU compatibility, but attempts to widen the scope of that competence were unsuccessful.

The Core Declines

In October 1997, at the start of the Jerzy Buzek government's tenure, the extent to which line ministries were mobilized in EU rule adoption by the core executive declined. The key contributing factor was the internal incohesiveness of the AWS-UW governing coalition that pushed the Buzek cabinet toward ministerial-type government. Not without significance was also a relative lack of domestic and external incentives for the strengthening of the existing core executive institutions. Under such conditions, party political configurations led to a general downgrading of central coordination and control and largely prevented ministers from responding promptly to revealed organizational deficiencies.

The Impact of Party Configurations

The AWS and the UW—two parties that formed the coalition supporting the Buzek government—were in many ways strange political bedfellows. The UW was a strongly liberal party headed by Leszek Balcerowicz, who was finance minister in the first noncommunist government of Tadeusz Mazowiecki. The AWS was a diverse mixture of trade unionists, Christian democrats, and conservative nationalists, headed by the head of the Solidarity Trade Union, Marian Krzaklewski. Despite such fundamental differences, the two parties came together, mainly based on historical postdissident lineage. The programmatic incohesiveness of the AWS-UW coalition was also marked in the area of EU-related domestic alignment. Although both the AWS and the UW were committed to European integration in principle, major differences persisted at the level of practical policy choices. The AWS opted for a gradual alignment sensitive to the interests of large state enterprises and lent a sympathetic ear to reports from socioeconomic interests about difficulties in complying with EU requirements. The UW was much more euro-enthusiastic, advocating a much quicker adaptation that would benefit the emerging small- and medium-sized private sector.

It must also be noted that, at the start of the Buzek government's tenure, ministers did not consider EU accession a top priority for the cabinet. The negotiations had not started until spring 1998, and the EU institutions had not yet exerted strong pressures on the Polish government. The cabinet's and prime minister's interest was firmly with national politics and the four ambitious reforms launched in local government, health care, education, and social insurance (interview 14, pp. 6–7; interview 15, p. 5). These issues received most attention in parliament, the media, and within linkage institutions with socioeconomic interests, while EU accession was only beginning to stir some political interest. It must also be noted that euro-sceptic factions inside the AWS further pushed the cabinet's policy on Europe toward the lowest common denominator (interview 15, p. 5).

The combination of party configurations and weak internal and external incentives led to a decline in the position of the "European" core executive. The position of the KIE chairman deteriorated after Buzek conceded to his party's pressure to appoint Ryszard Czarnecki to the post. Although a full cabinet member, Czarnecki commanded little authority among his ministerial colleagues, mainly on account of his young age, relative political inexperience, and limited expertise in European affairs. A UKIE official said,

> Minister Czarnecki [. . .] found it extremely difficult to mobilize other ministers. [. . .] He was just one of cabinet ministers and, although he was responsible for EU affairs, he had no expertise in this area. A situation in which minister Czarnecki would arbitrate a conflict between, say, Balcerowicz [finance minister and deputy prime minister] and Tomaszewski [home minister and deputy prime minister] was simply unthinkable.
>
> (interview 27, p. 5)

Further, despite inheriting a weakly institutionalized position in EU transposition, Czarnecki had limited personal incentives to push for more powers in this area. As a leader of a euro-sceptic faction in the AWS, Czarnecki wished to improve the UKIE's legitimacy within government by, inter alia, making it known that he considered transposition commitments undertaken by the previous government too ambitious (interview 20, p. 5).

Czarnecki's position as the KIE chair was checked by Bronisław Geremek, foreign minister and senior member of the UW, who frequently contested the former's policies (interview 20, p. 4; interview 27, p. 5; interview 38, p. 1). Their conflicts were, of course, as much political as structural. The KIE removed one of the most prestigious policy areas from the Foreign Ministry's remit and turf wars between the KIE chairman and the foreign minister were to some extent inevitable (interview 27, p. 5).

Inside his own secretariat, Czarnecki was also kept in check by Piotr Nowina-Konopka, a UW-nominated deputy minister. A public conflict with Nowina-Konopka was later a major contributing factor in Czarnecki's dismissal in mid-1998 (Subotić 1998).

More significantly, unlike Hübner, Czarnecki could not rely on the prime minister's support. EU integration was not a major priority for Buzek, not least because he had little personal experience in foreign affairs (interview 20, pp. 1–2; interview 36, p. 2). Buzek himself was also sceptical about the relative benefits of the integration process and, early in his term, considered renegotiation of the Europe Agreement (interview 15, p. 5). Perhaps, more importantly, Prime Minister Buzek suffered from a weak political stature. His leadership was undermined, first and foremost, by the incohesiveness of his own party, the AWS. Marked programmatic differences and ongoing internal disputes within the AWS pushed Buzek into a constant balancing act between different factions of his own party. His role as prime minister was further weakened by the presence of the AWS leader Krzaklewski outside the government. Buzek's authority in cabinet was often challenged by Balcerowicz, who was also the leader of the AWS' coalition partner, the UW. Having no independent power base, the prime minister was frequently held hostage by deals struck between Krzaklewski and Balcerowicz (Zubek 2001, 2006).

Organizational Fragmentation of the "European" Core

Rather than strengthening the role of the "European" core, the AWS and the UW were thus more interested in shackling the KIE chair and in downgrading the competencies of the UKIE and the KIE committee. This was most evident in the organizational fragmentation of the core when, after protracted political bargaining between the two coalition parties, the chief negotiator and his accession coordination machinery were placed outside the KIE and the UKIE. Buzek and Czarnecki were opposed to placing the chief negotiator within the UW-dominated Foreign Office (MSZ), but the attachment within the UKIE was contested by the UW leaders (interview 34, p. 2). The main candidate for the job, Jan Kułakowski, former ambassador to the EU, also rejected the latter option (interview 49, p. 1). A high-level UKIE official said, "Kułakowski himself did not agree [to the UKIE attachment], since he believed the problems that the negotiations entailed would be of the kind that he could be effective only if he were deputy foreign minister or was located close to the prime minister" (interview 34, p. 7).

In the end, a compromise solution was chosen, and Kułakowski was appointed cabinet plenipotentiary at secretary of state level within the KPRM. The chief negotiator stood at the head of a Negotiation Team that comprised undersecretaries of state nominated by line ministries, though appointed in a personal capacity by the prime minister. Kułakowski had two deputies at secretary of state level, one from the Foreign Ministry and the other from the UKIE. The team's permanent secretary was an undersecretary of state from the UKIE. The team was assisted by an interministerial committee for the accession negotiations that had operated at undersecretary level since mid-1997 to screen domestic legislation for negotiations problems. The committee was led by the KIE chairman, and Kułakowski became its deputy chair (see figure 4.1).

The separation of the UKIE from the chief negotiator led to intense interorganizational rivalries. Having lost his bid to have the chief negotiator

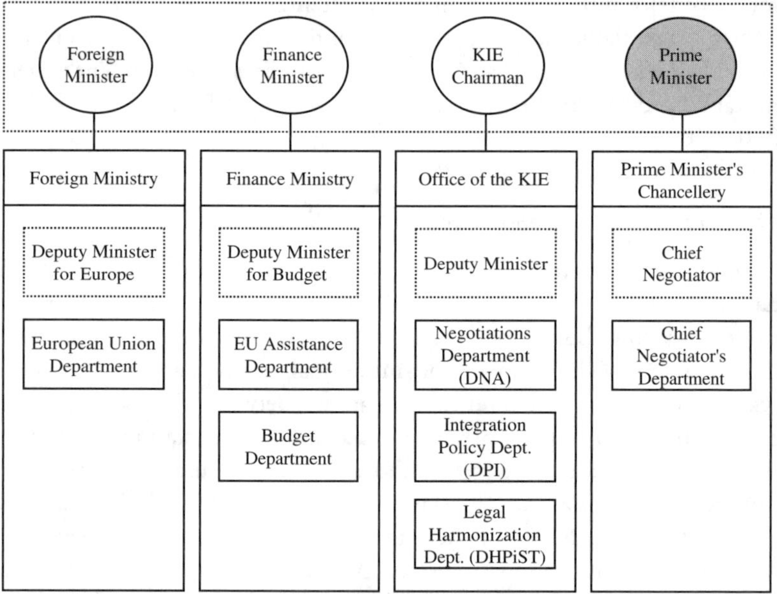

Source: Own compilation.

Figure 4.1   Individual and collective actors in EU affairs within the Polish core executive in 1998

as his deputy, Czarnecki aspired to control his staff at operational level (interview 34, p. 6; interview 30, p. 3). A KPRM official said, "[The relations] were terrible. The Christian Democrats' appointees [at the UKIE] wanted to have the widest possible control over us but had no professional justification, for these people had limited expertise in EU affairs. They took every chance to incapacitate us. It was a fierce fight" (interview 30, p. 3). The rivalry was also evident in Czarnecki's refusal to second some of the UKIE personnel to Kułakowski. Since mid-1997, the UKIE had had a Department for Accession Negotiations (DNA), providing administrative support to the interministerial committee for accession negotiations. As Kułakowski was not able to retain a large staff at the KPRM for budgetary reasons, he asked for the DNA personnel to be placed under his control (interview 30, p. 5). It was only after Buzek's intervention that Czarnecki reluctantly agreed to delegate one section of the DNA to work directly for the chief negotiator, though it remained organizationally part of the UKIE (cf. Official Communication SJK/7-37/98 1998).

The hybrid organizational arrangement fuelled further rivalries between the UKIE and the KPRM. The seconded section, called the Centre Supporting the Accession Negotiations (CONA), though formally part of the DNA, became increasingly alienated from the rest of the UKIE, working more and more closely with Kułakowski's small team in the KPRM (cf. Internal Memo DNA/1632/98 1998). It quickly marginalized the remaining part of the DNA—in November 1998 it already employed 14 staff, while the rest of the DNA had four personnel, including the director. A UKIE minister said,

> This [institutional arrangement] posed many problems. In formal terms the [CONA] answered to the UKIE management, but at an operational level it was accountable to minister Kułakowski. But any attempt to exercise the formal lines of accountability was considered an attack on the chief negotiator, and the CONA management or Kułakowski complained that we put pressure on them. [. . .] [L]ater [. . .] Kułakowski was aware that the CONA worked without any supervision and had become alienated in the sense that it only did what it wanted.
>
> (interview 15, p. 11)

The complex organizational matrix inhibited information flows between the CONA and the rest of the UKIE (interview 13, p. 12). An official of the Department of Integration Policy (DPI) said, "[The cooperation] was not too good. The [CONA] had an odd status: we were all on the same budget but they answered to the chief negotiator who was in the KPRM. Even our minister sometimes did not have any influence over what they did. This gives you some idea how hard it was for someone like a department director to be able to affect their work (interview 8, p. 7).

The interparty competition and a general malaise in EU affairs further prevented ministers from addressing organizational problems that were revealed in the process of transposition. The KIE chairman was, for example, hampered in his role as facilitator of EU transposition by weak institutional linkages between his secretariat and other central agencies within the core executive. This was particularly apparent in the UKIE's relationship with the KPRM. During the semiannual planning cycle, the chancellery's Cabinet Agenda Department did not verify whether line ministries included transposition commitments in their inputs into the cabinet legislative plan (interview 7, p. 13; interview 2, p. 5). A chancellery official said, "Cooperation with them [UKIE] is limited. There is also limited information with regard to the decisions made in the KIE committee. [. . .] Our role has been limited to routing of documentation from the UKIE to the cabinet" (interview 4, p. 11).

There was also limited communication with the Finance Ministry led by Balcerowicz. The transposition planning process was weakly coordinated with the budgetary cycle. A UKIE minister said, "The translation [of transposition commitments] into the budget was delayed in time [. . .] unfortunately the two processes were not correlated. The work on the national programme for the adoption of the *acquis* was finalized in mid-year, at a time when the discussions on the next budget only started" (interview 16, p. 1). Furthermore, since 1994 the Finance Ministry had blocked proposals to introduce EU-related expenditure into the formal budgetary classification, concerned that this might legitimize ministerial bids for more budgetary resources (Komisja ds Układu Europejskiego 1994, 1996). In effect, line ministries had subsumed EU-related expenditure under existing budget heads, which made it difficult for the centre to control what resources were in fact allocated to transposition (cf. Official Communication SekrMinPS/1296/99 1999).

Finally, besides problems resulting from the UKIE-KPRM divide, there were also organizational tensions within the UKIE itself (see figure 4.2). The key issue was limited cooperation between the two main departments involved in legal adaptation. The DPI, employing 19

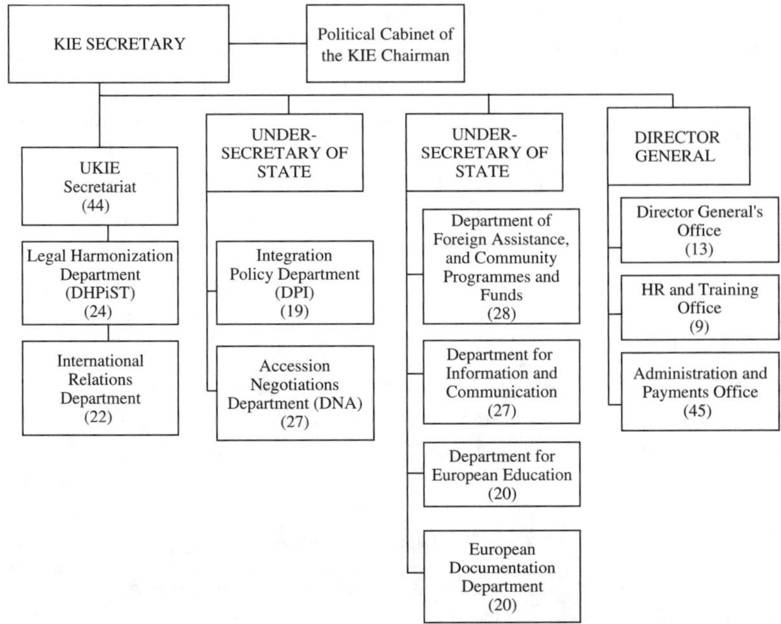

Source: Own compilation based on Executive Regulation No. 6 of the KIE Chair of June 3, 1998 and Executive Regulation No.1 of the KIE Secretary of September 30, 1998; staff figures were supplied to the author by the UKIE Secretariat.

Figure 4.2 UKIE's organigram in December 1998 (staff levels in brackets)

staff, mostly with an economics background, was the lead department for supporting interministerial coordination. Its brief covered, in particular, the planning and monitoring of adaptation action at ministry level. The other department was the Department of Legal Harmonization (DHPiST), staffed with 24 lawyers, which had a more analytical profile and concentrated mainly on checking all government-initiated drafts for compliance with the EU law. To a large extent these two departments worked independently. A UKIE official said, "There were no stable, binding procedures requiring the two departments to work together closely. And, if there are no such procedures or similar frameworks, then bureaucratic units have a tendency to work and function autonomously" (interview 26, pp. 9–10).

The weak cooperation was most evident during interministerial consultations. Acting on behalf of the KIE chairman, the DHPiST prepared a legal compatibility assessment, while the DPI provided more general comments on the compliance with national transposition commitments. Despite a complementary character of these tasks, the two departments had developed no standard operating procedure for communication at an operational level (interview 25, pp. 5–7; interview 8, pp. 10–11). In effect, the two opinions frequently provided competing assessments (cf. Internal Memo DHPiST/173/98 1998). The relationship between the DHPiST and the DPI was hindered, in large part, by different professional profiles of their staff and personal ambitions of their directors (interview 26, p. 10). The sympathies of the UKIE leadership also mattered. Under Czarnecki the rivalry between the DHPiST and the DPI was further fuelled by the KIE chairman's close collaboration with the DHPiST and his relative mistrust of the undersecretary of state supervising the DPI (interview 25, pp. 5–7; interview 40, p. 1).

The Impact on Authority and Information Rules

Problematic political leadership combined to dampen the central control over the process of EU transposition. In late 1997 and early 1998, this was clearly evident when the Buzek government set out to prepare the NPAA. In response to the EU-formulated accession partnership, Polish ministries, for the first time, had to plan transposition of the entire Community legislation. In December 1997 the KIE committee approved a list of adaptation priorities to be addressed and a general template that ministries had to follow in the preparation of the program (cf. UKIE Internal Document 10/12/1997 1997). But the KIE chairman and the UKIE left ministries much freedom in the practical "who, when and what" of transposition (interview 8, p. 5; interview 46, p. 5). Responsibility for identifying EU measures and domestic legislative actions was firmly with line ministers. The UKIE only collated and checked their inputs for compliance with the preagreed format. A UKIE official said,

> The first NPAA [. . .] contained information that a particular ministry wanted it to contain. Ministries were not required to identify all EU legal measures for each priority they addressed [and] [. . .] identified only those EU measures that they thought they would be able to transpose, given the cabinet legislative plan and the like. So [commitments] were a bit accidental. For instance, if a ministry was working on a new energy

law, it would decide to implement this and that [directive] on the margins of that new law.

(interview 21, p. 3)

The ministries alone were responsible for making provisions within their budgets to implement the NPAA. The same decentralized rule applied to the NPAA's integration with the cabinet's semiannual legislative planning cycle (cf. Official Communication SekrMinRCZ/2047/w/98/DPI-TBG 1998).

Most importantly, the Czarnecki-led KIE departed from a practice that slowly had evolved under Cimoszewicz that the committee had competence to process EU-related legislation. Draft transposing measures were prepared by line ministries and then routed through the standard interministerial procedures and cabinet committees together with nontransposing legislation. This change was part of a more general downgrading of the KIE's status. The committee's predicament was revealed in the low frequency of its meetings, the secondary rank of its participants, and the general nature of its agenda. Between October 1997 and June 1998, the KIE met on a monthly basis and held only eight sessions. Each meeting lasted approximately 2.5 hours on average. Its agenda was dominated by formal presentations of reports and documents rather than real decision making. To salvage the KIE's authority, the prime minister attended and chaired the committee meetings, despite Czarnecki being formally in the chair (interview 20, p. 3). Even so, the KIE evolved toward a monthly debating forum, attended mainly by junior ministers, civil servants, and numerous guests, including academics and parliamentarians (interview 14, p. 4; interview 15, pp. 4–5). A close observer said,

> The KIE did not have any legislative initiative. All in-coming draft laws were only screened [for EU compatibility] by the UKIE and the Foreign Office. The KIE's role was a mere formality. [. . .] The KIE heard reports. [. . .] It had no control powers or powers to take initiatives.
>
> (interview 36, p. 4)

Denied the opportunity to set the legislative agenda within the KIE committee, the KIE chairman and the UKIE confined their role to reactive comments on draft legislation within interministerial consultations. Like all other ministries, the KIE received draft legislation for comments and could review its compliance with transposition commitments (interview 8, p. 11; interview 46, p. 7). But the UKIE's position in the process was on a par with other ministries, and its opinion had the status of one ministry's comment on another's draft.

A slightly more authoritative instrument was provided by the EU compatibility assessment, a procedure under which the KIE chairman screened all legislation for compliance with the Community law. Based on the authority of the cabinet byelaws, such assessments had to be attached to all cabinet submissions. However, their effectiveness as a transposition guidance was limited, since they focused on legal conformity per se rather than on implementation of transposition commitments (interview 45, p. 8). A UKIE lawyer thus summarized the approach adopted in the compatibility assessment,

> We [the DHPiST] concentrated more on legal implementation rather than on planning legal adaptation. [. . .] [I]n all honesty, we did not care when, in what sequence and by whom such adaptation will be carried out. For us, it was the result that mattered. We made sure that changes that must be made were made in compatibility with the EU directives. The deadlines and timing were of secondary importance to us.
>
> (interview 13, p. 2)

The UKIE staff were rarely involved in the lawmaking process at operational level. Only sporadically did they participate in interministerial conciliation committees (cf. Internal Memo DPI 12/10/1999 1999), while legislation-focused task forces involving the UKIE staff were the exception rather than the rule (interview 52, pp. 7–8). A high-level UKIE lawyer admitted that the DHPiST had interacted with line ministries only when the latter had disagreed with their compatibility assessment (interview 25, p. 10). This passive role of the UKIE's legal services was confirmed by an Agriculture Ministry official, who said, "They [UKIE lawyers] maintained—which was probably true—that they had too much work to be able to help us or offered to help us at such future times that we were able to solve the problems ourselves by then (interview 42, p. 4).

Transposition work at line-ministry level was not subject to weekly or monthly monitoring procedures that could mobilize ministerial officials on a regular basis. When adopting the NPAA in May 1998, the KIE committee asked its chairman to report on progress only once a year. Part of the problem was that the transposition commitments contained in the NPAA provided too general an indication of the transposition tasks and the timetable for their implementation. A minister said, "The national programme [NPAA] was not liable to week-to-week or month-to-month monitoring given that transposition deadlines were identified with yearly precision" (interview 15, p. 7).

Admittedly, the UKIE Secretariat did track legislative changes on the margins of parallel processes (interview 15, pp. 6–7; interview 27, p. 1; interview 46, p. 5). This was chiefly done during the preparation of the Polish input into the Commission's regular progress report (interview 8, p. 1). The first such report was to be published in autumn 1998 and, already in midyear, line ministries were asked by the UKIE to prepare the necessary information (cf. Official Communication SekrMinJP/355/w/98/DPI-ES 1998). Another opportunity, although perhaps less effective, was provided by the meetings of the Europe Agreement institutions, at which Polish ministries presented the Commission with an update on transposition (interview 46, p. 1). The final monitoring channel was a bimonthly updating by line ministries of the Harmonogram Database, which since early 1996 had been maintained by the TAIEX office in Brussels (interview 21, p. 6). Besides such institutionalized processes, the UKIE Secretariat also undertook ad hoc interventions in crisis situations (interview 46, p. 5). While taken together these information channels ensured that the UKIE had a fairly good idea about the progress of transposition—they had the effect of mobilizing ministerial officials in irregular, at best six-monthly, intervals.

The KIE chairman and the UKIE had also limited institutional levers to sanction noncompliance if transposition delays were detected. Neither the KIE committee nor the cabinet considered transposition progress on a regular basis, which made it difficult for the KIE chairman or the prime minister to provide positive or negative incentives to non-compliant ministers. Enforcement was thus undertaken only in crisis situations through the KIE chairman's ad hoc interventions with the prime minister. A UKIE official said,

If one of our experts at the department saw there was a problem, for example, a particular draft law was scheduled for the end of May, and came April no work was under way, he or she would alert his or her boss and the department director who would, in turn, check what the status was, and if that did not help, we would take the matter up [to the minister].

(interview 46 , p. 5)

The effectiveness of such interventions was, however, adversely affected by the KIE chairman's weak political position and his gradually deteriorating relationship with the prime minister (interview 20, p. 3). This lack of enforcement from the center was recalled by an Economics Ministry official, who said, "I remember my surprise when a large number of tasks that had had to be undertaken in a given year or within some time brackets were subsequently deferred to a new deadline, [and this was done] completely without any consequences (interview 19, pp. 7–8).

Finally, after the accession negotiations were launched in March 1998, the core did not mobilize line ministers and their departments to translate the screening lists and negotiation positions into specific legislative blueprints. In large part, this lack of control seems to have stemmed from the confidential nature of negotiation documents. A UKIE official said, "In the beginning we adopted very restrictive rules as to the accessibility of negotiation-related documentation. Most of it was confidential and so it did not reach ordinary staff. And certainly this was a mistake. [. . .] [The documents] were only distributed to the members of the negotiation team at junior minister level" (interview 30, p. 6). In effect, by retaining the monopoly of negotiation-related information, the core made it difficult for ministerial staff to integrate negotiation commitments into their day-to-day work. An internal document thus summarized the situation: "The draft negotiation positions are prepared and analyzed by a small group of people and so the exact nature of negotiation commitments is not generally known to ministerial staff. As a result, when preparing programmes and draft laws central government staff do not take account of negotiation commitments" (UKIE Internal Document 12/07/1999 1999).

It is also important to note that transposition commitments fell between two stools within the core executive. Kułakowski's negotiation team focused initially on technical administrative support to line ministries during the screening process. An official at the DNA said,

Our role was that of pure organizational support. We focused on mundane but necessary things such as arranging travel, routing and consulting documents. And this is where our job ended. [. . .] At the start of the negotiations we were involved in the technical support of interministerial consultation meetings where screening lists A and B were discussed. [. . .] We were responsible for the flow of the entire [screening] documentation, i.e. sending lists to ministries, electronic communication, collating documents, attending the interministerial meetings. [. . .] We also kept all records.

(interview 32, p. 1)

When the negotiations were extended to cover the most sensitive issues, Kułakowski's focus shifted to the identification of the key negotiation problems (UKIE Internal Document 1998a). His team became more actively involved in shaping the nature of Polish negotiation commitments, in particular by developing arguments to substantiate ministerial requests for transitional periods (interview 30, p. 6). It also tackled regulatory and budgetary impact assessment (interview 10, p. 1; interview 58). But it had limited interest to assess legislative consequences of the negotiations. Some analytical work in this area was conducted in the DNA, but the DNA's reports were rarely practical enough and were not used as transposition guidance for ministries (interview 11, p. 2). In effect, the chief negotiator's team did not maintain regular monitoring or enforcement of the transposition commitments made during the negotiations. A UKIE official said,

> In my assessment the DNA had an important role to play when it came to the preparation of negotiations sessions, instructions, explanatory notes, etc. But they completely lost interest the moment a session was closed. They did not mind what happened afterwards. Of course there were certain crucial issues that captured their interest but these were [selected] issues that made it to the headlines.

(interview 46, p. 6)

Neither did the UKIE become involved in mobilizing ministries to make good on their screening and negotiation commitments. For one thing, the UKIE too had problems with accessing confidential negotiation documents. In September 1998, a UKIE junior minister wrote to the chief negotiator indicating that negotiation documents were not passed to the UKIE, which made it difficult to monitor the implementation of adaptation commitments (Official Communication SekrMinMKF/644/98/os 1998). The communication problems persisted and were again signalled by the UKIE the following year (cf. Internal Memo DHPiST/141/99 1999). Also, one needs to note that the UKIE did not play a prominent role in the formulation of the negotiation positions, which, counter to the formal procedure established in July 1998, were first approved by

Kułakowski's Negotiation Team and only then passed on to other ministries, including the UKIE, for interministerial consultations. In effect, the interministerial committee for the preparation of the accession negotiations, formally chaired by the UKIE head, was bypassed (Internal Memo DNA/355/99 1999).

Most significantly, the UKIE did not develop any regular procedure for integrating the screening and negotiation commitments into the NPAA. A DPI official said,

> We relied on institutional memory of our staff. Someone who had attended a negotiation session looked into his or her notes and suggested that the NPAA should be supplemented with this or that task. [. . .] We [also] received all formal protocols and instructions. There were also many personal contacts. [. . .] So it was informal cooperation, informal exchange of information.
>
> (interview 46, p. 6)

The situation was not much improved by an arrangement that each negotiation chapter had a central note-taker who attended all screening and negotiation sessions. These staff were recruited from three different central agencies—the UKIE, KPRM, and the Foreign Office—and hence provided little added value for coordination within the core executive. The KIE committee discussed transposition mainly in the context of the NPAA (cf. UKIE Internal Document 1998b). Similarly, the DPI continued to focus predominately on the NPAA as the bearing mark for EU transposition. The NPAA was thus quickly losing relevance as the key guidance instrument in EU transposition. The same was true of the transposition annex to the NPAA, which the UKIE's legal department, DHPiST, prepared in the second half of 1998. The DHPiST did not incorporate the specific issues disclosed during the screening sessions, but based it on much less precise original formulations made in early 1998. Unsurprisingly, the annex was quickly discarded as adding little value (interview 15, p. 15).

To summarize, between September 1997 and July 1998 (when Czarnecki resigned), the position rules relating to the KIE committee and the KIE chair remained unchanged. What changed, however, was the opportunity that existed under the Cimoszewicz government to invoke the formal and informal authority and information rules attached to the position of the prime minister. As demonstrated earlier, that possibility disappeared for two reasons. First, the Buzek government departed from the practice of prime ministerial chairmanship of the KIE committee and appointed a cabinet minister to the KIE chair. Second, and perhaps more importantly, the prime minister's weak political standing frequently prevented him from invoking his formal prerogatives, even though, in practice, he often presided over the KIE meetings.

Under these circumstances, ministers and departments faced only the limited authority and information rules attached directly to the position of the KIE chair and the KIE committee. These, however, had not been well institutionalized, as shown at the start of this chapter. Worse, the external and domestic incentives as well as the institutional setting did not facilitate the development of such rules. For one thing, neither Czarnecki nor Buzek had strong personal incentives to act as a political entrepreneur for such new rules. In any case, both had too weak a standing to make such an attempt likely to succeed. Moreover, the intracoalition conflicts prevented ministers from entering into collective commitments to new rules within the KIE. In fact, the KIE committee became less and less operational as the frequency of the meetings dropped, the agenda grew ceremonial, and ministers began to send junior deputies. Also, the ability of the KIE chair and the KIE committee to extend selective incentives and monitoring was undermined by a competition with the chief negotiator and the negotiations teams, fragmentation of resources such as personnel and finance, and organizational conflicts at departmental level within the UKIE. Finally, the accession negotiations had only just started and there was no pressure from the EU that would provide ministers incentives to develop new rules.

As a result, the authority and information rules attached to the position of the KIE chair/secretary and the KIE committee remained limited, both in number and in scope, throughout the period. The dearth of institutional incentives was most evident with regard to authority rules. In a departure from the practice that developed under the Cimoszewicz chairmanship, the KIE committee did not work on transposing legislation. Its involvement in the legislative process was limited to passive screening for EU compatibility performed by the KIE chair. Neither the KIE committee nor its chair had any authority to encourage ministers and departments to actively contribute to the transposition record. Also, the rivalry between the UKIE and the chief negotiator's team prevented the development of authority rules that would encourage the translation of screening tables into legislative commitments.

The situation looked slightly better when it came to information rules. But, although the KIE committee and the KIE chair were involved in planning and monitoring transposition, the applicable rules provided rather lightweight constraints on ministers and departments. In planning, only general templates were provided to ministries, and programs were collated from ministerial inputs without much substantive involvement by the KIE chair or the KIE committee. In monitoring, progress was comprehensively assessed by the KIE committee only once a year, with no weekly or monthly checks at the operational level.

The Neglected Core Persists

Between July 1998 and December 1998 a significant, albeit unsuccessful, attempt was undertaken to provide for new authority and information rules that would enhance intraexecutive incentives that ministers and departments faced in EU transposition. The opportunity for institutional change within the core executive arose when Prime Minister Buzek assumed the KIE chairmanship, following the departure of minister Czarnecki in July 1998. Czarnecki's position in cabinet had been on the decline since early 1998, not least because the smaller coalition party, the UW, lobbied for the prime minister to chair the KIE, an arrangement that would allow more maneuvering space to the UW-nominated foreign minister (interview 20, pp. 2–3; Rzeczpospolita 1998). But Czarnecki was more generally perceived as a weak Europe minister, and he was dismissed after Poland had lost a significant share of the Phare resources (Groblewski 1998; Subotić 1998). Standing at the KIE's helm, the prime minister appointed a new undersecretary of state within the UKIE, Maria Karasińska-Fendler, who became a provisional KIE secretary.

Having carried out a stocktaking exercise, Karasińska-Fendler alerted Buzek in September 1998 to serious transposition delays that had accumulated under Czarnecki. A UKIE minister said,

> Based on ministerial reports [Karasińska-Fendler] had the implementation of the NPAA measured in a single table with pluses and minuses where a law had been adopted or not adopted. The table generated a major turmoil in cabinet because it turned out that ministers undertook commitments but were not able to deliver.
>
> (interview 36, p. 5)

The new KIE secretary proposed to Buzek that the negotiation team be replaced with a smaller committee of state undersecretaries from the UKIE, Foreign Office, and the Economics Ministry (interview 36, p. 11). The KIE secretary further recommended that junior line ministers be required to produce—after each screening session—a detailed list of legislative initiatives that had to be undertaken to transpose relevant EU measures. The UKIE would then integrate the list with the NPAA on a regular basis (Bielecki 1998). In addition, Karasińska-Fendler wanted to establish a "rolling" catalogue of outstanding legislative drafts (KIE Protocol 8/1998 1998; UKIE Internal Document SS/2/1/009 1998). Finally, she proposed to reorganize the UKIE by dismissing around 150 people (interview 36, 11). Karasińska-Fendler's proposals were largely in line with similar suggestions made at the time by Chief Negotiator Kułakowski and other members of the Negotiation Team (cf. KPRM Internal Document 17/12/1998 1998; KPRM Internal Document SS/2/1/034 1998).

These proposals, however, remained largely unimplemented, culminating in Karasińska-Fendler's resignation in December 1998. There seem to have been two principal factors that contributed to the collapse of her reform plan. The first factor was Karasińska-Fendler's lack of wider political legitimacy within the government. Owing to an internal coalition deadlock, she was appointed only a provisional KIE secretary at undersecretary of state level. After Prime Minister Buzek had assumed the KIE chairmanship, the UW evoked an unwritten rule that guaranteed that if the minister came from one party, his first deputy had to be nominated by the other coalition party (interview 16, p. 7). As Buzek was a member of the AWS, the UW wanted to nominate his deputy, the KIE secretary (Sarjusz-Wolski 1999; Wielowieyska 1999; Subotić 1999b). The AWS failed to honour this arrangement, and the UW blocked a permanent appointment to the post. Karasińska-Fendler's provisional status and a relatively low rank within the administration proved a major handicap. A UKIE minister thus summarized Karasińska-Fendler's predicament: "[She] had no political power base and nobody supported her, neither the SLD, nor the Solidarity [AWS]" (interview 36, p. 3). A high-level UKIE official confirmed,

> There is a natural restraint when someone who is a provisional appointee contacts a full minister [. . .] also for a person who holds a position equivalent to an undersecretary of state it is more difficult to negotiate

> with a cabinet minister. [. . .] I think this is one of the reasons why the secretariat [the UKIE] was not able to achieve what it planned to do. [. . .] [O]ur authority to convince others or to impose what we had planned was inadequate.
>
> (interview 16, p. 8)

The second, and perhaps more important, factor was Karasińska-Fendler's inability to rely on the full support of the prime minister (interview 36, p. 7). Buzek, who despite becoming the KIE chair continued to have a weak political position within his cabinet and party, had neither personal motivation nor sufficient authority to back Karasińska-Fendler's proposals. Also, at the end of 1998, his government was finalizing work on the legislation introducing the social and economic reforms that were to be launched from January 1999. Buzek's attention was thus firmly on domestic politics (interview 36, p. 2). A minister said, "The most serious problem then was that [Karasińska-Fendler] could not convince the prime minister that, while he would not win elections on European integration alone, he would be certain to lose them [if his government failed on that issue]. But because this was not a political priority, [Karasińska-Fendler] was a redundant minister" (interview 36, p. 7).

This episode demonstrates that, between June and December 1998, the position, authority, and information rules that the core executive had at its disposal to induce ministers and departments to contribute to EU rule adoption remained unchanged in their scope and substance. This was despite Karasińska-Fendler's entrepreneurship undertaken in the face of mounting evidence of transposition delays. Her failure to trigger institutional change raises two important points. First, it shows that the outcome of entrepreneurship in institution building was heavily dependent on the prime minister's support, the preferences of the main coalition parties, and Karasińska-Fendler's own political and institutional standing. In a situation where such conditions were not favourable, the KIE secretary's mission could hardly succeed. Second, it is interesting to note that, although Buzek assumed the KIE chairmanship, his weak political standing largely prevented him from exercising the formal and informal prerogatives attached to the prime ministerial position. This was in stark contrast to Prime Minister Cimoszewicz in the years 1996–1997. Hence, the weak institutionalization of the rules attached to the position of the KIE committee and the KIE chair could not be compensated by strong incentives extended by Prime Minister Buzek. In any case, due to an overloaded schedule of any premier, his interventions could only be ad hoc and limited to specific issues.

External and Domestic Conditions Change

The conditions that had until then prevented the reinforcement of the authority and information rules began to change from early 1999. As a result, both Prime Minister Buzek and Chief Negotiator Kułakowski emerged as key entrepreneurs seeking to develop institutional levers with which to mobilize ministers to adopt transposing legislation.

The Prime Minister as Rule Entrepreneur

In spring 1999, EU transposition attracted the close attention of Prime Minister Buzek. There were a number of reasons for the prime minister's new interest—most notably, (i) a gradual evolution of his personal stance on EU affairs, (ii) the prospect of an impending crisis in accession negotiations, and (iii) domestic political calculations within the AWS-UW cabinet. The first point to note is that Buzek's personal preferences as prime minister evolved from relative indifference to increasing engagement in EU affairs. A UKIE minister said, "Since he took the office, the prime minister had undergone a major personal transformation, that is, he changed from a largely unknown politician with a rather simplistic worldview to a politician who appreciated Poland's position in the external world" (interview 15, p. 13). In this, Buzek was aided by his advisors. A senior advisor recollected,

> Arkuszewski [the *chef de cabinet*] managed to organize a really exceptional exercise—a personal workshop in European integration for the prime minister. We took him away for one whole day. [. . .] And three people lectured the prime minister on what the European Union was. [. . .] We covered it all, from the Treaty of Paris to the present day, going through all the EU policies one by one.
>
> (interview 35, p. 2)

In large part, the prime minister's new interest in EU-related affairs was also a function of the negotiation dynamic that, in early 1999, had reached an advanced stage. Increasingly drawn into the accession process, Buzek soon realized that the slow pace of domestic adaptation was becoming Poland's chief liability and, if unaddressed, it might seriously undermine the country's bid for EU membership (interview 29, p. 13; interview 15, p. 5; interview 16, p. 4). Most significantly, his attention was caught by alarming signals from the EU (interview 49, p. 4). A UKIE official said,

> There were official visits by European Commissioners who directly said what they thought about the situation. [. . .] There was an exchange of letters, perhaps not yet at political level but no longer at official level, for example, communications from Poland Director at DG Enlargement to the KIE secretary or minister [Jarosław] Pietras, the secretary of the negotiation team. All these contributed [to increased awareness of the prime minister].
>
> (interview 46, p. 2)

The decisive moment came at the end of April 1999, when a negative assessment was repeated by the European Commission during the seventh meeting of the Association Committee. The Commission clearly stated that, unless Poland improved its adaptation record, it would not be admitted in the first round of enlargement and would lose a substantial share of the financial assistance (UKIE Internal Document June 1999 1999, p. 2). A UKIE minister said,

> In April 1999 we had a meeting of the association committee where the Commission indicated that it would take an extremely critical position [in the forthcoming progress report on Poland]. And that information reached the prime minister—it managed to get through all the organizational shields that usually surround the prime minister and reached him. And the prime minister decided to take this up.
>
> (interview 15, p. 13)

But equally important were domestic signals indicating that EU transposition lagged behind. Most significantly, the revision of the NPAA in March 1999 revealed serious holdups in the transposition process (interview 16, p. 4) (Apanowicz 1999). As a follow-up, the UKIE provided a detailed report to the prime minister and identified a list of priority areas where immediate action had to be taken (cf. KIE Protocol 03/1999 1999).

The prime minister's final conversion to EU transposition came when he saw the opportunity for using integration with Europe as a way of injecting new impetus into his government. By mid-1999, the socioeconomic reforms that formed the core of the AWS-UW coalition had been well advanced, and the Buzek government looked for new challenges (cf. Paradowska 1999a). The introduction of fresh policy issues was also hoped to prop up the waning popularity of the government. Although the coalition parties were split on what the government should concentrate on, both the AWS and the UW agreed that EU integration had to be addressed (cf. Paradowska 1999b). A UKIE minister said, "Looking for [new] objectives for his cabinet [Buzek] identified European integration as an objective that he was able to realize, and one that would both let him avoid a crisis and achieve something" (interview 15, p. 13). Accordingly, in September 1999, the prime minister identified EU-related legal adaptation as one of five major priorities for the last two years of his cabinet's term (Gazeta Wyborcza 1999; Official Communication SekrMinPS/1768/99/DPI-mk 1999).

Additional Rule Entrepreneurship by the Chief Negotiator

Buzek's interest in transposition was matched by an increasing attention that the chief negotiator and his staff paid to the process of internal adaptation. Around the early 1999, when the negotiations started to cover the most crucial chapters of the acquis communautaire, Kułakowski and his team began to realize that the slow pace of transposition was adversely affecting their ability to achieve further progress (interview 27, page 2). A close observer said,

> The chief negotiator did not have any influence over the cabinet, did not have any lever to force full ministers to implement what the members of the negotiation team at a deputy minister rank declared. All were under the illusion that the negotiations would last long, and so they did not have to rush things, there being so much other more important business. And at some point we realized that there were a large number of things which we had promised to do but which were lagging behind.
>
> (interview 30, p. 3)

Kułakowski's new interest was also a direct result of a significant change in the negotiation tactics on the part of the EU. Since the early 1999, the European Commission had started to place more emphasis on the pace of adaptation as a measure for assessing the candidate country's progress toward accession. The Polish ambassador to the EU wrote,

"The emphasis has clearly shifted from measuring negotiation progress by the number of closed chapters to measuring progress by the degree of [internal] adaptation, and the pace of accession negotiations is now determined by the pace of internal alignment in the candidate countries" (Official Communication SJK/456-406/99 1999).

Realizing that further progress in the accession negotiations was not viable unless the transposition backlog was dealt with, Kułakowski's Negotiation Team started looking internally for ways in which to influence the transposition process (interview 27, p. 2). A member of Kułakowski's staff thus captured this new dynamic, "We tried to save the negotiations. We understood very quickly that unless we gave them a major shake-up, found some way to give a jolt to the structures responsible for transposition, then in some areas we would have major problems. And so this was a very pragmatic decision" (interview 35, p. 4).

The Failure of Existing Rules as a Window of Opportunity

In mid-1999 both Prime Minister Buzek and Chief Negotiator Kułakowski realized that, without the creation and enforcement of new authority and information rules, it would not be possible to extend effective selective incentives and monitoring to ministers and departments. This realization came as a result of two related events. First, in spring 1999, Buzek failed to secure a prerequisite for change to institutional rules—the appointment of a permanent KIE secretary and the head of the UKIE. That post had been vacant since December 1998 and, as the KIE chairman, the prime minister was interested in solving the protracted impasse. In line with his new interest in EU transposition, Buzek made it known in March 1999 that he wanted Kułakowski to become the KIE secretary, thus merging the UKIE and KPRM teams (cf. Kublik 1999; Subotić 1999b).

But the UW refused to accept this arrangement and put forward Jerzy Osiatyński, a former UW finance minister, for the KIE secretary. In return, the UW offered to give up the post of culture minister. The AWS initially agreed but later changed tack, fearing that the UW would in effect have full control over foreign policy (Subotić 1999a). Consequently, Buzek suggested that the UW nominate Jacek Saryusz-Wolski, former cabinet plenipotentiary for European integration in 1991–1996, but the UW leaders refused. A minister said,

Mr Saryusz-Wolski is not a member of the Freedom Union or a person recommended by our party. [If he were to be appointed as the KIE secretary] we would need to receive back the post of the culture minister or an equivalent post. This would be a good solution. But the problem is that prime minister Buzek wants the UW to nominate Mr Saryusz-Wolski.

(Sarjusz-Wolski 1999, p. 3)

As a result the situation within the UKIE did not improve. Buzek appointed Saryusz-Wolski his personal advisor at the KPRM, and the deadlock continued, precluding any further change. In the event, in April that year, Buzek appointed Paweł Samecki as yet another provisional KIE secretary at state undersecretary level.

The second event came when, in mid-1999, Buzek tried, and failed, to mobilize his ministers in the area of EU transposition through the existing institutional framework. Seeking to avoid an openly negative assessment in the forthcoming Commission's progress report, the prime minister convened three KIE meetings devoted entirely to transposition in May and June (KIE Protocol 05/1999 1999; KIE Protocol 06/1999 1999; KIE Protocol 07/1999 1999). A list of most pressing issues was prepared on the basis of assessments from the UKIE, Kułakowski, and the Polish ambassador to the EU (UKIE Internal Document 28/06/1999 1999; UKIE Internal Document DPI 16/06/1999 1999). At the accession conference in Brussels in June, the Polish foreign minister made a firm commitment to submit outstanding legislation to parliament by July (UKIE Internal Document 16/06/1999 1999). Inviting the ministers responsible for major delays to the special KIE meetings, Buzek asked them to present realistic action plans. The KIE imposed specific deadlines on ministers and asked the UKIE to monitor implementation. A few ad hoc meetings were convened between Buzek and individual ministers to resolve the most contentious issues.

But this attempt largely failed (Apanowicz and Bielecki 1999). Although some transposition activity was registered in June–July, it did not translate into a new sustainable dynamic. The prime minister did not convene a KIE meeting in June that was to review the implementation progress, perhaps knowing he would need to openly admit defeat. The failure proved to Buzek and Kułakowski that, without new rules, the process of transposition would be difficult to accelerate. This mood was best captured by one government minister, who said, "Buzek was scared, he was really terrified by the situation and he wanted to change this. But he had too high a position to do it himself and he did not have the right people" (interview 29, p. 13).

In summary, a change in external and internal opportunity structures transformed the preferences of the key core executive actors—the prime minister and the chief negotiator—who identified EU transposition as an area in which rapid remedial action was necessary. At the same time, the mid-1999 attempt to bolster the pace of EU transposition demonstrated that, without new institutional rules, personal leadership was not sufficient to produce desired outcomes. The impending transposition crisis also provided a new opportunity for Buzek to use the issue strategically to bolster his standing within the governing coalition. As a result, in mid- 1999, Buzek and Kułakowski emerged as political entrepreneurs for the development of new authority and information rules. In organizing his cabinet for addressing the collective action problem in the improvement of the transposition record, Prime Minister Buzek knew that he could capture a leader's profit. If successful, he would, first, avoid a collective bad of a major transposition debacle and, second, emerge as a true leader within his own party. In supporting Buzek, Chief Negotiator Kułakowski and his staff were acutely aware that any reinforcement to the existing rules would benefit them directly since they would be able to revitalize the accession negotiations.

The Core Reforms Hastily

Having realized that institutional levers they had at their disposal were insufficient for generating a new legislative dynamic, Buzek and Kułakowski started to look for ways in which to institutionalize a more forceful role of the center in EU transposition. Since an internal coalition impasse continued to block change within the UKIE Secretariat, it was the KPRM that, in the following months, emerged as the dominant institutional actor in EU transposition. In June 1999, Prime Minister Buzek asked Wojciech Arkuszewski, his former chef de cabinet and the then secretary for parliamentary affairs at KPRM, to become involved more closely in the coordination of transposition legislation.

A political old hand, Arkuszewski commanded great personal authority among both the AWS and UW ministers and high-level civil servants (interview 35, p. 5). Furnished with an appropriate mandate, he could use his staff and organizational resources located at the KPRM's

Department of Parliamentary Affairs and Department of Coordination to plan and monitor transposing legislation (interview 27, p. 2; interview 33, pp. 5–6). In contrast to the UKIE Secretariat, both these departments were closely involved in the regular legislative process within the executive and parliament and, hence, were able to rely on well-developed personal networks within the governmental administration. Last but not least, the organizational proximity between Arkuszewski's and Kułakowski's staff quickly locked these two teams in regular cooperation (interview 39, p. 6). A member of the chief negotiator's team, characterizing Arkuszewski's position, said, "It was a combination of three elements: he had personal authority, in some cases he could invoke the prime minister's authority and he could invoke our [Kułakowski's] authority" (interview 35, p. 5).

Arkuszewski's first move was to establish a detailed catalogue of all outstanding transposition measures, a catalogue that, for the first time, linked commitments made during accession negotiations and those undertaken in the NPAA (Internal Memo DPI/7/12/1999 1999; Official Communication MJP/859/99/TN 1999; Official Communication SekrMinPS/1497/99/DHP/ap 1999). In planning transposition, Arkuszewski and his staff were assisted by two junior ministers in the UKIE and members of Kułakowski's team (interview 16, p. 4; interview 27, p. 1). A close observer thus recollected the process:

[Arkuszewski] asked the deputy director of the Audit Department in the Prime Minister's Chancellery [. . .] and two secretaries to collect data. [He] first wrote to all deputy ministers to ask what had to be transposed and when. And then [he] put all that information into a single database. [. . .] This data was incomplete but in a sequence of fierce arguments [he] was able to find out the rest. [. . .] The UKIE maintained their data in such a way that it had no practical implications [. . .] nobody really knew what exactly had to be done. [. . .] The UKIE sent [Arkuszewski] long lists of things to do but these catalogues did not agree with the information [he] received from ministries. A large part of our work was to clarify which drafts were which.

(interview 29, pp. 9–10)

By developing a detailed listing of pending transposing laws, the core executive actors were able to gain a clear and complete picture as to what remained to be done, when, and by whom. Arkuszewski started from short listings of most pressing issues ("The List of Nine") and gradually moved to more medium-range planning instruments such as "the List of Sixty-Seven" and the plan for the first half of 2000 (Official Communication SWA-45-39/99 1999). Arkuszewski and his staff soon operationalized the listing or—in their own words—"made it fit for effective governing" (interview 29, p. 10). As well as providing for precise (monthly) deadlines, they specified, by name and ministry, the junior ministers responsible for preparing individual measures and prioritized all transposing legislation using a one-to-five star categorization (Official Communication SWA-10-28/99 1999; Official Communication SWA-45-39(3)/1999 1999). In effect, each ministry's transposition record became readily measurable and visible to all actors concerned.

Arkuszewski was asked by Prime Minister Buzek to extract the EU-related provisions from those draft laws whose preparation was in progress and have them compiled into special "transposition bills" (cf. KIE Protocol 18/1999 1999). The progressive operationalization of the transposition planning instrument was appreciated by both Kułakowski and the UKIE staff. A UKIE minister said,

> Thanks to the newly forged partnership between the Prime Minister's Chancellery and the UKIE, we were able to prepare a more advanced document, a plan which assigned accountability to specific people who now bore [personal] responsibility for both delays and successes. So I would say that, yes, the UKIE did have a good idea of what should be done but at the same time the prime minister's chancellery played a central role by assigning a higher priority [to transposition] and pushing things through. By the authority of the prime minister's staff the chancellery held much greater sway than a regular office [such as the UKIE] which, no matter how important, had simply none of the chancellery's influence and powers of persuasion.
>
> (interview 16, p. 4)

Detailed planning was soon matched by close monitoring and evaluation. Arkuszewski harnessed the KPRM's authority and technical resources to monitor progress in line ministries on a week-to-week basis (interview 27, p. 2; interview 33, pp. 5–6). The KPRM parliamentary secretary himself became involved in monitoring. A close observer noted, "[Arkuszewski] made up a list of outstanding issues and started ringing ministers. And so he spent six months on the phone, talking to ministers from morning to evening" (interview 29, p. 7). The regular monitoring from the KPRM shifted the attention of junior ministers in line ministries from non-EU to EU-related legislation. Arkuszewski's position within the KPRM and his close linkage to the prime minister helped ensure more effective enforcement. If delays were detected, he was able to take the matter directly to the prime minister. A KPRM official said, "[Arkuszewski] talked individually to people responsible for a particular issue at a given ministry [. . .] [and if consensus could not be reached] went to the prime minister and told him [he] had a problem" (interview 29, p. 14). The parliamentary secretary had also sufficient authority to cut through long-drawn-out conflicts that in many instances blocked interministerial consultations for long years (interview 29, p. 12).

As parliamentary secretary at KPRM, Arkuszewski was also able to alert the prime minister to the fact that transposition bills had to be assigned sufficient legislative time. In early January 2000, he criticized the draft cabinet legislative program as "completely unrealistic," given the number of transposition commitments to be fulfilled in the course of that year (interview 7, p. 8; Wielowieyska 2000). In a letter to the head of the KPRM, Arkuszewski contended that line ministers had proposed to submit over 200 draft parliamentary laws in the year 2000, whereas the parliament was able to adopt only approximately 100 per year (Official Communication SWA-20-1/2000 2000). More importantly, the draft program omitted a large number of transposing drafts that had to be adopted. He recommended that the cabinet assign most of the legislative time remaining until the 2001 parliamentary elections to priority EU-related legislation. In the event, Arkuszewski's intervention was only partially successful, but he succeeded in ensuring that the proportion of time assigned to EU transposition bills did indeed increase (cf. KPRM Internal Document RM-20-1-00 2000).

Arkuszewski's institution-building actions were complemented by new initiatives undertaken by Chief Negotiator Kułakowski and his staff. Three types of new institutional rules must be mentioned in this context. First, at the chief negotiator's request, the Negotiation Team introduced in July 1999 a new procedure for preparing draft negotiation positions (Official Communication SJK/456-315(1)/mcm/99 1999; UKIE Internal Document 12/07/1999 1999). From mid-1999 junior ministers responsible for negotiations in line ministries were required to provide detailed timetables for the transposition of the EU legislation within their remit. Analogous programs had to be provided for all negotiation positions that had been already adopted (cf. Official

Communication DWZ.V.078/88/99/PKM 1999; Official Communication IE60/sjr/ask/725/99 1999; Official Communication IE/WHP/1383/EP/99 1999; Official Communication MI-1/22.21/1139/KM/99 1999). The data from the timetables were cross-checked with Arkuszewski's listings and entered into the rolling catalogue of outstanding transposition commitments. Second, the meetings of the Negotiation Team began to monitor progress in the preparation of transposing legislation. A close observer said,

> At the time the Negotiation Team played a role that was largely disproportionate to its original mandate. It often replaced the KIE committee, that is, tackled adaptation and other alignment issues. [. . .] [T]here were numerous matters that landed on the agenda of the Negotiation Team even though they should not have been discussed there.
>
> (interview 39, p. 3)

Furthermore, Kułakowski's staff at KPRM used the December 1999 Helsinki summit's decision to review progress in legal adaptation to undertake an internal stocktaking exercise (cf. KPRM Internal Document 2000). In doing so, they had line ministries prepare detailed reports on how far they had progressed in EU transposition. These reports provided a fundamental basis for transposition monitoring undertaken by the chief negotiator from January 2000 (cf. UKIE Internal Document 1998a; Official Communication SKJ/458-11/BZ/00 2000). Kułakowski's staff at the KPRM also developed more short-range monitoring tools. An official said, "We started implementing monitoring instruments which we did not have at the start [. . .] for example lists of outstanding negotiation commitments. And we tried to get the cabinet or the KIE committee to adopt them in some form or the other so that they had some binding force [for ministries]" (interview 30, p. 5).

Finally, the chief negotiator's involvement helped coordinate transposition planning with the budgetary process, not least because the Finance Ministry provided a budget line for the implementation of the negotiation positions, while this was not the case for the UKIE-led NPAA (cf. Official Communication SJK/4561-5/99 1999; Official Communication SJK/4561-9(1)/MDW/2000 2000). The chief negotiator's increasing interest in EU transposition also meant that budgeting for transposition started to be discussed in the subcommittee for the budgetary implications of the accession negotiations, a committee that worked predominately for the Negotiation Team.

To summarize, between autumn 1999 and spring 2000, a major institutional change occurred within the core executive that resulted in the development of new position, authority, and information rules. As regards position rules, the parliamentary secretary, chief negotiator, and the Negotiation Team took the place of the KIE chair, KIE secretary, and the KIE committee, respectively, as the key organizational vehicles for administering selective incentives and monitoring in the area of EU rule adoption. The new rules mandated the emergence of both collective and hierarchical relationships. The meetings of the Negotiation Team provided the main collectivity-enhancing mechanism. The hierarchical relationship existed in two dimensions. First, it arose in the relationship between State Secretary Arkuszewski and senior/junior ministers. Second, it existed between Chief Negotiator Kułakowski and the members of the Negotiation Team. The new position rules came with new authority and information rules. The change with regard to authority rules relied mainly on Arkuszewski's strong position within the KPRM, his high standing within the AWS party, and his closeness to the prime minister. Arkuszewski harnessed his institutional authority to sanction junior ministers who failed to contribute to EU rule adoption. If his personal intervention was not successful, ministers knew he could at any time take the matter directly to the prime minister. Arkuszewski also used his authority to facilitate interministerial consultations by seeking to resolve disputes.

The largest improvements, however, occurred with regard to information rules. A detailed transposition plan was prepared that made it possible to assign responsibility if contributions to the collective record were not made. For the first time, the plan prioritized tasks and imposed deadlines on ministers and departments. Regular week-to-week monitoring was undertaken by Arkuszewski's team, and progress was also double checked within the collective framework of the Negotiation Team. The team introduced further information rules by requiring ministers to submit reports on transposition progress. Although the new position, authority, and information rules brought real constraints on the behavior of ministers and departments, it must be noted that most of these rules were weakly institutionalized. Not having been formalized in legal texts, they were underwritten mainly by the personalities that called them into existence. In large part, the weak institutionalization of the rules contributed to their rapid transformation in spring 2000, as is demonstrated in the next section.

The Core Rebounds

The Resolution of the Coalition Deadlock

The KPRM lost its central role in EU transposition after Arkuszewski resigned in mid-March 2000. Besides a general disillusionment with Buzek's record in office, Arkuszewski's resignation was prompted by an increasing realization that, by becoming closely involved in EU transposition, he was creating a structure parallel to the UKIE Secretariat, which, in many respects, added to, rather than alleviated, coordination problems within the centre. A close observer said,

> [Arkuszewski] came to the conclusion that what he was doing was partly destructive since he was in essence providing an interim cover for a vacancy in the position of the KIE secretary. [. . .] And it was that vacancy that was a major problem. [. . .] In [his] view a full KIE secretary had to be appointed.
>
> (interview 29, p. 14)

Following Arkuszewski's resignation, the planning and monitoring system reinforcing the KPRM's role in transposition quickly unravelled, not least because it heavily relied on Arkuszewski's personal commitment and authority. The new parliamentary affairs secretary at the KPRM simply lacked the necessary political clout and personal influence to underwrite it further.

Having lost Arkuszewski, who over the previous nine months had been responsible for accelerating EU transposition, Prime Minister Buzek realized that, if the slowly emerging new legislative dynamic were to be maintained, he quickly had to find new personal and institutional support. This was all the more important because he was already alerted to the risk of a slowdown in transposition (cf. Official Communication SekrMinPS/920/2000/TN 2000). Against this backdrop, the prime minister made yet another—though this time successful—attempt to unblock the appointment of the KIE secretary and the head of the UKIE.

There were three main factors that helped to resolve this long-standing impasse. First, Buzek was able to use the media and parliamentary pressures for a solution to the UKIE issue. Following the publication of an unfavourable Commission report in autumn 1999 and an intense parliamentary debate in mid-February 2000, the Sejm (the lower house of the Polish parliament) passed a resolution requiring the government to "more clearly correlate the competencies and functions of the Committee for European Integration, Government Legislative Centre and departments responsible for transposition in individual ministries" (Sejm RP 2000). In an article published in the daily press, the speaker of the Sejm and, at the same time, a high-ranking member of the AWS called for an end to the deadlock over the UKIE leadership (Plażyński 2000). A UKIE official said, "From July 1998 the UKIE had not had a permanent leader and so it was evident to anyone who wanted to know that things were not right. [. . .] So it was natural to expect that this had to be changed. [. . .] I think it was the protracted limbo that led to change—that is the main explanation" (interview 16, p. 7).

The second factor was that the prime minister's support for Saryusz-Wolski, the main candidate for the KIE secretary since early 1999, increased significantly after the latter had proved his worth as the prime minister's advisor. A close observer said, "I think that over time Buzek became convinced that Saryusz-Wolski was the right person for the job. By spring 2000, Saryusz-Wolski had become Buzek's right-hand man in EU affairs and the prime minister knew he could trust him" (interview 60). Finally, both the AWS and the UW began to realize that, if a major crisis were to be avoided, the UKIE needed a strong leadership that could be provided only by a person with high political and professional authority. In the event, the domestic pressures, Buzek's strong support for Saryusz-Wolski, and the converging preferences of the coalition parties made the UW drop its objections. In effect, in April 2000, Buzek nominated Saryusz-Wolski as the KIE secretary and the head of the UKIE.

Saryusz-Wolski was highly respected both within the UKIE and among EU-related personnel in line ministries. For one thing he was a renowned expert in EU affairs and vice rector of the College of Europe, an academic who "had a long-term vision and understood the integration processes within a broader context" (interview 46, p. 3). More significantly, Saryusz-Wolski was an experienced minister having served as the government plenipotentiary for European integration, with undersecretary of state rank within the Office of the Council of Ministers (later transformed into the KPRM). Most of the key civil servants within the UKIE had owed their jobs to him (interview 60). Saryusz-Wolski also had a forthright, strong-minded personality and was well known for his assertive management style (interview 29, p. 14; interview 27, p. 4).

Significantly, Saryusz-Wolski's authority hinged on staunch support from Prime Minister Buzek. Speaking of Saryusz-Wolski's ability to rely on the prime minister's support, a UKIE official said,

> Saryusz-Wolski was in close contact with Buzek. [. . .] He held great influence over the prime minister and—though he met with significant resistance from his colleagues in other ministries—I think ministers were aware that he could easily make their life difficult by informing the prime minister which minister was not doing what he or she was supposed to be doing.
>
> (interview 46, p. 3)

Saryusz-Wolski was skilful in reinforcing the image of his close relationship with the prime minister. Although nominated to the UKIE, he retained a small office close to Buzek's office at the KPRM where he had the benefit of a private line to the prime minister (interview 52, p. 4; interview 60).

This episode demonstrates that the mounting accession crisis acted a catalyst for the resolution of the long-standing deadlock over the appointment of the KIE secretary and the position of the UKIE. Thanks to pressures arising from within the accession process, by early 2000, both the AWS and the UW realized that their individual costs of compromise would be much smaller than the collective bad of a failed EU accession. Not without significance for achieving this result were the incentives and opportunities arising inside the domestic arena. National actors both channelled and amplified external EU pressures, but also guided the government's response toward specific changes to intraexecutive institutional rules whose deficiency was widely perceived as the main source of the problem. The domestic pressure reverberated all the more strongly since, rather unexpectedly, the electoral fate of the AWS-UW cabinet and that of its individual parties became linked to their ability to deal with the accession crisis.

The Creation and Enforcement of New Rules

Although building on some of the earlier instruments, Saryusz-Wolski and his staff developed a new institutional framework for planning, monitoring, and enforcing EU transposition, one that moved the onus for coordination from the KPRM and the Negotiation Team to the UKIE and the KIE committee. For one thing, Saryusz-Wolski was quick to reorganize the UKIE, notably by creating internal structures that functioned largely in parallel to the existing ministerial departments and were staffed with people he brought into the office. A UKIE official said, "The UKIE was in a complete organizational mess. It was over-staffed and many of the personnel were ill-qualified political appointees from Czarnecki's Christian Democrats Party. But Saryusz-Wolski did not have the time and the energy to deal with all this. He simply by-passed it" (interview 60). He placed loyal staff in strategic positions within the UKIE—his political cabinet, the UKIE Secretariat, and the director general's office. Most importantly, Saryusz-Wolski appointed a junior minister for transposition, Cezary Banasiński, with an explicit coordination brief. Banasiński bypassed the UKIE's existing lawyers and established a new Department for European Legislation (DLE) with 12 staff. Its management was handpicked by Saryusz-Wolski and Banasiński from the DNA. A UKIE official said, "[Banasiński] created a elitist department where people worked much more than eight hours a day, had the highest pay in the UKIE and treated their work as a public mission rather than a bureaucratic job" (interview 17, p. 2; see figure 4.3 for the UKIE's internal organigram in December 2000).

In transposition planning, Saryusz-Wolski further operationalized instruments that had been earlier developed by Arkuszewski and Kułakowski. Several days before his nomination, the KIE committee had adopted a list of all outstanding transposition commitments to be fulfilled before the date of accession and had recommended it for adop-tion by the full cabinet (cf. KIE Protocol 07/2000 2000; interview 15, p. 14). As KIE secretary, Saryusz-Wolski used that list to select measures that had to be adopted in 2000 if the Commission were to note progress in its forthcoming regular report. In May 2000, the KIE adopted a for-mal resolution asking line ministers to prepare all such parliamentary drafts by June and September 2000. The resolution had a binding force and was published in a reactivated *Official Journal of the Committee for European Integration*, which significantly increased its standing in the eyes of junior ministers and civil servants (UKIE Internal Document 2000b). In preparing the KIE resolution, the UKIE Secretariat, for the first time, used external time constraints to impose formal transposition deadlines on ministries (interview 11, p. 8). The catalogue of outstand-ing transposition drafts replaced all previous lists created by Arkuszewski

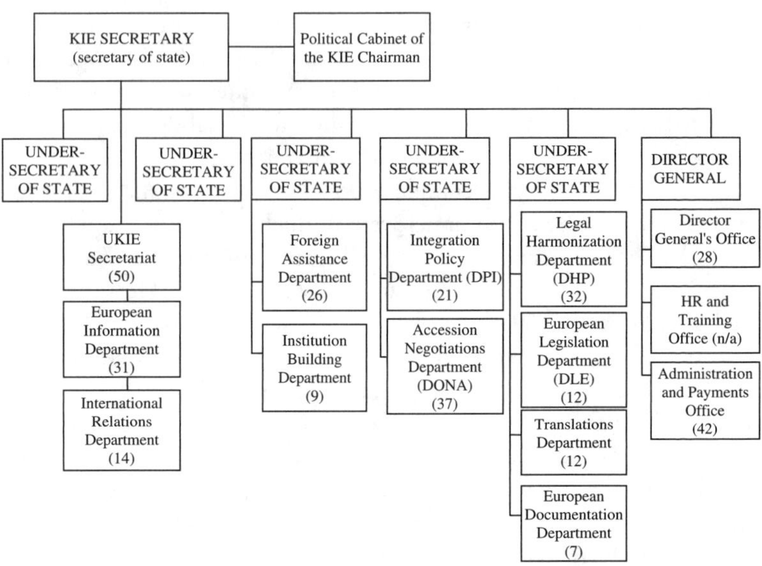

Source: Own compilation based on Executive Regulation No. 2/2000 of the KIE chair of September 21, 2000 and Executive Regulation No. 3/2000 of the KIE chair of December 29 2000; staff figures were supplied to the author by the UKIE Secretariat.

Figure 4.3 UKIE's organigram in December 2000 (staff levels in brackets)

and Kułakowski. A new list for the year 2001 was adopted by the KIE committee in November 2000 (KIE Protocol 16/2000 2000; Official Communication SekrMinJSW/1797/2000 2000).

More significantly, Saryusz-Wolski transformed the KIE into a committee dedicated to work on EU-related legislation (cf. UKIE Internal Document 2000a). A close observer said, "[Saryusz-Wolski] made the KIE committee function in that same way as KERM [cabinet economic committee] or other standing cabinet committee, that is, work on legislation. Every week we pushed through two to four draft laws. This meant that EU-related laws by-passed the regular cabinet committees and were debated by the KIE" (interview 14, p. 8). From October 2000, the KIE committee started to meet weekly, and the prime minister continued to chair the meetings (see figure 4.4). The KIE was shadowed by meetings at lower levels. Saryusz-Wolski wanted to organize a regular pre-KIE meeting at undersecretary of state level, but this was soon

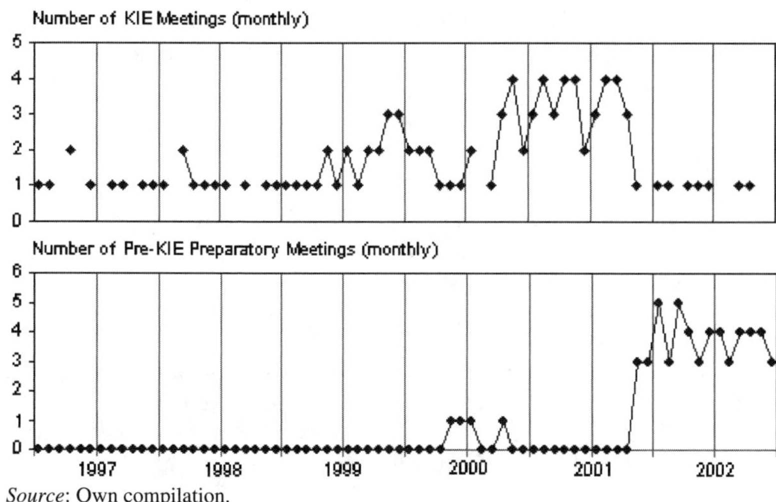

Source: Own compilation.

Figure 4.4 Number of KIE meetings between 1997 and 2002 (based on KIE protocols)

replaced by ad hoc conferences at director and minister level. A UKIE minister said,

> At the start we tried to create a pre-KIE meeting but we quickly gave up. [. . .] This forum was disregarded by ministries and was attended not by junior ministers but department directors. As a result, it had limited decision-making powers so we quickly replaced it with a weekly full KIE meeting. The technical coordination role was fulfilled by *ad hoc* conferences at director level. [. . .] These conferences were organized by the UKIE only with the ministries concerned. [. . .] And so if something could not be resolved at the KIE meeting, then the committee directed that by such and such time tomorrow the ministries concerned would meet together with the UKIE representative and would prepare a solution.
>
> (interview 14, p. 10)

The ad hoc conferences also served to control time. If a disagreement blocked progress on an issue, the KIE asked undersecretaries of state from the UKIE and line ministries to find a solution by a specific deadline, lest the matter be passed on to cabinet (interview 11, p. 13).

The responsibility for transposition monitoring moved from the Negotiation Team and the KPRM to the KIE committee and the UKIE.

From July 2000 legislative progress started to be verified at the beginning of each KIE session. A system was introduced whereby, once a week, all line ministries were subject to close scrutiny, their legislative record was debated and checked draft by draft (interview 14, p. 8). A UKIE official said,

> The regular KIE meetings were used to check legislative progress. So between 50–90 percent of the KIE agenda was occupied by EU-related legislation. [. . .] It looked as follows. The ministry responsible introduced a draft and then minister Banasiński presented a preliminary EU compatibility assessment. If there were problems, they were dealt with at the KIE or were referred to separate meetings with the ministries concerned. [. . .] If drafts were delayed, ministries were questioned and then regularly monitored. Once in a while a list of outstanding drafts was prepared to show which ministries did not comply with their commitments.
>
> (interview 12, p. 3)

The KPRM continued to offer assistance in monitoring legislative progress and, at some point, a list of outstanding parliamentary and secondary laws started to be made available at every cabinet meeting (interview 17, p. 3). The regular verification had a clearly mobilizing effect on line ministers and their staff. A UKIE official said, "All [ministerial staff] got used to the fact that regular requests for information and verification of implementation from the UKIE set the pace of the process" (interview 12, p. 5).

Like Arkuszewski, Saryusz-Wolski and Banasiński combined close monitoring with strict enforcement. In the latter they heavily relied on the prime minister's support. A close observer said, "The UKIE informed on ministries by writing reports for the prime minister that, for example, ministry X was late by six weeks. Then the prime minister would raise the issue with the minister during a cabinet meeting or would call a junior minister and ask why something had not been done and demand immediate action" (interview 16, p. 6). Another official concurred,

> If delays were identified, letters were sent from the KIE secretary to ministers, and if delays persisted, meetings were organized with the prime minister. [. . .] Besides the premier, such meetings were attended by the minister concerned, his deputy for EU affairs, [Saryusz-Wolski]

and his UKIE staff. [. . .] If there were still delays, the prime minister would send reprimands to his ministers which we [the UKIE] had drafted.

(interview 14, p. 8)

To ensure effective enforcement of transposition commitments, Saryusz-Wolski wanted the prime minister to chair all KIE sessions, knowing that with Buzek's presence the KIE decisions and their implications were much more significant (interview 16, pp. 6–7). Buzek also made it known in his cabinet that he considered transposition record an important benchmark for assessing a minister's performance in office (interview 35). This new rule allowed Saryusz-Wolski and Banasiński to place additional pressure on line ministers and their staff (interview 26, p. 14). A UKIE official said, "Banasiński was able to use arguments to the extent that any delays or errors could have negative personal consequences for the ministers responsible for transposition in a given area. [. . .] He would say to a minister, "If this issue is not dealt with, then I will need to refer it up to the cabinet, and then you would have to provide an explanation personally to the prime minister" (interview 26. p. 14).

Besides the monitoring and enforcing role, the UKIE began to operate as a facilitator of transposition. Banasiński's team moved beyond passive compatibility checks in their legal work. A UKIE official said, "The DHP [old legal department] focused on compatibility assessment [. . .] but did not actively initiate legislative work which was really essential at that stage. And this is what the DLE [new department] did. They looked at the [transposition] process from a different perspective—what remains to be done to achieve legal alignment" (interview 27, p. 4). Banasiński and his new legal staff became actively involved in all interministerial meetings involving transposition legislation. The DLE lawyers guided drafts through the legislative process and chaired or otherwise facilitated ad hoc conciliations mandated by the KIE. They also started to be seconded to line ministries to help with drafting (interview 16, p. 6; interview 17, p. 2; interview 25, p. 18). A DLE lawyer said,

Our role was not limited to issuing a compatibility assessment. We became involved at very early stages, already when the main tenets of a particular draft law were being discussed. [. . .] [E]ither [we] were approached by the ministry for legal assistance and I seconded a lawyer

> to that department for some time or we took the initiative and approached
> the ministry to point out some problems and offered out assistance.
>
> (interview 11, p. 14)

In some cases, where a ministry was not able to deliver on time, the DLE drafted the transposing measure themselves (interview 17, p. 1; interview 18, p. 5; interview 45, p. 5). In this, it was helped by the Government Legislative Center, a new institution established in early 2000.

Significantly, the UKIE's facilitation of EU transposition often went beyond simple drafting and extended to assistance with substantive policy choices (cf. Official Communication SEkrMinCB/336/2000/mk 2000). Frequently, the DLE lawyers developed alternative policy solutions or demonstrated the level of discretion that a particular ministry had in regulating a particular issue (interview 12, pp. 1–2). A UKIE official said, "When policy problems arose, [. . .] [Banasiński] proposed optional solutions to the prime minister and informed him of the position taken by the minister" (interview 11, p. 13). To reinforce his capacity to offer such policy advice, minister Banasiński forged strong links with the UKIE's Accession Negotiations Department (DONA), which provided similar analysis principally for Kułakowski (Internal Memo 06/07/2000 2000; interview 12, p. 5; interview 39, p. 5; interview 49, p. 4). A DONA official said, "Banasiński needed us to provide non-legal advice on policy issues. [. . .] He was interested in economic analysis or some other comprehensive impact assessments for a particular directive" (interview 32, p. 9). The information he received from the DONA enabled Banasiński to rise above the legal arguments and embrace the political context (interview 25, p. 19).

Finally, the core executive actors provided close guidance to line ministries on the methodology of EU transposition. Banasiński joined forces with the Legislative Council to develop a set of original legislative tools for the transposition of the Community measures into the Polish legal order (interview 17, p. 3). Departing from a modernization or "creative transplant" approach to transposition, the UKIE developed a new model of a "European" parliamentary law (Subotić 2000). The special "EU-related" laws allowed Banasiński to technically separate transposition-related amendments from non-EU-related provisions that lowered the potential political salience of parliamentary bills. In many ways, after the AWS-UW coalition collapsed in mid-2000, the new "EU" parliamentary law became a necessity for the new minority Buzek cabinet because the opposition made its support for transposition conditional on a clear separation of EU-related provisions (interview 15, p. 13). Furthermore, the KIE's internal byelaws were amended to specify new formal requirements that had to be fulfilled by line ministries in preparing such special EU laws (cf. UKIE Internal Document 2000a).

Although the institutional rules described above remained unchanged until the parliamentary elections in September 2001, numerous political observers and government officials noted that the position of the KIE secretary and the UKIE declined vis-à-vis line ministries toward the end of the Buzek cabinet's term (interview 52, p. 2; interview 60; interview 6). This seems to have been primarily due to changes in the preferences of Prime Minister Buzek and line ministers that occurred in response to the forthcoming elections. In early 2001, Buzek and his ministers realized that the AWS was heading for an electoral defeat; this may have dampened their resolve to support controversial legislation. Perhaps, more importantly, the close and direct relationship between Buzek and Saryusz-Wolski faltered in 2001 as the prime minister's chef de cabinet started to wield more influence (interview 7; interview 52, p. 2). A public disagreement in May 2001 regarding the preferred date of membership further undermined Buzek's confidence in Saryusz-Wolski, as did the latter's decision to join a newly established party, the Civic Platform (Pszczółkowska 2001). Last but not least, another contributing factor was the natural reluctance of central government officials to engage in policy making before an impending change of government. All in all, the UKIE's grip on the process of transposition lessened toward the end of the Buzek government's tenure.

In summary, the period from spring 2000 to autumn 2001 brought another major change in position, authority, and information rules. As regards position rules, the resolution of the intracoalition deadlock over the appointment of the KIE secretary made it possible to activate the institutional rules related to the KIE chair, KIE secretary, and the KIE committee. As a result, from spring 2000, these rules replaced those relating to the parliamentary secretary, chief negotiator, and the Negotiation Team as the main organizational vehicles for extending selective incentives and monitoring to ministers and departments in the area of EU rule adoption. There were also new position rules that became important. The full cabinet became increasingly involved in monitoring progress in transposition, and a position of a junior minister for EU transposition was established within the UKIE.

Besides the position rules, a substantial change occurred at the level of authority rules. The KIE secretary and the transposition minister were able to administer sanctions by asking the prime minister for direct intervention. They could also "name and shame" noncontributing ministers and departments within the KIE committee or the full cabinet. Furthermore, from mid-2000—after the UW had withdrawn from the coalition—Prime Minister Buzek's authority to reward and sanction ministers increased substantially in what was now a minority single-party cabinet. Apart from administering sanctions/rewards, the KIE secretary and the transposition minister started facilitating ministerial contributions to EU rule adoption by helping them to resolve interdepartmental conflicts and providing methodological guidelines. In this context, it is important to note that the UKIE finally translated the screening and negotiation commitments into detailed legislative advice on what issues needed to be addressed through specific legislation.

The authority rules were also enhanced within the KIE committee and the cabinet. The KIE started to function as a dedicated cabinet committee working on EU-related legislation. It met weekly and, through regular review mechanisms, exerted peer pressure on ministers and departments. It further developed a set-aside mechanism by referring conflictual issues for resolution to smaller working groups. It is also interesting to note that the new authority rules led to a reinterpretation of the position of the KIE committee. The hierarchical relationship between the KIE (as a supreme administrative organ) and the non-KIE ministers gave way to a more collective relationship as the committee began to function as just another cabinet committee.

As for information rules, the institutional solutions developed between autumn 1999 and spring 2000 were further enhanced within the framework of the new position rules. A rolling catalogue of outstanding legislation was maintained by the UKIE's transposition minister, who insisted on making the data on required legislative action as detailed as possible. Progress was verified at the start of each KIE session and, with time, also at the full cabinet meetings. The progress in EU rule adoption was visible to all KIE members, and responsibility for delays or omissions was easy to allocate. Finally, it must be mentioned that, unlike under the previous institutional regime, at least some of the new authority and information rules were institutionalized into legally binding KIE resolutions. This said, the operational force of many of the authority rules was heavily dependent on the personal relationship between Buzek and Saryusz-Wolski, and hence these rules may have been less effective in constraining ministers and departments when that relationship started to break down in 2001.

The Core Consolidates

Pressures for Further Institutional Change

In late 2001 the new Miller government consolidated the UKIE's central role in planning, monitoring, and enforcing the transposition of the Community legislation. Determined to achieve further progress in EU accession negotiations, Prime Minister Miller—like Buzek in the second part of his term—put his personal and institutional authority behind the UKIE. It must be noted that, in contrast to Buzek, Miller had a higher capacity for strong prime ministerial leadership. This was mainly because he combined his post with the leadership of the largest parliamentary party—the SLD. The SLD clearly dominated the cabinet and was in a close programmatic alliance with one of its coalition partners, the UP. Moreover, Miller was a seasoned political actor with extensive parliament and government experience going back to the communist time and had served as labour minister and the minister-head of the URM under the 1993–1997 SLD-PSL government. All this meant that prime ministerial leadership in EU affairs improved further from the late 2001.

The new government introduced organizational changes to consolidate the capacities of the "European" core executive. Several factors occasioned the redesign of institutions. The people who were instrumental in creating and underwriting the existing institutional configuration (Kułakowski, Saryusz-Wolski, and Banasiński) had left the government. The new actors—Cimoszewicz as foreign minister, Hübner as KIE secretary, and Jan Truszczyński as chief negotiator—brought with them new ideas on how European integration should be handled organizationally at the center of government. Not without importance was their previous government experience: Cimoszewicz had been prime minister in 1996–1997, Hübner had been KIE secretary under Cimoszewicz, and Truszczyński had been the Polish ambassador to the EU under the Buzek government. More significantly, their perception of what had to be changed was shaped by the evidence of institutional failures under the Buzek government, resulting in particular from internal fragmentation within the "European" core executive (interview 38, p. 1). Problems were most evident in the organizational separation of competences for accession negotiations, foreign affairs, and internal adaptation. A close observer said,

> The rationale for change was to avoid a situation that was characteristic for the previous government, one in which functions and competences in European integration were split among the Foreign Office, the Prime Minister's Chancellery and the UKIE. This split was damaging because, despite good interpersonal relations, it often resulted in policy discrepancies which is inevitable when three institutions deal with the same issues and do not operate within clearly defined boundaries.
>
> (interview 37, p. 1)

Another important factor was that the government changeover offered a critical juncture for dealing with Saryusz-Wolski's organizational legacy within the UKIE. Entering the office after the 2001 parliamentary elections, the new KIE secretary, Hübner, had much greater leeway in shaping the internal structure of the UKIE than her predecessor in April 2000. As a result, she quickly moved to bring down the parallel structures that Saryusz-Wolski had erected within the UKIE, and sought to integrate them with the rest of the secretariat. Finally, it is important to note that the core executive institutions had to be adjusted to the new coalition character of the SLD-PSL-UP government and, perhaps more importantly, to the much greater institutional authority of the prime minister, who, for the first time since 1989, combined his office with the leadership of the largest parliamentary party.

In a first step, the organizational units responsible for accession negotiations and internal adaptation institutions were integrated. A UKIE official said,

> The idea was to integrate the three institutions—KPRM with Kułakowski, UKIE and the Foreign Office—which under the previous government were responsible for European integration. Since it was difficult to initiate radical structural changes when the new government was being formed, a decision was taken to pool competences with one person and channel all actions [. . .] through one institution. And that was done and this is what the UKIE is for.
>
> (interview 11, p. 10)

Hübner, as the new KIE secretary, combined her position with that of deputy foreign minister, while the chief negotiator was moved from the KPRM to become her immediate subordinate in the MSZ. Integrated through Hübner's double institutional role, the UKIE and the MSZ's EU pillar started to operate under the banner of a "European secretariat." Further integration occurred at the department level. The chief negotiator's staff from the KPRM and the UKIE's Accession Department merged with the MSZ's EU department. Regular meetings of all directors from the UKIE and the MSZ started to be held to reinforce the team spirit and facilitate information sharing (interview 15, p. 12). An official said,

> There were two types of meetings. First, there were weekly briefings of all department directors [from the UKIE and the MSZ EU pillar] on Friday afternoon where we had a *tour de table* in which every director briefed everyone else on what priorities they had. [. . .] The idea was to let everyone know what was happening in the system and, at the same time, to deal with issues that required improvement or resolution. Such meetings were chaired by minister Hübner or minister Pietras. And the second type of meetings were those of the senior management of the European secretariat, that is, minister Hübner, Truszczyński, Pietras, Kozek. [. . .] These meetings were also attended by directors who a had special coordinating role—director of the DOKIE [Department Supporting the KIE Committee] and director of the EU department in the MSZ. [. . .] These meetings were held ad hoc and their frequency fluctuated with events.
>
> (interview 37, p. 2)

Owing to an informal arrangement, Hübner, Pietras (UKIE state undersecretary), and Truszczyński could issue direct instructions to departments both within the UKIE and the MSZ (its EU pillar), circumventing the regular interministerial channels (interview 38, p. 6). Within the UKIE, the DLE merged with the DHP, forming a European Law Department (DPE), the UKIE's second largest department, employing 36 staff (see figure 4.5). Significantly, the DPE senior management was recruited from the DLE rather than the DHP, thus ensuring that the department retained its active profile in EU transposition. Further, Hübner refrained from appointing a minister for transposition but split Banasiński's competences between state

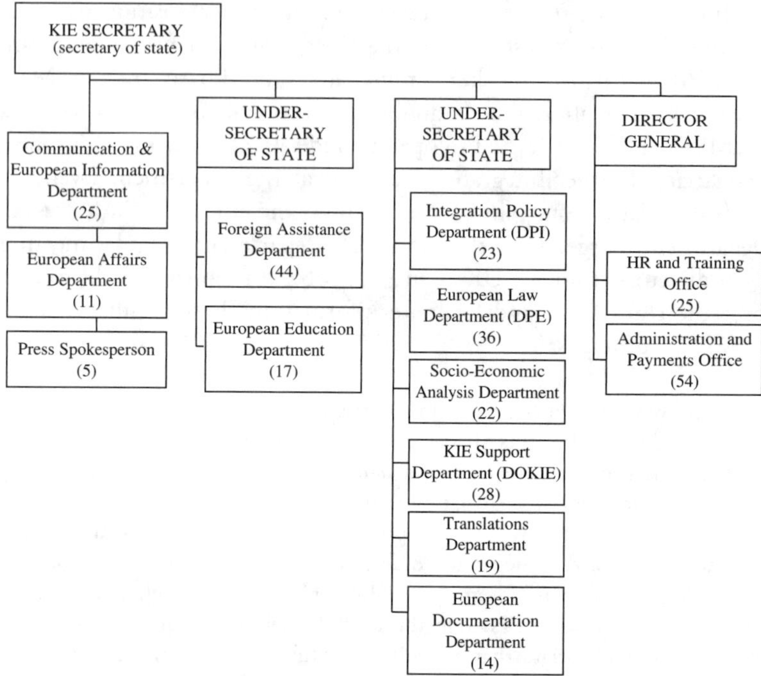

Source: Own compilation based on Executive Regulation No. 1 of the KIE chair of January 18, 2002 and Executive Regulation of the KIE chair of January 21, 2002; staff figures were supplied to the author by the UKIE.

Figure 4.5   UKIE's organigram in January 2002 (staff levels in brackets)

undersecretary Pietras, the DPE director, and the newly established DOKIE. A UKIE official said,

> At the moment there is no special minister for transposition, and there is only minister Pietras, so we have had to organize our work differently. The concern was not to place the entire coordination burden on Pietras or the DLE director. [. . .] So under Banasiński we [the DLE] reviewed the implementation of the timetable, while now [. . .] this is done by the Department Supporting the KIE Committee (DOKIE). [. . .] [T]his is because it is the KIE committee that accepts the timetable and the full cabinet that approves it.
>
> (interview 11, pp. 6–7)

A principal role for the DOKIE was to ensure cohesive action within the UKIE by integrating the inputs from the DPE lawyers, DPI economists, and the Foreign Assistance Department. A UKIE official said,

> This department has no competences [. . .] besides technical coordination. But this is where many very important issues come together [. . .] and [our] role is to ensure cohesion in the work of [UKIE] departments. There are three departments which deal with legislative issues: Department for Integration Policy [. . .] European Law Department [. . .] and the EU Department in the Foreign Office. [. . .]. And there has to be a single place where [their opinions] come together. Our department fulfils this role since all documents come here and leave from here. [Our director] does not intervene directly in the work of other directors. [. . .] But whenever we see a problem, we take it up to minister Pietras and he decides.
>
> (interview 27, p. 7)

Finally, the weekly KIE meeting at cabinet minister level was replaced by a weekly meeting at junior minister level chaired by the KIE secretary (ZPKIE). This was essentially an evolutionary change as in many ways the ZPKIE confirmed what became the norm in the last months of the Buzek government. A UKIE official explained,

> The ZPKIE was established as a response to the situation that obtained in the last few months of the previous government when the prime minister would come to the KIE meeting which was not attended by even one full cabinet minister and where directors often filled in for junior ministers. [. . .] And so we decided to have a formal meeting at a level that would make it possible for the KIE secretary to chair it.
>
> (interview 15, p. 8)

Besides practical considerations, the personal preferences of Prime Minister Miller were also crucial for stimulating the change (interview 27, p. 6). A close observer said, "Buzek would chair the KIE even though it was attended only by undersecretaries of state. [But] Miller said he wanted full ministers at the KIE" (interview 11, p. 12). In the event, ZPKIE's ascendancy marginalized the full KIE, which met only eight times between October 2001 and December 2002. The latter's role was now more ceremonial, though it sometimes debated strategic issues relating to accession negotiations (interview 37, p. 6). The ZPKIE, in turn, became a nodal point for processing all EU-related legislation. Although additional review by other standing cabinet committees did occur, most transposing drafts were routed only through the ZPKIE committee. Hübner and Pietras retained the practice developed under Saryusz-Wolski of organizing ad hoc director conferences to tackle most sensitive issues (interview 37, p. 5; interview 41, p. 5; interview 46, p. 8). This time, however, there was an increasing tendency for such meeting to involve only experts and ministerial officials. A UKIE official said, "There are no [ad hoc] meetings at the state undersecretary level but there are frequent meetings at the expert level which have the same function. The only difference is that decisions that have to be approved by a minister are [later] passed on to a given minister or state undersecretary" (interview 12, p. 8).

In sum, changes at the center of government occurred chiefly in response to a shift in domestic political circumstances. The urgent need for crisis management that was so marked in the second half of the Buzek term had all but disappeared by the time the Miller cabinet took over in late 2001. The parallel structures within the UKIE were thus either dismantled or more firmly embedded in general structures. Perhaps, more importantly, the extensive evidence of interorganizational rivalries between the UKIE Secretariat, the Foreign Office, and the chief negotiator, which troubled the Buzek cabinet even in 2000–2001, provided the new government with a powerful motivation to push for consolidation of the core. The SLD's dominance inside the cabinet made such consolidation possible, though it is interesting that it was achieved in large part through personal rather than structural means. Finally, Miller's personal preference for a close prime ministerial control in EU affairs provided a further incentive for tightening the "European" core's grip over ministerial departments.

More Institution-Building

In transposition planning the DPE continued to maintain the rolling catalogue of outstanding transposition measures, while paying more and more attention to the adoption of secondary laws (cf. UKIE 2002b). The catalogue became further operationalized to provide for monthly deadlines for the adoption by the KIE and the full cabinet. A UKIE official said, "I think a positive development was to specify planning and monitoring with monthly precision. There are now short-range plans for May, June, July etc. which specify a fixed amount of legislation that must be adopted" (interview 26, p. 14). Unlike under Buzek and Saryusz-Wolski, the UKIE no longer unilaterally imposed transposition deadlines but, based on negotiation positions and the NPAA, put forward proposals that were now much more widely consulted (interview 11, p. 8). Perhaps, most significantly, the UKIE integrated legislative, institutional, and financial commitments in a single document. This work was undertaken by the DPI (interview 8. pp. 2–3). In November 2001, a systematic action plan (*bilans otwarcia*) was prepared for the following nine months, one that prioritized work from the point of view of accession negotiations, legislation, and financial assistance (UKIE 2001). In mid-2002, a new edition of the action plan (*bilans przygotowań*) was prepared and, in many respects, it replaced the NPAA as a fully operational rolling catalogue of all integration-related actions to be undertaken before accession (UKIE 2002a).

Progress in transposition continued to be monitored on a weekly basis. All the ZPKIE sessions started by examining transposition progress, and ministers were asked to provide explanations for holdups. A UKIE official said, "A report is presented at the ZPKIE stating which laws were planned for adoption by the cabinet in a given month and which were in fact adopted. And [if a law has not been adopted] [Pietras] asks for explanation and each minister must provide an answer" (interview 12, p. 7). The UKIE developed a rigorous system for collecting the information on transposition progress (interview 19, p. 7). The system of regular data collection was supported by dedicated IT software developed by the DOKIE (interview 38, p. 3). An official from one line ministry's EU department said,

> [We] sent the entire list of all legislative commitments to other departments [. . .] on Friday afternoon, directors reported back to [us] by Tuesday, and on Wednesday we could send the file to [the European Law Department] at the UKIE. Based on our files the UKIE prepared a report which was presented at the ZPKIE on Friday. [. . .] After the ZPKIE approved the report, it was passed on to cabinet ministers on Monday, and during the Tuesday cabinet meeting minister Hübner informed the prime minister which ministers were overdue with legislative work.
>
> (interview 43, p. 6)

To bolster the ZPKIE's authority, Prime Minister Miller introduced a permanent point on the full cabinet's agenda devoted entirely to reviewing transposition progress. This new instrument provided the KIE secretary with an opportunity to regularly "name and shame" ministries that do not deliver on time or at all (interview 12, p. 8).

The direct involvement of the prime minister and the weekly review of transposition progress at cabinet level were crucial for facilitating enforcement by the UKIE vis-à-vis the line ministries (interview 37, p. 5). A line ministry official said, "[If delays are identified] there is always a risk that the issue may be raised at the cabinet meeting. No minister likes to be told in cabinet that one of his documents [. . .] is overdue" (interview 41, p. 3). The implicit threat of raising an issue at the cabinet meeting enabled the UKIE to use ad hoc director conferences as a time-control mechanism as did the pre-2002 KIE. In such situations the UKIE would ask line ministries to come up with a resolution by a particular deadline lest the matter was referred to the cabinet (interview 38, p. 5).

Another official confirmed, "The most common instrument is a strong appeal made in the presence of other ministers to a minister who is in delay. This may be done rather harshly at times [. . .] and pressure is brought to bear" (interview 37, p. 5). This said, in late 2002, Hübner and Miller concluded that the ZPKIE needed further institutional reinforcement. The first step was to increase the status of the transposition timetable by passing a formal cabinet resolution that contained it (interview 39, p. 8). The other instrument was the organization of trilateral meetings attended by the prime minister, Hübner, and the minister concerned at which delays and problems were discussed (interview 39, p. 9). Hübner used Miller's presence at such meetings to increase the authority of the commitments that ministers made. A UKIE official said, "[At a meeting with the prime minister] one tends to be careful with what one says. I can agree on a deadline with ministers from some ministry but it will be easy for them to write to me some time later and defer the deadline by two months. But when one talks to the prime minister, one accepts much greater responsibility for what one says" (interview 46, p. 4).

Finally, the UKIE continued to fulfill the role of a transposition facilitator. This was chiefly done at the expert level and mostly had the form of legislative and drafting assistance by the DPE lawyers. The DPE was also aided by the Government Legislative Center. A UKIE official said,

> [Our] staff got engaged in areas where the line ministries had largest problems, weakest professional staff and most pressing deadlines. Our staff were seconded there, and frequently were given competence to work

and co-draft the laws. The good thing about it was that such drafts received our compatibility acceptance at that early stage and most often there were no problems later.

(interview 26, p. 15)

The facilitation was also undertaken at political level by minister Hübner or Pietras within the context of the ZPKIE. A close observer said, "Usually we know in advance that there is some dispute. So [minister Hübner] or minister Pietras is ready with some pre-prepared alternative solutions. Having long experience with these kind of problems, they are both able to convince our side or the other" (interview 27, p. 7). There is, however, some evidence that, unlike under Buzek and Banasiński, assistance provided by the UKIE under Hübner was more successful on drafting issues than on substantive policy choices. When political issues were at stake, the ZPKIE often lacked the necessary authority to resolve them and matters were referred to the cabinet standing committee or the full cabinet (interview 25, p. 14).

To sum up, in 2002, the position, authority, and information rules that the core executive actors used to mobilize ministers and departments to adopt cooperative strategies in the area of EU rule adoption were further reinforced. As for position rules, the Miller government integrated some of the loosely bound position rules within a tighter hierarchical framework. The chief negotiator was made directly accountable to the KIE secretary, who, in turn, was subordinated to the foreign minister. This change made it possible for the KIE secretary to better manage selective incentives and monitoring, taking into account not only the internal but also the external implications of EU rule adoption. Another transformation of the position rules occurred when the KIE committee was replaced by the ZPKIE, a junior committee at undersecretary of state level. Although, as observed earlier, this change was a formal endorsement of what had become the norm since the end of the Buzek government, it was likely to have further enhanced the collective relationship among junior ministers who became permanent members of the committee. Finally, the position of the minister for transposition was removed and its competences were distributed among other junior ministers and directors within the UKIE and the Foreign Office.

As regards the authority rules, like Saryusz-Wolski, the KIE secretary was able to refer matters to the prime minister for direct intervention. The trilateral meetings between the prime minister, KIE secretary, and the minister concerned provided a further opportunity to sanction, reward, and enforce the behaviour of departments. As before, the UKIE junior ministers and departmental staff facilitated the adoption of transposing legislation, though perhaps more so at an administrative rather than political level. The authority rules were enhanced also within the ZPKIE and the full cabinet. The ZPKIE provided a collectivity-enhancing instrument for exerting peer pressure on ministers and departments. The set-aside technique was maintained, though this time referrals were made more to the technical rather than the political level. Significantly, Prime Minister Miller introduced a permanent point on the cabinet agenda that made it possible for the KIE secretary to "name and shame" ministers at a level higher than the ZPKIE. The information rules were also further enhanced. Besides those developed under Buzek and Saryusz-Wolski, two new ones require special mention. The transposition plans were extended to cover processes parallel to transposition. Perhaps, most importantly, reporting requirements for individual departments expanded substantially as ministries were expected to provide detailed feedback to the UKIE every week using dedicated IT software.

Conclusion

This chapter has mapped the institutional rules that the Polish "European" core executive had at its disposal to provide incentives and opportunity structures to ministers and departments in the area of EU rule adoption. They have demonstrated that, between 1997 and 2002, six broad configurations of such rules were present (see table 4.1). Between autumn 1996 and mid-1999, the core adopted three distinct configurations, each characterized by rather limited institutional levers for mobilizing departments in EU-related lawmaking. The development of more robust rules was precluded by, most notably, weak leadership from the prime minister and the KIE chair as well as the intracoalition conflict over the organization of the KIE and the UKIE. Between mid-1999 and the end of 2002, the core executive assumed three configurations, each characterized by highly developed institutional levers for mobilizing ministers to contribute to compliance. The new rules were developed through political entrepreneurship of the prime minister and the KIE secretary as well as through collective commitments made by ministers with the KIE committee and the ZPKIE. Table 4.1 summarizes the evidence of the cross-temporal variation in the configuration of the explanatory variable.

Table 4.1 A summary of variation in the explanatory variable

Period	Position rules	Authority rules	Information rules	Overall assessment
Autumn 1996–autumn 1997	KIE committee KIE chair/prime minister (PM) KIE secretary	• Ad hoc sanctions and rewards by PM • Ad hoc facilitation by the KIE committee • The KIE chair/UKIE does not participate in lawmaking besides EU compatibility assessment	• Transposition plans collated from ministerial inputs • Twice-yearly monitoring	Limited mobilization from core
Autumn 1997–mid-1998	KIE committee KIE chair	• Limited ad hoc sanctions and rewards by PM • The KIE committee and KIE chair/UKIE do not participate in lawmaking besides EU compatibility assessment	• Transposition plans collated from ministerial inputs • Twice-yearly monitoring • Ad hoc monitoring on the margins of parallel processes	Limited mobilization from core
Mid-1998–mid-1999	KIE committee KIE chair/PM KIE secretary	• Limited ad hoc sanctions and rewards by PM • The KIE committee and KIE chair/UKIE do not participate in lawmaking besides EU compatibility assessment	• Transposition plans collated from ministerial inputs • Twice-yearly monitoring • Ad hoc monitoring on the margins of parallel processes	Limited mobilization from core
Mid-1999–spring 2000	Negotiation Team Parliamentary secretary chief negotiator	• Parliamentary secretary and PM provide sanctions • Parliamentary secretary facilitates transposition • Chief negotiator works closely with the parliamentary secretary	• Parliamentary secretary imposes a detailed program with deadlines • Parliamentary secretary monitors daily • Negotiation Team requires progress reports from ministers	High mobilization from core

(Continued)

Table 4.1 (*Continued*)

Period	Position rules	Authority rules	Information rules	Overall assessment
Spring 2000–mid-2001	KIE committee Full cabinet KIE chair/PM KIE secretary Minister for transposition	• KIE secretary, transposition minister, and PM provide sanctions • Transposition minister facilitates transposition • KIE committee is involved in work on legislation • EU compatibility assessments extended to cover negotiation commitments • A set-aside mechanism for conflictual issues	• Transposition minister provides a detailed catalogue of legislative actions • Transposition plans specify in detail what issues need to be addressed • The KIE (and often the full cabinet) verifies progress at the start of each session • Individual record is clearly visible to all concerned	High mobilization from core
Autumn 2001–end 2002	ZPKIE committee Full cabinet KIE chair/PM KIE secretary	• KIE secretary and PM provide sanctions • UKIE staff facilitate transposition • ZPKIE committee is involved in work on legislation • Trilateral meetings held between PM, KIE secretary, and minister concerned • EU compatibility assessments extended to cover negotiation commitments • A set-aside mechanism for conflictual issues • ZPKIE provides peer pressure on ministers • KIE secretary to "name and shame" ministers at full cabinet meeting	• Cabinet adopts a detailed catalogue of legislative actions • Transposition planning extended to cover parallel processes • The ZPKIE and the cabinet verify progress at the start of each session • Individual record is clearly visible to all concerned • Detailed weekly reporting requirements for all ministries	High mobilization from core

CHAPTER 5

Impact of Executive Institutions on Rule Adoption in Poland

This chapter brings together the data on Poland from the two preceding chapters. It finds, first, that the variation in core executive rules has been, over time, consistent with changes in the EU rule adoption record. To further substantiate such congruence, the chapter provides process-tracing evidence of causal mechanisms that linked the two variables. The analysis also finds that incentives and opportunity structures originating outside the executive had some—though perhaps less systematic—effect on EU rule adoption.

Consistency with Theoretical Predictions and Causal Mechanisms

The picture that emerges from the data presented in chapters 3 and 4 indicates that the theoretical predictions formulated in Chapter 2 find confirmation in the empirical evidence (see table 5.1). The impact of rule configuration one (1996–1997) is not discussed since transposition of EU legislation per se had not started until mid-1997 and, even then, was immediately interrupted by parliamentary elections in September 1997.

The Impact of Configuration Two: Autumn 1997–Mid-1998

Between late 1997 and mid-1998, limited core executive mobilization coincided with poor EU rule adoption. This is consistent with the theoretical prediction that collective dilemmas are likely to hinder rule adoption if institutional rules are absent that would allow the core

Table 5.1 Congruence of empirical findings with theoretical predictions

Period	Core executive	Theoretical prediction	Compliance record	Overall congruence
Autumn 1997–mid-1998	Limited mobilization from core executive	Unresolved collective dilemmas and low compliance record	• Low compliance with NPAA • Low number of transposition drafts • Declining level of substantive adaptation	+ + +
Mid-1998–mid-1999	Limited mobilization from core executive	Unresolved collective dilemmas and low compliance record	• Low compliance with NPAA • Medium number of transposition drafts • Declining level of substantive adaptation	+ +/− +
Mid-1999–spring 2000	High mobilization from core executive	Resolved collective dilemmas and high compliance record	• High compliance with NPAA • High number of transposition drafts • Declining level of substantive adaptation	+ + −
Spring 2000–mid-2001	High mobilization from core executive	Resolved collective dilemmas and high compliance record	• High to low compliance with NPAA • High to low number of transposition drafts • Increasing level of substantive adaptation	+/− +/− +
Autumn 2001–end 2002	High mobilization from core executive	Resolved collective dilemmas and high compliance record	• High compliance with NPAA • High number of transposition drafts • Increasing level of substantive adaptation	+ + +

Source: Own compilation.

executive to extend selective incentives and monitoring to ministerial departments. Three causal mechanisms lend support to the above claim of consistency with theory. First, limited mechanisms for sanctioning and rewarding ministers for transposition could have hardly solved the problem of high opportunity costs that arises when ministers must comply with collective commitments that bring long-term benefits but entail short-term costs. At the planning stage, in the absence of central prioritization, ministers and line departments paid only limited attention to the practical necessities of transposition and the feasibility of plans. A UKIE official thus described the implications of such limited mobilization from the center:

> The way in which the timeline [for transposition] was specified was ridiculous. [. . .] But this problem arose because we did not have any way or institutional lever with which to discipline ministerial departments and make them commit, for example, to transposing this or that directive in 1998.
>
> (interview 19, p. 3)

Neither did the prime minister nor did the KIE sanction or reward compliance at the implementation stage. Hence, ministers and departments tended to devote only a small share of their resources to EU rule adoption, saving larger resource donations for more pressing and beneficial tasks. A high-ranking official at the PMO thus described the reason why compliance had been poor:

> It is likely that the emphasis on other policy issues such as [. . .] the four social reforms [. . .] led to the neglect of the active verification of adaptation tasks. [. . .] Some work was underway and had been begun in most areas, but there was likely to be an insufficient supervision over whether such work had been in fact completed.
>
> (interview 6, p. 13)

The limited mobilization thus caused the nominal number of transposing legislation to remain within a low range and the level of substantive adaptation to decline as new legislation was not compatible or partially compatible with the Community acquis.

Second, limited monitoring precipitated widespread shirking. The twice-yearly reporting cycle, combined with the poor precision of transposition programs, offered ministers and their staff ample opportunities to free ride on the efforts of other departments. This causal linkage was further confirmed by the UKIE minister, who said, "If one could report once a year that some things had not been implemented, and there were no consequences, then one had limited incentives to make any major efforts in that area" (interview 15, p. 6). Another official explained,

> The [transposition delays] occurred because the cabinet was not well organized. [. . .] When the council of ministers decided on something, ministers [often] forgot about that. [. . .] The implementation of the decisions was not exacted from them. Political decisions were made but these did not translate into action at the bureaucratic level.
>
> (interview 46, p. 4)

Unsurprisingly, the implementation of the NPAA commitments proved patchy and difficult, with only 16–31 percent of them actually realized.

Finally, limited facilitation from the center did little to lower coordination costs associated with EU compliance. Given the crosscutting nature of transposition as well as the high learning costs, the executive actors took much longer to work out compromises and push legislation through interministerial consultation and committees. Consequently, EU-related legislation was found to provoke prolonged debates at cabinet level, if it ever got pushed that far. Speaking about the causes of compliance problems, a lawyer at the UKIE Secretariat thus described what had been a major shortcoming in the center's role in 1997–1998,

> As well as urging them [ministerial departments] to adopt and change laws, we should have followed this up with concrete substantive assistance. For example, we could have provided more detailed guidance on what should be transposed by not only identifying the titles of directives but also by specifying which problems should be addressed in a given amendment. This would have been helpful since at that early time ministerial departments did not have strong legal expertise while such knowledge was concentrated within the UKIE.
>
> (interview 26, p. 9)

The cost of contributions to transposition was further increased since the core executive agencies kept most negotiation-related documents highly confidential and did not inform ministerial departments about the precise nature of transposition commitments. As a result, any ministerial official working in that area had to expend additional resources on simple identification of adaptation tasks. An internal government memo thus described the key reason behind delays in transposition:

> Draft negotiation positions are prepared and reviewed by only a small circle of people which means that the precise nature of the final commitments undertaken in these documents is not generally known to staff within the administration. This, in turn, means that those staff that prepare government programmes and draft legislation in individual ministries and central agencies do not take such negotiation commitments into account. [. . .] These problems cause adaptation commitments that Poland makes vis-à-vis the European Community to be implemented in an untimely manner.
>
> (UKIE Internal Document 12/07/1999 1999)

The Impact of Configuration Three: Mid-1998–Mid-1999

The efforts to bolster the pace of legal adaptation between mid-1998 and mid-1999 were taken without prior institutional change to the position of the core executive. This was because the intracoalition impasse over the appointment of the KIE secretary had prevented both Karasińska-Fendler and, later, Prime Minister Buzek from reinforcing the institutional levers available to the "European" core. The data on the rule adoption record demonstrate that the collective dilemmas continued to persist. This result is consistent with the theoretical expectation.

Three general causal mechanisms may be identified. First, despite a closer involvement by the prime minister, his practical ability to shift ministerial attention to EU transposition continued to be limited. This was because, as one would expect, Buzek could only intervene sporadically, while the operational responsibility for extending the threats of sanctions and/or prospects of rewards to ministers and departments was with the KIE secretary and the UKIE Secretariat. The latter, however, lacked the necessary institutional tool-kit to undertake such actions. In effect, ministers continued to commit only limited resources to EU transposition. Even if they did react to Buzek's new ambition, the new interest was likely to be short lived, given that the new agenda was not translated into action at the operational level. A minister said,

> Ministries made declaratory statements but then it was not the full minister who supervised concrete actions but a junior minister responsible for that area. And there was frequently a problem with the translation of that verbal commitment by the head of ministry into concrete action which was within the competence of a junior minister or department director. This problem persisted even when the prime minister started to chair the KIE.
>
> (interview 20, p. 3)

Second, the free-rider problem associated with EU rule adoption was left unaddressed as monitoring mechanisms remained provisional and ministers and departments had many opportunities to obfuscate the real extent of their contribution to the collective transposition effort. The passive compatibility checks by the UKIE did not provide the necessary incentives to ministerial departments. A UKIE minister said,

> "When a draft law was sent to the UKIE, the UKIE assessed whether it was compatible or not but did not check whether that same minister was supposed to draft ten or twenty other laws which were needed to close a given negotiation chapter.
>
> (interview 17, p. 1)

Another official confirmed, "The UKIE and the KIE committee's role was [. . .] to collate [documents from ministries] [. . .] but neither had the power to push a ministry to undertake work on a draft law if that ministry did not want to do that" (interview 13, p. 4). In effect, the implementation of the new transposition commitments continued to be patchy, with only two out of the six promised laws adopted on time and the overall score for the 1999 at 31 percent.

Finally, the KIE secretary and the UKIE continued to lack effective instruments to undertake facilitation at operational level. The UKIE lawyers did not take active interest in the lawmaking processes involving transposing legislation. In effect, coordination costs remained high.

The Impact of Configuration Four: Mid-1999–Spring 2000

From mid-1999, the institutionalization of stricter core executive constraints vis-à-vis line ministers lay foundations for a definitive shift in the rule adoption record starting from the year 2000. This finding is in congruence with the theoretical expectation outlined in Chapter 2. The core executive effect was mediated through a number of causal mechanisms. Thanks to the new instruments for sanctioning and rewarding that became available with the involvement of the parliamentary secretary and the chief negotiator in EU transposition, the Polish core executive was able to impose a stricter framework on the legislative priorities of individual ministers and departments. The center took over the transposition planning function from the line ministry level and harnessed it to the negotiation process. The close relationship between Arkuszewski and Prime Minister Buzek as well as the former's political standing within the AWS lent sufficient credibility to the threats of sanctions and prospects of reward. In effect, the nominal number of transposing legislation rose to a high level. A minister said,

> [Arkuszewski] would go to the prime minister and would say [he] had a problem. The prime minister would yell at the minister, and things started rolling. [. . .] The problem was that they were all stuck in a general malaise. And when one started pushing [. . .] redirecting the focus of line ministries on a given draft legislation, then the entire process started moving on.
>
> (interview 29, p. 14)

Second, the regular weekly monitoring from the PMO helped shift the attention from non-EU to EU-related legislation. Perhaps, more importantly, it also made the rule adoption record of individual ministers and their departments clearly visible and measurable. This limited any opportunities for shirking and free riding that hitherto dampened the incentives to contribute to transposition. A minister at the PMO thus described the nature of the problem and the effect of Arkuszewski's institution building,

> The problem is in the internal flow of documents since the same administrative machinery processes now five to six times as many documents as twelve years ago. [. . .] This is a very significant increase. The time that officials previously had available to work on a single

document must now suffice to deal with six to eight such documents. So how did they deal with this problem? [. . .] [H]e or she selected the document that they thought was the most important, and wrote "no comments" on the remaining ones. [. . .] The draft laws that officials wrote "no comments" on were then passed on further up, and were soon blocked for lack of agreement. [. . .] And so, if one wanted to deal with this problem [in transposition], then either one had to modify the system through which document passed—this [we] could not do—or ensure that some documents moved more quickly than others. The latter was simple. One had to draw up a list of required drafts and start calling ministers every week to remind them. [. . .] Of course [Arkuszewski] did not haven any special powers but it was enough for some junior minister to receive a regular call from the Prime Minister's Office for things to get moving.

(interview 29, p. 7)

The close monitoring improved compliance with transposition deadlines. As a result, the implementation of the transposition commitments rose to a high level of above 80 percent.

Third, the PMO became involved in the facilitation of transposing legislation, thus lowering the coordination costs. Arkuszewski had sufficient authority to cut through drawn-out conflicts that in many instances blocked interministerial consultations for long years. As a result, the average length of time the cabinet needed to pass transposing legislation dropped to between two and seven days (indicator 4). A minister at the PMO gave the following example,

The best case in point is the water law. [. . .] The work on that law started in early 1990s. But because there was some serious dispute with the environment ministry there was no progress for several years. [. . .] No one [at the center] took any interest in what was really blocking it and it was only [Arkuszewski] who intervened and made all the parties drop objections. [. . .] Two months later work was resumed on the law. It was enough to scold someone for things to start moving.

(interview 29, p. 13)

Although, on the whole, the empirical evidence seems consistent with the theoretical prediction, it is nevertheless interesting to note the speed with which the new institutions affected the behavior of line ministers and their staff. The emergence of new institutional rules preceded the change in the rule adoption record by only three to six months.

Some doubts may arise whether the new core executive institutions alone could have exerted so deeply transformative an impact on actor preferences and transposition outcomes over such a short period of time. One explanation may be that weakly institutionalized rules may create stronger effects than deeply entrenched institutions incentives, but this interpretation would run counter to much of institutional theory. Another explanation—which will be explored in the next section—is that ministers and their staff were concurrently subject to other mobilizing incentives originating outside the executive.

The Impact of Configuration Five: Spring 2000–Mid-2001

While the next wave of institutional change in spring 2000 had a significant effect on the configuration of institutional rules, it did not reduce the intensity and scope of the selective incentives, and monitoring the core executive extended to ministers and departments. Hence, in keeping with the theoretical expectation, configuration five had a largely consolidating effect on EU rule adoption, though its impact was not constant over time. The causal mechanisms at work were as follows. The problem of opportunity costs was tackled through the setting of clear transposition priorities by the KIE secretary and their formal endorsement through a resolution by the KIE committee. A UKIE official thus described what unblocked the compliance process: "The trick was rather simple and consisted in the detailed planning of transposition and then regular exacting of implementation from ministries (interview 52, p. 4). Another official confirmed,

> In my view the crucial contributing factor was that some organizations were forced to undertake efforts which they should have expended as a matter of course but had not. This change was achieved through institutional mobilization and coordination of the process; earlier [. . .] work [on transposition] had not been as centrally planned and vigorously enforced as later. So, in brief, the key element was to provide an overarching framework, plan the process, enforce, monitor.
>
> (interview 11, p. 16)

The commitment to the transposition priorities was sanctioned and rewarded by the prime minister with operational assistance from the KIE secretary and the minister for transposition. In effect, the nominal number of transposing legislation remained high throughout the year 2000.

The free-rider problem was addressed through close monitoring. Regular reporting to the KIE and the full cabinet made it difficult for ministers and departments to conceal the real size of their contribution to the collective compliance. An official said,

> The system of regular verification and the methodical processing of individual drafts [. . .] took us to the point where adaptation timetables which were adopted by the [KIE] committee [. . .] were implemented at 100 per cent or with only slight delay, whereas other government programmes had a 50 per cent or lower implementation record. The regular routine proved a very effective instrument of pressure.
>
> (interview 12, p. 3)

The impact of close monitoring by the UKIE was confirmed by a line ministry official who thus described the way in which central pressures entered lawmaking processes at the ministry level: "We organized regular meetings at ministry level to review draft legislation which was to be discussed at the KIE committee. [. . .] If any of our line departments was found to be in delay or otherwise in default, its representative was asked to provide explanation at that intra-ministerial meeting" (interview 19, p. 9). Unsurprisingly, compliance with transposition commitments stayed at high level, and the percentage of fully compatible domestic measures finally began to climb.

The coordination cost problem received perhaps the most attention. The close professional support from the UKIE lawyers at all stages of the lawmaking process helped to lower the costs of reaching consensus. The new time-control techniques provided a further incentive for junior ministers to solve problems at the lowest possible level and to avoid taking up matters in cabinet unless they were really of fundamental importance. The causal link between the UKIE substantive involvement and the rate of rule adoption was confirmed by a line ministry official, who said,

> They [UKIE lawyers] started to take interest in what was happening outside their secretariat. [. . .] Until then the legal department only provided written compatibility assessments. [. . .] But later UKIE lawyers started to attend interministerial meetings where many line departments were represented. This was a very good practice because it allowed us to solve a given problem right away.
>
> (interview 19, pp. 9–10)

The positive impact of configuration five faltered in 2001, despite there being no evidence of a major institutional reconfiguration at the center of government in that year. Does this observation run against the theoretical expectation? Not necessarily. It is possible to argue that, while the configuration of the authority and information rules remained intact, important changes occurred in the extent to which such rules could be invoked. Recent in origin, the new rules were underwritten by individuals rather than through valued internalized conventions. Hence, when the position of the prime minister and the KIE secretary declined in 2001, so did the operational force of the new rules they had created. The credibility crisis occurred because Buzek's authority crumbled as the AWS ministers realized that they were heading for an electoral defeat and, no matter what they did, the prime minister could not deliver reelection. This said, it is clear that the core executive variable alone cannot, in full, account for the rule adoption outcome in 2001. As will be seen in the next section, the effect of other variables, most notably the changes within the Polish party system on the eve of parliamentary elections in September 2001, must be considered to capture countervailing influences on the preferences of ministers and departments.

The Impact of Configuration Six: Autumn 2001–End 2002

In 2002, the consolidation of the position, authority, and information rules under the Miller government coincided with a second upward shift in the EU compliance. Several causal mechanisms were at work. First and foremost, Miller, the new prime minister, and his KIE secretary, Hübner, lent new credibility to the authority and information rules that had lost their operational force toward the end of the Buzek government's tenure. These included, among others, the prime minister's powers to sanction and reward ministers, transposition facilitation by UKIE lawyers, a set-aside mechanism for conflictual issues, and regular monitoring by the UKIE and the KIE committee. In a press interview, Prime Minister Miller said,

> After a few weeks into the government's term, I introduced a practice that all cabinet meetings should start with minister Hübner's presentation about the accession negotiations and related interministerial consultations. This was because I realized that not only the negotiation issues but also the adoption of draft laws, decrees and other decisions, was subject

to such controversies and line ministries were putting up such opposition, that progress could only be assured at the cabinet level.

(Paradowska and Władyka 2002)

A UKIE official confirmed, "[Progress] is reviewed weekly in cabinet. There is a permanent point on the cabinet agenda and the prime minister receives full information on who did not do what. This system is very effective [. . .] because insubordinate behaviour toward the prime minister is a serious problem. And everyone does their best to avoid it" (interview 12, p. 8). Besides hierarchical instruments, the Miller cabinet reinforced collectivity-based rules through the creation of the ZPKIE committee, which further helped the UKIE to enforce the transposition timetable (interview 41, p. 3; interview 46, p. 8). A minister said,

> A collective pressure in the form of appropriate decisions by the ZPKIE imposing deadlines for preparing transposition measures was an effective instrument because a deputy minister for European integration [at a line ministry] could apply not only his own pressure but also the collective pressure of the ZPKIE on his colleagues within the ministry.

(interview 37, p. 4)

Thanks to increased mobilization from the core, the rule adoption record returned to a high level. Compliance with transposition commitments rose to a higher level, as the nominal number of transposing legislation increased to between 13 and 29 drafts per quarter.

But, besides honing the legacy rules, both the prime minister and the KIE secretary introduced new institutions, which paved the way for additional improvements to EU rule adoption. First, the problem of high coordination costs was addressed by a combination of the deeper involvement of the UKIE technical level and more extensive punishments for unnecessary referrals to the cabinet. The coordination costs were further lowered through a practice of trilateral meetings between the premier, KIE secretary, and the minister concerned. Second, the new monitoring mechanisms combined with peer pressure within the ZPKIE committee to reduce opportunities for shirking and free riding. The written reporting system locked ministries in a rigid routine that allowed all holdups to be quickly identified and made visible to all the parties concerned. Another significant instrument was provided by the set-aside technique employed to manage the timely resolution of interministerial conflicts.

The new rules contributed to major improvements in EU rule adoption. The reliability of the NPAA legislative commitments rose substantially, especially at the monthly and quarterly levels. On the one hand, the exceptional character of such improvements was likely to have been due to a progressive institutionalization of the core executive rules that were employed to extend selective incentives and monitoring to departments. But, on the other hand, such a gradual institutionalization must have been made more difficult by a change of government, the arrival of new political actors, and the organizational changes to the PMO, the UKIE, and the Foreign Office. Hence, it seems that, again, the effect of other contextualizing variables must be explored to more fully explain the size of the changes in the transposition record.

Contextualizing the Impact of the Core Executive

This section analyzes the depth of the causal relationship between core executive and EU compliance by exploring the influence of incentives and opportunity structures originating outside the executive: (i) the EU institutions, (ii) political parties, and (iii) nonexecutive state and non-state organizations.

The Impact of EU Incentives

The theoretical expectation outlined in Chapter 2 is that, where institutional rules exist that enable EU actors to extend selective incentives and monitoring to Polish ministers and their staff, then such rules should facilitate the resolution of collective action problems and the adoption of EU rules. Indeed, since mid-1998, the EU had developed an increasing array of institutional levers that should have allowed it to make the collective dilemmas in transposition much less pronounced. These rules included, first and foremost, sanctions and rewards within the technical assistance programs. The EU provided financial resources to the Polish government on the condition that it demonstrated progress in legal adaptation. Such conditionality was particularly emphasized during the Seventh Association Committee in April 1999. An internal government document noted that "the EU delegation [. . .] made it clear that the financial assistance for Poland in this [internal market] area was conditional on further legislative progress" (UKIE Internal Document June 1999, pp. 10–11). Besides conditionality, the

Commission had more direct instruments to extend selective incentives. One such instrument was provided by personal interventions by EU officials with Polish ministers. This took the form of letter exchange and personal contact. The members of the Negotiation Team personally travelled to negotiation sessions in Brussels and were subject to direct pressure from the EU officials. Also, Poland had many visits by the EU officials who held talks in line ministries and put strong pressure on ministers (interview 49, p. 5).

From mid-1998, the European Commission had acquired institutional tools to facilitate EU rule adoption through the screening process. At multilateral screening sessions, held jointly with other acceding countries, the Commission provided Polish officials with educational guidance on how the acquis should be understood and implemented. Between 1998 and 1999, over 80 such sessions were held in Brussels (KPRM 1999). Such close exchanges with the Commission services and member states' officials provided incentives for domestic ministers and their staff to identify individual benefits in transposing legislation. The ongoing negotiation process allowed the Commission to develop new instruments to exert pressure on Polish government ministers and departments. For one thing, the Commission could take advantage of the natural competition among acceding states and harness peer pressure to mobilize Polish decision makers. But, most importantly, it could affect the Polish government by the threat of reopening, or delaying the closure of, negotiation chapters. A Commission official thus explained its logic:

> I remember one chapter [. . .] where they [Poland] promised to adopt by a particular date some law that would go in this and that direction. There had been experts working together with them, sitting around the table and telling them what exactly had to be done, so they said "ok we will do it" and that was taken as a commitment in the negotiation draft common position and the common position. We closed the chapter provisionally but six months later the experts who had been working on that chapter became alarmed realizing that they [Poland] were not going to do what they told us. The big alarm bell started ringing, the member-states were informed and [they] asked us what the Commission was going to do now as Poland was not doing what it had promised. So we sent very high level letters to whatever minister was in Poland telling them that if you were not going to rectify the situation, we would be obliged to re-open the chapter.
>
> (interview 51, p. 3)

The European Commission also had instruments to function as an external monitor for Polish ministers keeping a watchful eye on their progress in EU compliance. The Commission had the opportunity to "name and shame" Polish ministries in its regular progress report. The accession negotiations offered the Commission further opportunities to undertake monitoring. During the negotiations, the Commission developed new monitoring tools ranging from general tables to specific transposition databases (Official Communication SekrMInJSW/5558/2000 2000; Official Communication SekrMinJSW/7041/2000 2000). The Commission services could also act as competitive agenda setters in domestic law-production since Polish ministries often sent draft legislation to Brussels for a final check before adoption (interview 10, p. 2; interview 51, p. 5). A Commission official said,

> If there was good cooperation, dialogue and confidence, then the ministry would send the draft to us for opinion, especially, when the directive was not easy to transpose. [. . .] But the member states themselves also wanted to see the draft and to provide comments. This happened very, very frequently.
>
> (interview 53)

These EU incentives were likely to have an impact on EU rule adoption. The process-tracing material reveals that the EU incentives did play a role in shaping the actions of ministers and their departments. It has been argued, for example, that the absence of EU mobilization in 1997 and 1998 may have adversely affected the individual preferences of ministers and their staff. A line ministry official said,

> The perception that these tasks should be undertaken was not very high among government officials. [. . .] This [lack of awareness] was perhaps due to the limited importance of the negotiations process [in their work]. It is understandable that when the [accession] process went slowly, then nobody here was in a hurry to carry out these tasks.
>
> (interview 19, p. 8)

The incentives originating from the accession negotiations may have further contributed to improved EU rule adoption in 2000. An official said, "Later [after the negotiations had started] when the effects of one's work were immediately visible, then the commitment of staff increased (interview 16, p. 8). A crucial function in changing expectations of ministers and their staff was fulfilled by the screening of domestic legislation that opened the negotiations process. For the first time, Polish ministerial officials came into intensive contact with the Commission officials and, where necessary, had to supply information on how they intended to transpose EU measures. By addressing the problem of high opportunity costs of transposition, the screening had a clearly mobilizing effect on line ministries (interview 21, p. 4). A UKIE official said,

I think [the negotiations] introduced a significant change. [. . .] The line ministries became closely engaged in the screening process, since the Polish delegation was composed of line ministry officials responsible for a particular policy area. The delegation was headed by a line minister who bore responsibility for political and technical positions that were taken. And so all became stakeholders in the process, all became involved.

(interview 26, p. 5)

The institutional levers originating within the negotiation process clearly shaped the calculations of ministers and their staff. The Commission's threat of reopening or delaying the closure of negotiation chapters was a particularly effective instrument (interview 16, p. 9; interview 7, p. 12). An official confirmed,

The Commission employed instruments that shaped the actions of Polish actors. It could always exert political pressure by declining to close or open a particular negotiation chapter. And then we looked what the problem was and [. . .] some official had to quickly work to close the gap.

(interview 52, p. 4)

It has also been argued that domestic actions were responsive to monitoring by the European Commission. This causal link was confirmed by a UKIE minister, who said,

The EU was very good at verifying our compliance with transposition commitments. If we declared that we would do something is six months, then the EU would come back in six months time and ask if we have done it. [. . .] This was an important element of pressure on our administration.

(interview 16, p. 9)

Perhaps, most importantly, the EU contributed to the improvement of the Polish compliance record by threatening Poland with ejection from the first round of enlargement in mid-1999. As a result, the mounting evidence of serious delays in transposition combined with a credible external threat produced a widespread sense of national crisis in late 1999. If Poland had been denied EU membership, this would have been considered the most serious setback in foreign affairs for decades. The special circumstances are likely to have made it incumbent on ministers and their staff to contribute to transposition as a patriotic obligation. That EU membership was considered at the time as an objective of utmost national importance is attested to by unprecedented written agreements concluded by, on the one hand, the executive and parliament, and, on the other hand, by all major political parties (Pakt 2000; Trójporozumienie 2000). A PMO official said,

> The acceleration of transposition work in 2000 reminded me sometimes of the 1989–1990 transformation when the cabinet was caught in a fever of legislative work. Many drafts were submitted to cabinet spontaneously in response to developments in the accession negotiations.
>
> (interview 7, p. 12)

The above evidence demonstrates that EU incentives were likely to have an effect on the behavior of individual ministers and hence to affect rule adoption. Indeed, the EU effect may help to explain, for example, the rapid nature of the change in rule adoption patterns in early 2000. This is because, by gradually redirecting the attention of Polish governmental ministers to EU transposition since the late 1998, the Commission may have created conditions favorable for a strong and immediate reversal in the path of compliance that occurred once the core executive had been strengthened. This linkage would thus help to explain the puzzle indicated in the preceding section of weak institutions having quick and strong effects. Having said that, it must be noted that the process-tracing evidence in Chapter 4 demonstrates that the EU incentives alone were not sufficient to unblock transposition in mid-1999. It was only after the new core executive rule had been in place that the trajectory of the legal adaptation changed. Furthermore, the EU incentives are not able to explain the sudden decline in compliance in the year 2001. Even though the ongoing accession negotiations provided the European Commission with a growing array of new institutional levers, the dynamic of EU rule adoption declined that year.

The Impact of Party Constellations

Another variable that needs to be considered here is the incentives and opportunity structures originating within political parties. The theoretical prediction presented in Chapter 2 is that where party-based rules exist that allow party leaders or the coalition as a group to extend selective incentives and monitoring to individual ministers and their staff, then such rules should facilitate the resolution of the collective dilemmas and, hence, should contribute to better rule adoption. In the period under investigation, Poland had three governments, each characterized by a different configuration of party discipline and intracoalition cooperation. The AWS-UW government (autumn 1997–mid-2000) was characterized by limited rules for party-based mobilization (cf. Zubek 2001; Rydlewski 2000, 2002). Although the UW had fairly well-developed internal party controls, the AWS—the senior coalition member—was a loose conglomerate of small parties and had extremely scant institutional levers with which to mobilize its members toward collective policies. More significantly, major policy differences in the area of EU-related domestic alignment prevented the coalition from developing internal party-based rules for coalition management in that area.

The minority AWS cabinet established after the UW withdrew from the coalition in June 2000 was characterized by limited internal party controls within its supporting party. For a brief spell, in the second half of 2000, Prime Minister Buzek was able to reinforce his grip on the party when he replaced Krzaklewski at the AWS' helm (interview 35, pp. 6–7). Yet, that improvement turned out to be rather short lived. Already, in 2001, the AWS began to disintegrate and the internal discipline declined substantially. The internal dissention within the AWS was mainly caused by a widespread realization among its members that their party was heading for an electoral defeat in the forthcoming parliamentary elections. As a result, many of the AWS's constituent parties began to dissociate themselves from the government, starting to run independent election campaigns. The AWS's disintegration was further facilitated by a parallel split within the UW. In January 2001, a large number of UW members set up a new party, the Civic Platform, which acted as a magnet for many AWS members.

The SLD-UP-PSL government was able to rely on relatively well-developed internal party controls and institutional procedures for intercoalition cooperation (Zubek 2006). The SLD and the PSL had a highly centralized internal organization inherited from the apparatus of their communist predecessors. Miller, SLD leader, further tightened his grip over the party after the SLD had transformed from a coalition of several parties into a unitary political party. The internal cohesiveness of the SLD, the UP, and the PSL facilitated the development of more centralized coordination mechanisms under the Miller government. The SLD entered into a stable electoral coalition with the UP, and the two parties were widely expected to run together in the next elections. Although there were major policy differences between the SLD and the PSL, they had governed together in 1993–1997 and were quick to develop institutions that would facilitate cooperation, including party summits and coalition management conferences.

The empirical evidence confirms that the party-based configurations had some direct impact on actions of individual ministers in the area of EU-related legal adaptation. The direction of that relationship is consistent with the theoretical predictions made in Chapter 2. It has been pointed out, for example, that the absence of cooperation within the coalition adversely affected the tempo of transposition in 1998–1999 (interview 46, p. 4). An official confirmed that individual parties often bound their ministers to realize party ideal point policies:

> The coalition nature of the government had an impact. Many different interests collided here, and [legal adaptation] did not always match the interests of the environment or agriculture minister because their own party opposed a particular solution. [. . .] So it all depended on [personal] relations between ministers, particularistic interests, and on whether EU requirements ran with or against one's preferences.
>
> (interview 26, p. 5)

The party configurations are perhaps less well placed to explain the acceleration of transposition in early 2000. The new compliance dynamic emerged despite the fact that there were no major changes in internal party controls or interparty cooperation. There is some evidence, however, that the temporary improvement in Buzek's ability to control the AWS in late 2000 may have positively affected the compliance process to some extent. A senior advisor at the PMO said,

> After the Freedom Union had left the government [. . .] the cabinet's operation became smoother for a while [. . .] the government was more

cohesive, the decision chains became shorter and so certain decisions could be taken more quickly, though we did not succeed every time because that government was not cohesive in ideological terms.

(interview 35, p. 7)

The disintegration of the AWS in 2001 may also largely account for the decline in the rule adoption record. The lower enforceability of party-based sanctions and rewards was certain to produce increased shirking on the part of line ministers and their staff. This was especially likely given that relative benefits from private interest actions became more attractive for ministers who wished to individually avoid the collective electoral fate of the AWS. Another contributing factor was that Saryusz-Wolski, the KIE secretary, joined the new Civic Platform in 2001, which eroded his relationship with the prime minister and, consequently, his ability to rely on the latter's authority in relations with line ministers. Finally, under the SLD-PSL-UP government, the reinforced party-based lines of accountability facilitated the resolution of the collective dilemmas in the compliance with EU legislative commitments. Prime Minister Miller combined premiership with the leadership of the SLD and was able to heavily rely on party-based lines of accountability to sanction and reward his ministers, though his powers in this area were somewhat constrained by the coalition nature of his government.

The Impact of Parliament and Nonstate Organizations

Two other variables that need to be considered here are institutional incentives originating from parliament and nonstate actors. With regard to the former, there is evidence that parliament had shaped the actions of ministers in the transposition of EU legislation. In 1997–1998 ministers and departments were subject to limited mobilization from parliament. The parliamentary committee on European integration (PKIE) dealt with legal adaptation only a few times a year when it reviewed the government's reports. The actual work on transposition was decentralized and conducted by individual sectoral committees. That limited mobilization from parliament was likely to contribute to poor compliance. A parliamentary observer was sceptical about the effects of parliamentary work during that time:

The parliament did not block or hinder [transposition] but perhaps the Sejm did not fully grasp what it was all about. [. . .] Since 1995 the

Europe Agreement Committee, later the European integration committee, had moved into this area with difficulty, and every year devoted one session to transposition but it was more of a ritual than real decision-making.

(interview 18, pp. 2–3)

The impact of selective incentives and monitoring may be also traced in 1999–2000. The change in the rule adoption record from the start of 2000 had been preceded by an institutionalization of new constraints on the executive by the Polish parliament (interview 18, p. 6). In October 1999, the KIE in the lower chamber debated the Commission's progress report and, dissatisfied with what it found, required the executive to present a list of all transposing laws that had to be implemented until mid-2000 and to take rapid remedial action to accelerate the pace of legislative work (Sejm RP 1999). Parliament's most vital contribution to improving EU rule adoption came in the first half 2000. In February–March 2000, the lower and upper chambers passed resolutions asking the government to prioritize transposing legislation and to prepare a detailed legislative program (Sejm RP 2000; Senat RP 2000). In mid-2000 the lower chamber set up a special parliamentary committee to work exclusively on transposition, which mobilized government ministers to prepare and submit relevant draft legislation (interview 1; interview 33) and monitored this work. An official said,

It was parliament who demanded outstanding drafts to be calculated, required detailed lists [of planned legislative activity] to be developed, identified delays in the submission of such drafts, and forced the government to take action. So this is a clear success of the [European Law] committee.

(interview 18, pp. 8–9)

The parliamentary incentives are perhaps less useful in explaining the improvement in compliance patterns in 2002. The upward shift in that year was not associated with the institutionalization of any new constraints from parliament. Indeed, one could argue that such parliamentary mobilization declined as the lower chamber decided not to set up a special committee to work on EU transposition only.

As regards the impact of nonstate actors, the picture is rather mixed. It is possible to argue, on the one hand, that the Polish executive operated within a dense network of socioeconomic entanglements and that such embeddedness may have hindered the process of compliance since many sectoral groups were able to persuade ministers to delay costly adaptation. That the executive-society linkage is rather porous in Poland is well documented (Staniszkis 1999; Hausner, Marody, et al. 2000; Staniszkis 2000; Pedersen and Zubek 2004). The causal linkage between such embeddedness and rule adoption patterns has been identified by some interviewees. For example, a line ministry official said,

> I think that there was a strong pressure from different lobbies [. . .] miners, steel workers, farmers. [. . .] These lobbies are part of the electorate [. . .] and, if a government has the prospect of a four-year term, if it is that lucky, then not everyone wants to [. . .] risk their political future. And so, it required a lot of effort to push some things through.
>
> (interview 39, p. 3)

On the other hand, the years 1998–2002 did not bring any moves toward greater executive autonomy that could contribute to improved transposition in situations where domestic constraints blocked policy change. Neither was institutional connectedness reinforced in such a way as to generate new incentives and monitoring facilitating EU rule adoption (interview 31; interview 57). In sum, the impact of institutional incentives originating from parliament and nonstate actors, though evident, seems to be slightly less pronounced that in the case of the previous two contextualizing variables.

Conclusion

This chapter has assessed the consistency of the theoretical predictions outlined in Chapter 2 with the empirical data presented in chapters 3 and 4. In doing so, it has found that the variation in EU rule adoption has been, over time, causally related with the changes in core executive rules. Between late 1997 and mid-1998 the limited core mobilization contributed to a poor legal alignment by failing to address the collective action dilemmas that impinged on the adoption of EU transposing measures. Between mid-1998 and mid-1999, despite prime ministerial efforts, the failure to reinforce the core executive rules prevented the Polish cabinet from improving its rule adoption record. It was only the institutionalization of stricter core executive constraints vis-à-vis line ministries in mid-1999 that pushed EU rule adoption onto a new trajectory. The chapter has also found that the effect of the core executive variable is contextualized by the incentives and opportunity structures originating outside the executive. The EU incentives are particularly helpful in explaining the rapid character of the shift in EU rule adoption from 2000. The party constellations are best placed to account for the slowdown in rule adoption in 2001.

CHAPTER 6

Core Executive and Rule Adoption in Hungary and the Czech Republic

The preceding chapters have shown that variation in core executive institutions shaped Poland's rule adoption record over time. This chapter examines if the core executive variable is capable of explaining cross-country variation in EU rule adoption. In doing so, it selects two countries that vary on core executive institutionalization—Hungary and the Czech Republic—and checks whether the outcomes of rule adoption in these countries are consistent with the expectations of the core executive model. The chapter first maps the emergence of the Czech and Hungarian "European" cores. It shows that core executive reinforcement advanced furthest in Hungary but failed to make similar progress in the Czech Republic. The chapter then presents comparative data on the success of rule adoption in Hungary and the Czech Republic. The data demonstrate that Hungary performed better at EU rule adoption than the Czech Republic, which confirms the expectations of the core executive model. The chapter closes by assessing the effect of EU conditionality, political party configurations, socioeconomic interests, and executive-legislative relations.

Core Executive Institutions in Hungary

Pressures for Institutional Change

At the start of the postcommunist transition, Hungary—like other Central European states—had weak capacities for effective policy and political coordination at the center of government (Goetz and Wollmann 2001; Dimitrov, Goetz, and Wollmann 2006). Under communism, this task had been routinely performed by the party's central administration, and the latter's demise left the government without a true center. The process of creating a core executive around the Hungarian cabinet and prime minister started already in the early 1990s (cf. Ágh 1999, 2001a; Schiemann 2004; Brusis 2006). The constitutional amendment of 1990 reinforced the powers of the prime minister, paving the way for the emergence of a prime ministerial government. The Council of Ministers' Office was transformed into a PMO and was endowed with extensive control and coordination powers. Interministerial consultations became gradually institutionalized. A newly established weekly conference of administrative state secretaries—chaired by the head of the PMO—reviewed all cabinet submissions, while political coordination was reinforced by creating ministerial-level cabinet committees.

The institutionalization of the core executive received a new impetus with a widely perceived "performance crisis" of domestic institutions in the mid-1990s (Ágh 2001a; Dimitrov, Goetz, and Wollmann 2006). A worsening fiscal balance forced the Horn cabinet (1994–1998) to reorganize the budgetary process whereby more stringent constraints were imposed on the spending discretion of ministers and departments (cf. Brusis and Dimitrov 2001; Dimitrov, Goetz, and Wollmann 2006). The new framework included, inter alia, a consolidated budget, multi-year planning, and centralized financial accounts. Learning from the experience of the fiscal crisis and the institutional changes that followed, the Orbán government (1998–2002) extended the core executive upgrading to nonbudgetary policy making. A full cabinet minister was placed at the head of the PMO, whose capacity for strategic analysis and monitoring was upgraded (Brusis 2006, pp. 71–74). Specialist ministry desks were set up to monitor closely the policy-making process at departmental level. The PMO was given a more active role in strategic policy prioritization and agenda setting (Zubek 2007).

The crisis of governance also extended to the "European" structures in the Hungarian government. The increased intensity of the EU-Hungary relations, after the decision to move toward enlargement had been taken at the 1993 Copenhagen summit, presented new coordination challenges. Until 1996, EU affairs were coordinated by two separate units: the Office of European Affairs in the Ministry for Trade and Industry and the EU Department in the Foreign Office (cf. Vida 2002; Lippert and Umbach 2005). In the mid-1990s, the Hungarian decision makers became increasingly aware that the "two-centered" coordination solution was insufficient to respond effectively to the new adaptation tasks. Vida writes, "This structure necessarily entailed rivalries between the two ministries and diminished the effectiveness of management of European affairs" (2002, p. 59). In a parallel development to the Polish executive, such external and domestic pressures led to an overhaul of the "European" core executive in Hungary at the level of position, authority, and information rules.

Position Rules

The overall coordination of EU affairs was entrusted to the Hungarian Foreign Office and, in particular, its State Secretariat for Integration (SSI) (cf. Vida 2002; Ágh and Rozsas 2003; Nunberg 2000; Lippert and Umbach 2005). The SSI was established in 1996, following a merger of the Office of European Affairs in the Ministry for Trade and Industry and the EU Department in the Foreign Office. It housed departments dealing with trade and economic relations, political cooperation, technical aid and assistance, and legal harmonization. At its heart was the EU Coordination Department, which provided the support for accession delegations and internal coordination fora. The SSI became the State Secretariat for Integration and Trade after external economic relations were added to its brief in 2002. The foreign minister was placed in charge of all matters relating to the preaccession process and, once negotiation talks started in March 1998, headed the Hungarian delegation. He was assisted by the head of the SSI and the head of the Hungarian mission in Brussels, who was chief negotiator (Lippert and Umbach 2005).

In the area of legal approximation, the key role was assigned to the Hungarian Ministry of Justice (MJ) (Vida 2002; Ágh and Rozsas 2003; Németh 2000). From early 1995, the MJ prepared legal approximation plans, supervised their implementation, and supplied advice to ministries. It was in charge of developing methodological guidelines on how transposition should be handled in legislative terms. The MJ also ensured that all bills and secondary legislation were compatible with the acquis. This was done through a screening of all legal texts for EU compatibility. The MJ was responsible for ensuring the coherence of Hungarian translations of EU legislation. The ministry had a specialist General Department for Legal Harmonization, which took the lead in all transposition-related tasks within the ministry and in relations with other agencies. In 2002, the MJ appointed a special deputy state secretary to coordinate legal adaptation processes (interview 67, p. 3).

Two collective institutions were also established. The European Integration Committee brought together key cabinet ministers (foreign affairs, finance, economics, home, and justice). It was chaired by the prime minister and served as a briefing—and, if necessary, a conciliation—forum for cabinet ministers (Ágh and Rozsas 2003, p. 9). The committee did not meet during the Orbán cabinet but resumed its operation under Prime Minister Medgyessy (2002–2004). The other institution was the Interministerial Committee for European Integration (ICEI), which was a consultative forum for discussing EU-related government business (Vida 2002, pp. 60–61). It was chaired by the head of the SSI and composed of state secretaries and other high-level ministerial officials. The ICEI also established a network of expert groups, which helped with the screening of Hungarian legislation. They were chaired by respective ministries and were also attended by the representatives of the Foreign Office, MJ, and the Finance Ministry.

The new institutional framework survived throughout the accession process. Perhaps the most important change occurred in 2003 when Medgyessy appointed a minister for European affairs as part of a larger upgrading of the PMO's role in EU affairs. Three new departments were created in the PMO: National Development Plan, Regional Development, and Public Relations and Communication (Vida 2002, p. 64). Yet, none of the changes implied a major reorganization of institutional roles in the area of legal transposition. The stability of the structures responsible for EU rule adoption was stressed by one Hungarian minister, who said,

> It was a ten years' job. It did not matter which coalition was in power. The work could go on in a calm manner. [We] could prepare what was needed, and the work was concentrated in one hand. [. . .] The ministry of justice was not disturbed so it was a highly professional process.
>
> (interview 67, p. 4)

The institutional continuity can be ascribed to low party political conflict surrounding the institutionalization of the Hungarian "European" core. The Orbán cabinet focused mainly on domestic issues and was happy to leave in place the mechanisms created by the previous Horn government. Even Prime Minister Medgyessy, who adopted a more hands-on approach to accession-related business, exercised self-restraint in introducing institutional changes (interview 66, p. 6). The stability was further reinforced by the fact that the Hungarian cabinet delegated the new tasks to institutions that had already enjoyed much credibility as coordinators of horizontal policies. The Foreign Office had always played a leading role in the management of EU relations, while the MJ had a well-entrenched role in coordinating the executive lawmaking process.

The 1995–1996 reorganization of the Hungarian core executive created new position rules, providing an organizational vehicle for administering incentives and monitoring in the area of EU rule adoption. The rules mandated the emergence of both hierarchical and collective relationships. The hierarchical relationship arose through the delegation of powers to the Foreign Office and the MJ. Both these institutions can be viewed as agents/monitors retained by the Hungarian cabinet to facilitate rule adoption. The collective relationship was introduced through the European Integration Committee and the ICEI committee, two new institutions that complemented the cabinet and other interministerial fora in the collective management of EU-related legislation.

Authority and Information Rules

The position rules were complemented by authority and information rules. The MJ had the right to program legal approximation inside the Hungarian cabinet (interview 65, p. 7; interview 67, p. 2). It prepared, updated, and enforced regular national transposition programs. In 1995, the MJ formulated a five-year approximation program and started preparing detailed annual timetables for transposition. Once accession talks had been launched, the MJ coordinated its planning work with the Foreign Office and the ministry that led negotiations in a given policy area. The ICEI expert groups provided the technical platform where sectoral officials and horizontal coordinators worked out the details and timing of the adaptations to be undertaken (interview 62, p. 11). The final say was with the Foreign Office and the MJ, which brought legislative programs in line with the commitments made under the NPAAs and the information contained in the screening lists. A close observer said,

> The European content of the programme was prepared by the European state secretariat but then the ministry of justice had to identify the real requirements—if some change was necessary in a statute, governmental decree or ministerial regulation. These legislative issues had to be decided and it was the task of the ministry of justice.
>
> (interview 62, p. 11)

The MJ and the Foreign Office ensured that EU-related legislative tasks were incorporated into annual and half-yearly cabinet legislative programs. On initiating a planning cycle, the PMO received a detailed list of adaptation requirements from the Foreign Office, including a legislative program prepared by the MJ. These documents formed part of the guidelines that the head of the PMO sent to individual ministries when inviting bids for legislation. The MJ and the Foreign Office alerted the PMO if departments did not include preplanned EU legislation in their proposals to the cabinet program (interview 68, p. 5). Such issues were typically raised at the meetings of the administrative state secretaries at the PMO.

Thanks to a close linkage with regular legislative planning, EU rule adoption benefited from a relatively high centralization of cabinet programming in Hungary. In contrast to the Czech Republic (as will be seen later), the Hungarian core executive had provided much tighter guidance to ministries in legislative planning (Zubek 2007). For one thing, the cabinet program was as a rule constructed according to explicit prioritization criteria. Bills relating to the government manifesto, EU accession, and codification enjoyed priority; all other bills were committed to a reserve list. Once an item was placed on the program, ministerial implementation was subject to close scrutiny by the PMO and its ministry desks.

Besides mobilizing ministers and departments in transposition planning, the MJ adopted a centralized approach to drafting EU-related legislation. The ministry itself prepared the texts of many pieces of major EU-related legislation and was deeply involved in the drafting and legal review of the other measures. As one Finance Ministry official noted, "The general legislation was prepared by the minister of justice but VAT and other specialist bills were developed together with the finance ministry" (interview 63). In areas in which the MJ did not have sufficient expertise and had to rely on departmental lawyers, it nevertheless controlled the technical quality of the transposition process. Its General Department for Legal Harmonization formulated various guidelines and methodological norms outlining the philosophy of adopting the acquis into the Hungarian law (cf. Németh 2000).

In guiding EU rule adoption, the MJ mirrored its traditionally strong coordinating role in the Hungarian legislative process (interview 64;

interview 67). The minister for justice enjoys a veto over the legislative quality of a bill, as he or she had to sign off all bill submissions to the cabinet. To be effective in this role, the MJ is home to many sectoral divisions specializing in different areas of law, which act as clearing houses for draft legislation prepared by ministries. It also takes a lead in codification. An official described this task:

> The Justice Ministry has a special role in codification because all laws made by other ministries are sent to us because we have to see all drafts. [. . .] If a draft is in connection with [our brief] we have to see that draft.
>
> (interview 64, p. 1)

Given that the MJ enjoyed a highly institutionalized role in domestic legislative coordination, the EU-specific rules, in particular those relating to drafting methods, may be seen as extensions of the already robust authority and information rules attached to the Hungarian core executive.

Transposition work was subject to regular core executive monitoring (interview 61, p. 9; interview 65, p. 7). The Foreign Office and the MJ assessed how well individual ministers complied with EU-related legislative commitments. The foreign minister prepared regular quarterly reports to the cabinet on the status of accession negotiations and domestic adaptations (see also Vida 2002, p. 62). The report was submitted typically for information but—if it identified major problems and in the final stages of the accession talks—it was subject to cabinet discussion (interview 66, p. 4). The cabinet also held annual evaluations of the NPAAs. If necessary, monitoring was enhanced. Speaking about such situations, a PMO minister said, "The foreign minister had the duty to report to every cabinet meeting how we fulfil these requirements. And so we could see regularly if some ministry had problems which had to be addressed" (interview 61, p. 9).

If delays or problems were identified, the prime minister or the PMO minister asked the minister concerned to explain the situation at the cabinet meeting. If the reasons for the holdup were merely technical, the minister was asked to report to the cabinet in a few weeks on what had been done to remedy the situation (interview 66, p. 5). If such "name and shame" mechanisms did not work or contentious issues were involved, the PMO, its head, or even the PM became involved in resolving the problem. At times, the PMO had to take a lead in formulating the new policy. A PMO official explained,

> More generally [. . .] [the bureaucrats] did not want to do it. So they sent the bill for consultation with this and that ministry. They tried to postpone. And sometimes we had to change the priority, as it happened after we replaced [. . .] the agriculture minister. [. . .] And they were not able to manage so quickly and professionally, so we had to set up a working group inside the PMO. We took some advisors from the-outside. The prime minister participated in these meetings. We also invited the state secretary from that ministry and tried to revitalize the process.
>
> (interview 61, pp. 9–10)

To summarize, the Hungarian "European" core executive benefited from an extensive array of newly established and preexisting rules attached to the positions of the MJ, Foreign Office, and the PMO. The authority rules included, in particular, the right by the MJ and the Foreign Office to determine the form and the timing of EU rule adoption. In this, both these actors could rely on their long-standing institutional authority as horizontal coordinators inside the cabinet. The information rules took the form of the procedures for the translation of negotiation commitments into domestic legislative plans and regular monitoring and firefighting in EU rule adoption. These authority and information rules enabled the Hungarian core executive actors to extend effective incentives and monitoring to ministers and their departments.

Core Executive Institutions in the Czech Republic

Developments before 1998

In contrast to Hungary, Czech cabinets made few efforts to institutionalize central coordination capacities after the 1993 breakup of Czechoslovakia (cf. Nunberg 2000; Brusis 2004; Dimitrov and Zubek 2006). In formal terms, the prime ministerial powers over the cabinet and its members remained limited. The Government Office acted as a government registrar, providing mainly technical assistance to the cabinet as a whole. Policy development was firmly in the hands of individual ministries, while the onus of inter-ministerial coordination fell on a loose web of advisory councils and committees. The reasons for the weak institutionalization of the core executive were party political (Dimitrov and Zubek 2006, pp. 150–151). Enjoying supreme control of the ruling party—the Civic Democratic Party (ODS)—Prime Minister Václav Klaus found the establishment of a strong center of government unnecessary. In mobilizing his cabinet, he relied mainly on party lines as well as personal networks and loyalties. Klaus's distinctive antibureaucratic bias provided a further disincentive to institutionalizing administrative mechanisms for planning, monitoring, and enforcing collective cabinet actions.

The situation changed somewhat with the Zeman cabinet (1998–2002). Prime Minister Miloš Zeman appointed three deputy prime ministers with explicit policy coordination briefs—foreign, economic, and social affairs (cf. Nunberg 2000; Dimitrov and Zubek 2006). They were supported by newly established secretariats in the Government Office, held regular briefings with other ministers, and met as a government presidium before each cabinet meeting. The prime minister also appointed a fourth deputy prime minister to chair the Legislative Council (LC). The LC and its working groups—which had existed since the late 1960s—checked draft legislation submitted to the cabinet for drafting quality, constitutionality, and compliance with international law. While these changes may have improved coordination, the Czech executive continued to operate as a decentralized ministerial government. The main obstacle to a major upgrading of the core executive was a deeply entrenched tradition of far-reaching ministerial autonomy (cf. Dimitrov and Zubek 2006; Kabele and Linek 2004).

The limited institutionalization affected the development of the Czech "European" core executive. Some adjustments were made in 1994, when a Government Committee for European Integration and a Working Committee for the Europe Agreement were established at ministerial and senior official level, respectively. The Foreign Ministry and its then EU Section—created in 1996—provided the lead in managing the Czech-EU relations (cf. Šmejkal 1998, pp. 113–120). But the structures responsible for legal adaptation remained underdeveloped (interview 73; interview 79; interview 83). Before 1996, general guidance was provided by an independent Office for Legislation and Public Administration (Pavlik 2002, p. 26). The responsibility was then moved to the Justice Ministry, which, however, did not enjoy wider coordination functions in the legislative process (unlike in Hungary). An official thus described the state of affairs in EU rule adoption in 1998 when the Zeman cabinet assumed office:

> The department of EU compatibility did not work [. . .] maybe prime minister Klaus did not pay any attention to these issues. For example, we found the computer funded by EU for the translation of EU legislation still packed up in a box!
>
> (interview 73, p. 1)

Once in office, the Zeman cabinet began to address such institutional shortcomings not least because of the mounting criticism from the European Commission, which, in its regular report of late 1998, complained about a slow pace of EU rule adoption. As in Hungary, the external pressures contributed to domestic changes in the configuration of the Czech "European" core executive.

Position Rules

The overall coordination of EU accession was placed in the hands of the deputy prime minister for foreign affairs. In 1998–1999, this position was occupied by a minister without portfolio but was then merged with that of the foreign minister. In operational terms, accession negotiations were managed by the Foreign Ministry (cf. Pavlik 2002; Lippert and Umbach 2005). The first deputy foreign minister was in charge of EU affairs and headed the Section of European Integration (SEI). The SEI (created in 2000 from EU Section) housed departments dealing with communication strategy, common foreign and security policy, and the acquis communautaire (Lippert and Umbach 2005, p. 118). The key department was that for coordination of EU relations. It employed around 23 staff responsible for interdepartmental coordination and the accession process (Pavlik 2002, p. 32). After 1999, the first deputy foreign minister supervised the Department for European Integration in the Government Office. Once accession talks started in March 1998, he was also chief negotiator and led the Czech negotiation delegation.

In legal transposition, the principal coordination role was assumed by the chair of the LC. The LC chair was in charge of general executive lawmaking and had some coordination powers vis-à-vis ministers, in particular with regard to legislative planning and monitoring. In November 1999, the LC chair was entrusted with the coordination of

EU rule adoption inside the cabinet (Czech Government 1999). In early 1999, the EU Compatibility Unit was moved from the Justice Ministry to the Government Office and incorporated as a new department into the Section of the Deputy Prime Minister for Legislation (LC chair). It had three main sections: the analytical section that checked the compatibility of draft legislation with EU law; the approximation section that maintained a database of EU measures and the corresponding Czech legislation (the so-called ISAP); and the translation section that was responsible for translating or revising translations of EU laws (interview 83, p. 1).

Collective institutions were also reinforced. In 1998, a Negotiation Delegation was created. It was chaired by the deputy foreign minister for EU affairs and consisted of Foreign Ministry diplomats and high-level civil servants from key ministries. It was assisted by more than 30 working groups, each headed by an official from the ministry responsible for a given chapter (Pavlik 2002; Lippert and Umbach 2005). The standing of the Government Committee for European Integration was strengthened. In 2000, an amendment to the cabinet rules of procedure mandated that documents submitted to the committee would not undergo consultation in other interministerial fora. More importantly, the decisions by the committee stopped being subject to open debate at the full cabinet, unless a minister explicitly requested a discussion at the beginning of the cabinet meeting.

The 1998–1999 reorganization of the Czech executive created new position rules providing hierarchical and collective vehicles for administering incentives and monitoring in the area of EU rule adoption. The hierarchical relationship arose through the delegation of coordination powers to the Foreign Minister and the LC chair. Both these institutions can be viewed as agents/monitors retained by the Czech cabinet to facilitate rule adoption. The collective was enhanced by the reinforced Government Committee for European Integration and the coordination meetings at the Government Office, the institutions that complemented the cabinet in the collective management of EU-related legislation.

Authority and Information Rules

Unlike in Hungary, the core executive in the Czech Republic was not furnished with the authority to program EU rule adoption (interview 73, p. 2; interview 74, pp. 7–8). The principal role of the Government

Office was to ensure that each EU measure had been allocated a responsible ministry. The power to program transposition remained in the hands of individual ministries, who decided what legislative changes had to be made to comply with the acquis (cf. Czech Government 1999) The ministerial departments formulated legal adoption programs during the screening process together with the European Commission. Besides areas in which transitional exemptions were requested (where clearance from the Committee for European Integration and Foreign Ministry was required), the transposition of noncontentious acquis was left to the discretion of individual departments. A minister explained,

> After receiving the position papers, the EU asked us if we could specify the steps to achieve [transposition], if we foresee any problems, how we will establish the necessary institutions. [. . .] [T]his planning of individual steps was the responsibility of individual ministries.
>
> (interview 74, p. 8)

Once ministerial transposition programs had been formulated, they were logged in a centralized database (ISAP) at the EU Compatibility Unit at the Government Office (interview 83, pp. 7–8). The department was then able to use this information to check if—at a time when the Government Office collected bids to the government legislative program—ministries complied with their EU-related legislative commitments. Such checks became regular especially after the screening process had been completed (interview 74, p. 9). If the department found some measures to be missing, it alerted the LC chair (interview 78, p. 5). A ministry official explained, "There was this meeting with the head of the Legislative Council who asked us [why] there is this type of [EU-related] aim but no legislation" (interview 86, p. 2).

Unlike in Hungary, however, the "European" core executive in the Czech Republic could not rely on an established practice of centralized cabinet programming. The Czech legislative plans were typically constructed in a bottom-up fashion and were driven by sectoral lawmaking strategies. There was little scope for core executive prioritization, and the institutional powers of the LC chair were weakly developed (Kabele and Linek 2004). Ministries were legally responsible for the substantive content of legislation, while the center was concerned only with its legislative and technical quality (Linek and Kabele 2004, p. 7). In such circumstances, noninstitutional resources determined the extent to which the core was able to mobilize ministerial departments. The political standing and personal determination of the deputy prime minister for legislation emerged as key factors influencing the prioritization of EU rule adoption during legislative planning (interview 73, p. 5; interview 6; interview 7).

The strict, legally entrenched division of powers between the center and ministries meant that, unlike in Hungary, the Czech "European" core rarely, if at all, took the lead on the preparation of horizontal transposition measures. Policy formulation and initial legal drafting of all EU-related legislation were firmly in the hands of ministries (interview 73; interview 79; interview 83). This said, the core executive did exercise extensive control on the quality of EU-related legal drafting. The EU Compatibility Department developed a methodological guide for ministries, which was adopted as a formal cabinet resolution (Czech Government 1999). It also assessed EU compliance of all draft legislation during the interministerial review and before submission to the cabinet. On average, the Government Office redrafted one in two pieces of legislation (Linek and Kabele 2004). This strong role in legal quality review built on the established practice of the Government Office controlling the lawmaking process in technical terms (cf. Dimitrov and Zubek 2006).

EU rule transposition was subject to core executive monitoring. The key instrument in this area were quarterly and monthly transposition reports to the cabinet (interview 78, p. 5; interview 83, p. 3; interview 75, pp. 4–5). They were prepared by the EU Compatibility Department on the basis of sectoral reports received from ministries. An official said, "Every three months we prepared a report for the government regarding where there are [transposition] gaps [. . .] and every month some information for the government on how we fulfil our obligations" (interview 83, p. 3). These reports were discussed in the Government Committee for European Integration, its working committee, and the full cabinet. A minister said,

> The EU committee had regular meetings. [. . .] And the procedure was similar to a regular review of the government legislative plan during cabinet meetings. [The key focus was on] the ongoing changes to harmonize the Czech legislation with the EU law, which deadlines have been kept, and if not, what we should do. These were very working meetings which always set tasks and deadlines for individual ministries. The decisions were presented to the cabinet which routinely approved them.
>
> (interview 75, pp. 2–3)

The Czech government relied extensively on the monitoring by the EU (interview 73, p. 4; interview 74, pp. 8–9). The regular progress reports by the European Commission were scrutinized in detail and discussions were held in committees and the cabinet. The EU role was particularly important when it came to ensuring the completeness of EU rule adoption. A minister said,

> I would say the best monitor was the EU. We submitted the idea that we have this kind of plan for legislation. [. . .] And they gave us comments. We did not have a watchdog in the Czech government which would check that all directives have been transposed.
>
> (interview 74, p. 8)

There were limited sanctions for noncompliance at the administrative level. The EU Compatibility Department in the Government Office kept a record of progress in rule adoption but had no direct instruments to induce ministerial staff to initiate EU-related legislation (interview 73, p. 5; interview 83, p. 6). A minister said,

> I would say [. . .] the control was rather automatic. Staff in the Compatibility Department made these checks. [. . .] [F]or every ministry they had a contact person [. . .] [who] did the checking. Another question is how strong the leadership was to speed things up.
>
> (interview 74, p. 9)

This said, the EU Compatibility Department could alert the deputy prime minister for legislation if serious delays were detected. He would then contact ministers or deputy ministers directly and request explanation. An official in the Government Office said,

> We described the situation in our report and they had to speed up the work on some draft legislation. And then it went up to deputy prime minister for legislation. [. . .] [L]etters were sent to the ministers [by the deputy prime minister]. [. . .] [The letter] would say we have found out that you are in delay with some legislation and so please inform me [why this is so].
>
> (interview 83, p. 6)

The success of such interventions depended critically on the personal standing of the deputy prime minister for legislation (interview 73,

p. 5; interview 83, p. 7). Pavel Rychetský, who held the office between 1998 and 2003, was highly respected inside the cabinet and enjoyed good relations with Prime Minister Zeman and Vladimir Špidla, who was prime minister between July 2002 and July 2004. After Rychetský's departure in 2003, however, his office remained vacant for six months and the successors did not match his stature (interview 83, p. 7). If the deputy prime minister were unsuccessful in resolving the problem directly, he raised the matter with the prime minister and at a cabinet meeting. The extent to which the prime minister could induce individual ministers again depended on his personality, determination, and the political ability to dismiss ministers (interview 81, p. 5; interview 82, p. 4). A close observer explained,

> There was regular reporting to the government on the transposition of EU legislation. There was a list of laggards which was discussed within the government and if you saw a long line of [nontransposed] directives under certain minister, the prime minister, in particular Zeman, became interested. And he asked how it was possible that [for example] the minister of health had such a bad record. How come such a big delay? [. . .] Špidla was not pushing ministers as strongly as Zeman. He was softer, nicer to his ministers. The debate was calmer. Špidla did not threaten ministers to replace them because of their bad record the way Zeman did.
>
> (interview 74, p. 9)

Such "naming and shaming" in cabinet resulted in formal resolutions being passed that requested ministers to take prompt action within a fixed deadline. The implementation of these resolutions was subject to monitoring by the Government Agenda Department and the deputy prime minister for legislation (interview 83, p. 3).

To summarize, although—similarly to Hungary—the Czech cabinet delegated the coordination of EU rule adoption to preexisting institutions, the latter did not benefit from institutionalized authority rules. In effect, the Czech "European" core executive had limited powers in areas such as transposition programming, sanctioning of noncompliance, or preparation of horizontal transposing legislation. In such circumstances, the success in mobilizing ministers in EU rule adoption depended critically on noninstitutional resources such as personality or political position of officeholders. This said, the Czech core executive developed a rich array of information rules. The Government Office monitored rule adoption at administrative level, not least through the ISAP database.

At the political level, the prime minister and the cabinet held regular discussions of the Czech rule adoption record.

The Core Executives Compared

The comparative case studies demonstrate some similarities between Hungary and the Czech Republic. The similarities in institutional design are most marked at the level of position rules. Both core executives established the role of monitors for EU rule adoption. The task was delegated to the MJ in Hungary and the deputy prime minister for legislation/LC chair in the Czech Republic. In both countries, these institutions in turn set up specialized EU legal departments—the General Department for Legal Harmonization in Hungary and the EU Compatibility Department in the Czech Republic. Both countries also created collective institutions to deal with rule adoption. Ministerial committees included the Cabinet European Committee in Hungary and the Government Committee for European Integration in the Czech Republic. The similarities were also evident at the level of authority and information rules. Both "European" core executives had the power to monitor progress in rule adoption at ministry level. Ministries were required to submit monthly or quarterly reports on their transposition records, which were double-checked by the core. In both cases, the core executives also had some mechanisms at their disposal to mobilize ministers in EU rule adoption.

But, despite such similarities, the two cases also reveal important differences in core executive institutionalization. Whereas in Hungary the authority and information rules were highly institutionalized, this process was much less pronounced in the Czech Republic. Three dis-similarities are worth highlighting. First, in Hungary the "European" core executive operated as a central authority in the programming of EU rule adoption. The Hungarian MJ prepared detailed transposition plans and guided the process of EU rule adoption at ministry level. In the Czech Republic, programming of rule adoption was in the hands of ministries while the Government Office and its EU Compatibility Department performed a technical, record-keeping role. Second, the central legal department in Hungary was placed in charge of preparing horizontal or omnibus EU-related legislation. The Hungarian MJ itself drafted a large proportion of all transposing measures. The role of the Czech Government Office was limited only to performing quality checks. Third, in Hungary, sanctions for delays or rewards for compliance were extended already at administrative level. The MJ's legal departments maintained close regular contacts with the ministerial administration and could mobilize staff behind EU rule adoption at an early stage of lawmaking. In the Czech Republic, the EU Compatibility Department operated at arm's length and sanctions or rewards were available mainly at the political—mainly cabinet—level.

To a large extent, these differences reflect diverse trajectories of domestic executive development. In Hungary, institutional reforms aimed at establishing a stronger center of government began already in the early 1990s and continued throughout the decade. A major reinforcement of the Hungarian "European" core was thus a natural step in the same direction. Meanwhile, the overhaul of the Czech "European" core executive by the Zeman cabinet did not build on earlier institutional changes and was undertaken against a legacy of well-entrenched ministerial autonomy. In the country where core executive had been progressively strengthened (albeit not without problems), the "European" core emerged the strongest; where the center remained weak throughout the 1990s, the "European" core was less successful in acquiring substantial new powers. Deficits in executive institutionalization tended to enhance the impact of personalities. In the Czech Republic, the authority that Prime Minister Zeman and Deputy Prime Minister Rychetský commanded in cabinet had an important impact on the dynamics of EU rule adoption. EU-related legislative activity noticeably slowed down after the soft-spoken Prime Minister Špidla had taken over from Zeman, and Rychetský had left the cabinet. In Hungary, personal qualities of the key executive actors mattered less for the transposition dynamics.

Impact of Core Executive Institutions on Transposition Record

In line with the theoretical expectations formulated in Chapter 2, major differences in executive rule configurations should lead to variation in the success of rule adoption. One would thus expect that EU transposition would be more problematic in the Czech Republic than in Hungary. This is for at least three reasons. First, the limited powers of the core executive in the programming of EU rule adoption increased the likelihood of incomplete transposition by individual ministries. If departments were autonomous in both deciding what legislative action needed to be taken and implementing such decisions, then there were strong incentives to engage in some shirking behaviour, particularly where costs of adaptation were high. Second, the weak role of the Czech core in sponsoring horizontal or omnibus legislation may have led to problems in rule adoption where transposition required the joint action of many ministries. This is because rule adoption entailed high cooperation costs. Third, limited core executive mobilization at administrative level may have resulted in bureaucratic resistance or indifference to EU rule adoption. The reason is that the cost-benefit calculations of ministry officials were not tipped in favor of transposition.

To check such intuitions this section examines Czech and Hungarian transposition records at the time of EU accession. Two principal sources of information can be used for this purpose. First, the Secretariat General of the European Commission publishes regular data on the notification of national measures implementing EU directives. In August 2004, the Commission published data on new member states for the first time (European Commission 2004c). The second source of information is the Single Market Scoreboards published biannually by DG Internal Market. The scoreboards present the progress in notification of implementing measures for EU directives relating to internal market. The July 2005 scoreboard was the first to include systematic data on the new member states (European Commission 2005). These data are not, of course, without problems. They are based on self-assessment and, although the Commission monitors its credibility, some national governments may strategically overreport transposition. The data do, however, provide some indication of national rule adoption records.

The Secretariat General data for compliance records show significant variation among the new member states (cf. European Commission 2004c) (see figure 6.1). According to the Commission data for August 2004, the transposition deficit (measured as a number of non-notified directives) stood at from 30 (1.2 percent of all directives) in Hungary and 253 (10 percent) in the Czech Republic. These scores were—respectively—the second best and the worst result in all of the EU8. The data also reveal that Hungary and the Czech Republic belonged to different clusters among the new Central European member states. Together with Lithuania and Poland, Hungary formed a group of transposition leaders. These countries failed to notify only a few measures (under 50, or 1.6 percent of all directives). The Czech Republic—together with Slovakia—belonged to

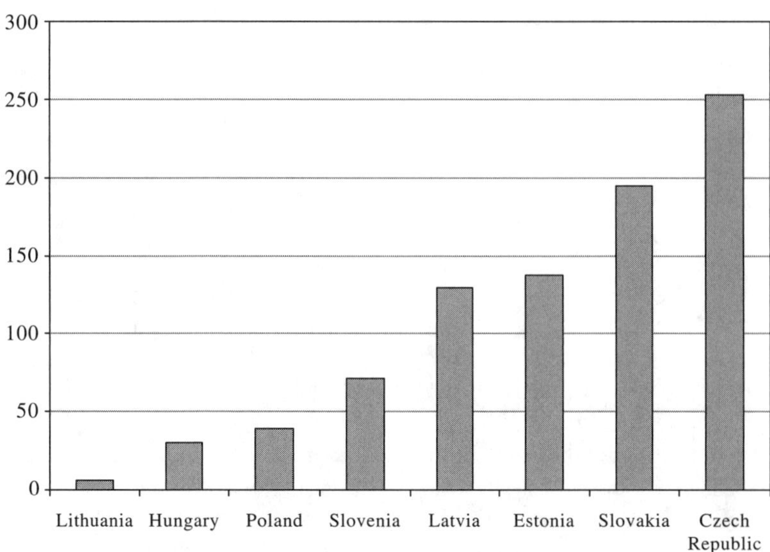

Source: Own compilation based on the data from European Commission 2004c.

Figure 6.1   Notification of transposition of EU directives (all), August 2004

transposition laggards. The number of nonnotified directives in these states exceeded 150 (or 7.8 percent of all directives).

The Internal Market Scoreboard data published in July 2005 show a similar variation in the notification of internal market directives (cf. European Commission 2005; see figure 6.2). The transposition deficit stood at 12 (or 0.7 percent of all directives) in Hungary and 57 (or 3.6 of all directives) in the Czech Republic. Again, these results were the second best and the worst score in EU8. The countries also belonged to similar—but not identical—clusters. Together with Lithuania and Slovenia, Hungary was a clear leader in the transposition of single market directives. The countries in this group had a transposition deficit of approximately 0.7 percent of all directives. In contrast, the Czech Republic was among the three countries with the highest deficit. The states in this group failed to notify between 2.4 to 3.6 percent of all single market directives.

The picture that emerges from these data confirms the theoretical predictions of the core executive model. The country that advanced the furthest in institutionalizing a strong "European" core executive had a

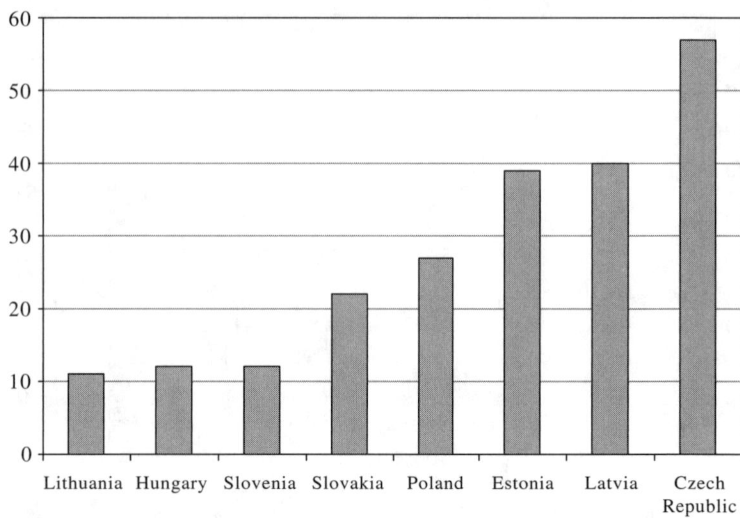

Source: European Commission 2004c, 2005.

Figure 6.2 Notification of transposition of EU directives (single market), July 2005

much better rule adoption record than the country in which this process did not make similar headway. It is interesting to note that the result holds when the Polish case is added to the analysis. Unlike in Hungary, the "European" core in Poland did not benefit from early and successful institutional reinforcement. At the same time, in contrast to the Czech case, the Polish core executive did undergo a major overhaul in the late 1999 and early 2000, acquiring new powers in programming transposition, sponsoring horizontal legislation, and mobilizing action at administrative level (see Chapter 4). As could be expected, Poland's transposition record at the time of EU accession was slightly worse than that of Hungary but much better than that of the Czech Republic. According to the Secretariat General data, Poland was one of the three compliance leaders with a deficit of 39 nonnotified directives (or 1.6 percent of all directives). In the Single Market Scoreboard, Poland occupies a lower position but still performs better than the Czech Republic.

Does this result still hold if one considers the impact of other factors? Chapter 2 identified three contextualizing variables: (i) opportunities generated by the EU, (ii) incentives provided by parties and coalitions, and (iii) incentives extended by domestic nonexecutive organizations. Let us check if any of these variables could have affected rule adoption, relying on secondary literature to establish the values that they take in each of the two ountries. First, a question arises if the variation in the rule adoption records may be related to different levels of EU incentives. This seems rather unlikely. Most research on Europeanization in Central Europe finds that, while the degree of EU conditionality varied over time, there was limited cross-country variation. Perhaps, more importantly, the studies that do find cross-country variation show that that Hungary and the Czech Republic faced similar intensity of conditionality (cf. Steunenberg and Dimitrova 2007). The impact of party configurations on transposition dynamics also seems at best limited. Both executives relied on fairly well-institutionalized supporting parties, and prime ministers could rely on rules attached to the office of party leader. If at all, party configurations may have had a more negative impact on rule adoption in Hungary than in the Czech Republic. The Orbán cabinet (1998–2002) was a coalition of three parties, a condition that may have hindered the effectiveness of party rules, while the Zeman government was a single-party government, which may have positively affected the ability of party leaders to control its members.

The situation looks slightly different when one considers the potential impact of nonexecutive actors. It can be expected that strong linkages between ministries and socioeconomic networks may exacerbate the collective dilemmas underlying rule adoption, while more autonomous executives would be able to solve such problems more easily. Meanwhile, the existing research on Hungary and the Czech Republic finds that the former has a much more autonomous executive than the latter (see Stark and Bruszt 1998). This suggests that differences in rule adoption records may be due to variation in the intensity of socioeconomic entanglements. However, this relationship looks less strong if one adds the Polish case to the analysis. As shown in Chapter 5, the Polish executive operated within a dense network of socioeconomic interests, as did the Czech Republic, and yet it had a better transposition record at the time of accession.

Besides the three factors discussed here, it is necessary to consider the possible effect of one more variable—the configuration of executive-legislative relations. The impact of this factor was not considered in previous chapters because the dependent variable was operationalized as cabinet compliance with EU-related legislative deadlines. It needs to be examined, however, if one analyzes national transposition records. It can thus be expected that the stronger the position of the executive vis-à-vis the parliament, the smoother the process of transposition. It is generally accepted that Hungary is closest to a majoritarian executive-dominated democracy while the Czech Republic resembles a consensual system with an influential legislature (see, for example, Olson and Norton 2007). Moreover, the latter state had a minority government in 1998–2002. The variation in rule adoption may have thus been caused, at least in part, by different executive-legislative configurations. It is, however, difficult to judge the relative strength of this effect in a two-country comparison. If one factors the Polish case into the analysis, it seems that, although important, executive position in parliament cannot fully explain the dynamics of EU rule adoption. Poland has as a dominant parliament and a proclivity for minority governments (cf. Goetz and Zubek 2007) as does the Czech Republic, but this was not reflected in the overall success of EU rule adoption.

Conclusion

This chapter has presented a comparative analysis of executive institutions and EU rule adoption in Hungary and the Czech Republic. It has found that the reinforcement of the "European" core executive advanced furthest in Hungary but failed to make similar headway in the Czech Republic. Using comparative transposition data, the chapter has shown that, in line with the theoretical expectations, Hungary performed better at rule adoption than the Czech Republic. The impact of other factors, in particular that of external incentives and nonexecutive actors, looks less robust. The results complement the longitudinal case study of Poland (chapters 3, 4, and 5) and provide further validation of the core executive model.

CHAPTER 7

Conclusion: Core Executives and EU Compliance

This concluding chapter teases out the broader implications of the study. This is done under three headings. The chapter first shows how the present findings contribute to a better understanding of the modalities of EU rule adoption in Central Europe. Second, it demonstrates that the core executive argument resonates well with the research on EU compliance in the old member states and may be used to improve the predictive power of the theoretical models employed in that research. Finally, the chapter argues that this study of EU rule adoption in Central Europe can inform our understanding of how governments may organize to produce policies that deliver general long-term benefits but impose sectoral short-term costs.

Understanding Europeanization in Central Europe: What Have We Learnt?

Lesson One: EU Rule Adoption Presented Challenges for Domestic Executives

The first lesson from this study is that the specific characteristics of EU rule adoption before accession presented significant institutional challenges for domestic executives in Central European states. The uncertainty about how much rule adoption had to be achieved to qualify for EU membership created incentives for ministers and their staff to shirk on EU-related legislative commitments. The diffuse and long-term nature of the benefits from rule adoption encouraged ministerial administration to commit resources to other uses that could bring concentrated and short-term political gains. The extensive need for coordination, across both time and sectors, pushed up the transaction costs of rule adoption, which provided a further bias against engaging in transposition work. These problems made it difficult for Central European executives to initiate and adopt EU-related legislation and had to be resolved before successful rule adoption could be achieved at the domestic level.

The national executives had to respond to these challenges by strengthening the capacities at the center of government. The book finds evidence of a move toward the institutionalization of "European" core executives in all of the three countries analyzed. In Hungary, the core was reinforced in 1996–1998—before the accession talks started—and remained almost unchanged until 2004. In Poland and the Czech Republic, some institutional changes were undertaken before the onset of negotiations, while the most significant overhauls occurred in 1998-1999, when the membership talks were already under way. In functional terms, the reforms were designed to solve the problems of free riding, opportunity costs, and coordination. The reorganizations had two common features. They created the position of a monitor/central authority for EU rule adoption whose primary task was to program, monitor, and—if necessary—induce ministerial compliance with EU legislative requirements. The other shared feature was the setting up of collective institutions to lower the costs of programming, monitoring, and coordination.

That the transposition of EU law prior to accession presented important challenges for domestic executives in Central Europe has not so far been appreciated by the research on EU rule adoption in Central Europe (Schimmelfennig and Sedelmeier 2005; Grabbe 2006; Vachudova 2005). Inspired mainly by international relations perspectives, this research has treated national institutions as black boxes and has paid limited attention to the internal life of executives. The present findings confirm, however, the results reported in the literature on the emergence of core executives in Central Europe (see Laffan 2003; Lippert and Umbach 2005; Dimitrov, Goetz, and Wollmann et al. 2006 for comparative overviews). This research shows that the three governments covered in this book are not exceptional in having sought to institutionalize a "European" core. Similar reforms were also undertaken in the other accession states in Central Europe (see Nakrosis 2003, Dimitrova and Maniokas 2004 for Lithuania; Scootla and Scootla 2004 for Estonia; Bilčík 2004 for Slovakia; Fink-Hafner and Lajh 2003 for Slovenia).

Lesson Two: Core Executive Institutionalization Influenced EU Rule Adoption

The second, and perhaps the most crucial, lesson is that core executive reinforcement was a key determinant of EU rule adoption in Central Europe (cf. Zubek 2005). This book has shown that the success of legislative alignment depended on the institutionalization of specific position, authority, and information rules, which could be used by core executive actors to mobilize and monitor ministers and their staff. If such rules were weakly developed, rule adoption proceeded unevenly; if they were well established, legal change tended to be timely and accurate. This relationship has been tested in a cross-temporal setting. The study has shown that the Polish ministerial administration failed to comply with self-imposed commitments to transpose EU laws as long as the core executive actors continued to possess limited institutional levers. The linkage was further examined in a cross-sectional analysis. It has been found that Hungary (where the reinforcement of the "European" core advanced furthest) achieved better legal alignment than the Czech Republic (where the institutionalization process did not make similar headway).

These findings underscore the importance of domestic variables for explaining the outcomes of EU rule adoption in Central Europe. The latter factors remained largely unexplored in the strand of the Europeanization literature, which has accorded primary explanatory power to EU conditionality. These accounts found domestic variables to have had little systematic impact on the success of EU rule transfer, though they did discover some influence on the timing of legal alignment (see Schimmelfennig and Sedelmeier 2004). The present results suggest that the effect of domestic variables may have been much more pervasive. The study finds that the organization of the national executive had an effect quite independent from external incentives and proved a useful explanation of the variation in the success of legal alignment. Tapping into the real-life mechanisms of legal change, it also makes it possible to formulate accurate predictions of postaccession compliance in the new member states.

This study adds to, and reinforces the findings of, the more nuanced conditionality-centered explanations of EU rule adoption in Central Europe (Grabbe 2006; Vachudova 2005; Dimitrova 2004). These accounts find that the scope of Europeanization effects has been determined not only by EU demands but also by domestic factors such as the reform fit, degree of political will, and institutional capacity. Perhaps the most relevant parallel is with the research by Mattli and Plümper (2004). These authors have argued that leaders in more democratic systems can be expected to have greater incentives to produce public goods such as EU-related regulatory alignment. In their analysis, they find that regime type was a key factor in accounting for differing rates of alignment with the EU requirements among the accession states. This result resonates well with the insights from the present study. A well-institutionalized core executive may be viewed as a mechanism that enhances democratic governance by mobilizing individual ministers and departments toward achieving collective rather than individual goals.

Lesson Three: EU Pressures Had Two Channels of Influence

The third lesson is that EU pressures had two—both contingent—channels of influence on EU rule adoption in Central Europe. The first channel was the direct shaping of the rule adoption decisions of ministers and departmental staff. The European Commission held frequent meetings with governmental decision makers in Central Europe in the framework of the Europe Agreement and the accession talks. These contacts enabled EU officials to monitor and induce adoption of EU rules at the domestic level. The study demonstrates, however, that the effectiveness of such direct EU mobilization for inducing rule adoption was conditional on domestic factors. In Poland, the mounting pressures from the Commission in 1998–1999 failed to produce a major shift in the dynamics of EU rule adoption. The latter occurred only after the Polish "European" core had been upgraded in the late 1999 and early 2000. Similarly, the predominant reliance of the Czech executive on EU monitoring and mobilization was not sufficient to remedy the shortcomings of its executive organization and resulted in relatively poor transposition record.

The second channel was an indirect influence through encouraging the emergence of strong "European" core executives. The acquis conditionality revealed a misfit between domestic executive arrangements in Central European states and the external challenge of legal alignment. In cases where a high degree of misfit resulted in transposition delays (particularly in Poland and the Czech Republic), the EU encouraged institutional reform by "naming and shaming" accession states. Such external pressures opened up opportunities for domestic entrepreneurs to push for core executive reinforcement. But the success of such latter action was contingent on domestic conditions, in particular coalition politics, prime ministerial preferences, and institutional legacies. In more general terms, it was also determined by the overall trajectory of executive development. In Poland and Hungary—where there was a more general move toward establishing a strong center of government— it produced deeper effects that in the Czech Republic, where such a general trend was not present. The EU pressures played a significant, albeit not a self-standing, role in empowering domestic entrepreneurs and necessitating institutional change.

These findings contribute to the conditionality-centered literature on Europeanization in Central Europe by identifying the channels through which external pressures may have affected the behavior of domestic decision makers. The "inside-out" perspective made it possible to tease out the different linkages between the national and EU levels that have been largely unacknowledged by existing research. More significantly, the study demonstrates that, regardless of the influence channel, the impact of external pressures was conditional on domestic factors. This result runs parallel to the findings from that Europeanization research which argued that EU rule adoption was shaped by an interaction of external and domestic factors (see, for example, Grabbe 2006). What this book contributes to such latter accounts is the integration of both types of variables within a theoretical framework. In doing so, it shows that domestic and conditionality-centered perspectives are complementary—rather than alternative—explanations.

Core Executives and Rule Adoption in EU25

Core Executives and Post-Accession Compliance

The core executive lens has been useful for understanding EU rule adoption before accession in Central Europe. But does this argument hold broader relevance? There is some evidence that this is the case. It can be argued, for example, that the model helps explain the patterns of postaccession compliance in the new member states. In line with institutionalist theory, one would expect the effect of well-established executive rules to persist beyond accession. Except where radical institutional changes were introduced after accession, the domestic executives should continue to have recourse to the position, authority, and information rules that facilitate ministerial responsiveness in EU-related legal alignment. Hence, the country's postaccession transposition record should—at least in the first few years of membership—shadow that achieved on joining the EU. The leaders may be expected to continue to excel in rule adoption, while the laggards should keep on underperforming. This pattern may of course change in the medium term as other new factors—not least of institutional or political nature—begin to influence the dynamic of transposition. But it should hold in the short term.

Preliminary evidence supports this expectation. Of the three countries covered in this volume, Hungary may be predicted to remain one of the leaders in EU transposition, Poland a good to middling performer, and the Czech Republic one of the shirkers. The data on notification of the single market directives in 2005–2007 seem to confirm this intuition (see figure 7.1). Despite some cross-time variation, Hungary and Poland clearly performed better than the Czech Republic. During the first three years of EU membership, the number of nontransposed directives stood at 12–15 and 14–27, respectively, in the former two countries and at 26–57 in the latter state. The Secretariat

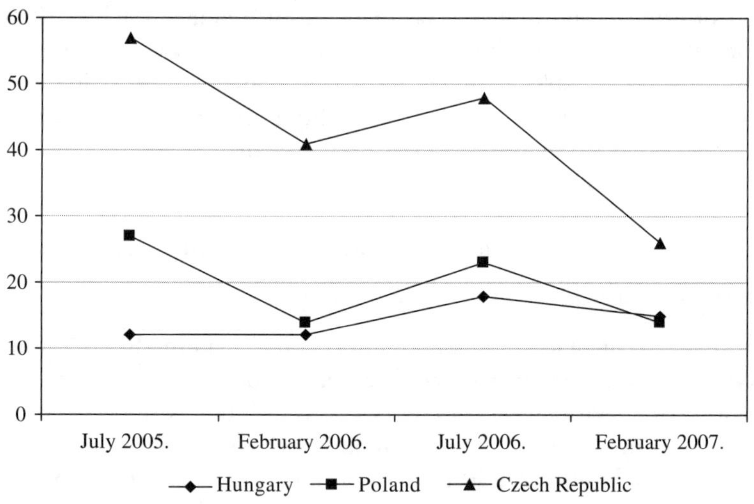

Source: Own compilation based on European Commission 2005, 2006a, 2006b, 2007.

Figure 7.1   Number of nonnotified single market directives, 2005–2007

General data on the notification of all directives show a similar trend. In line with the expectations, the countries that institutionalized forceful "European" cores before accession continued to have a superior transposition record.

In predicting the patterns of postaccession compliance, the core executive model fares much better than the conditionality-centered arguments. These explanations generally expected a major decline in the EU transposition record of the new member states after accession (cf. Sedelmeier 2007). They have argued that, since preaccession alignment was largely driven by the conditional incentives of EU membership, once the Central European states have joined, they can be expected to procrastinate further rule adoption. The data in figure 7.1 do not confirm such expectations. The number of nonnotified directives in Poland, Hungary, and the Czech Republic remained at a similar level or declined. The data for the other new member states show a similar trend (European Commission 2005, 2006a, 2006b, 2007). These results provide an additional support to the finding that the domestic factors underpin EU rule adoption in Central Europe.

Core Executives and Compliance in Old Member States

But is the core executive argument relevant beyond the study of EU rule adoption in Central Europe? Can it inform our understanding of compliance in the old member states? It must be noted, of course, that many of the assumptions on which the present argument is based do not necessarily hold for the old member states. By having much experience of the EU-level decision-making process, ministers from these states have opportunities for shaping EU laws in such a way as to maximize benefits and minimize adaptation costs. If there are clear benefits from transposition, they can also be reaped without delay. The member state administrations may also be expected to have found ways and means to lower internal coordination costs in rule adoption. This said, dilemmas similar to those impinging on preaccession rule adoption may arise in the old member states. If national ministers lose a battle at the EU level, they may have to implement policies that have a negative cost-benefit ratio. In such circumstances ministerial shirking can be expected and, if transposition were to follow, the executive must organize to address the problem.

Indeed, some studies on EU compliance in the old member states provide interesting parallels with the approach adopted in this study.

Two of these deserve special mention here. The first work is a cross-temporal analysis of the Greek transposition patterns by Dimitrakopoulos (2001). In his assessment, Dimitrakopoulos has emphasized the role of organizational factors within the central administration for shaping Greek transposition outcomes in the 1980s and 1990s. He writes,

> The process of transposition illustrates clearly that the Greek central government was, and partly remains, dominated by sectoral logics which transform the policy process into a power struggle between ministries and ministers. Repeated calls for a co-ordinated approach to transposition are frequently ignored by major actors, who seem to be more interested in pursuing their narrow goals rather than acting as parts of a larger body.
>
> (Dimitrakopoulos 2001, p. 616)

In his view a critical change in the transposition patterns occurred owing to the emergence of "steering" mechanisms that helped to overcome the fragmentation of the Greek central administration. The steering levers enabled ministerial decision makers to influence EU transposition and implementation in the desired direction (Dimitrakopoulos 2001, p. 613). It is interesting to note the striking parallels between Dimitrakopoulos's analysis of the obstacles to transposition in Greece and the arguments made earlier about the Central European cases. Furthermore, it is hard to overlook the similarity between the concept of "steering" and that of selective incentives and monitoring employed in this research.

The other relevant contribution is Hallerberg's recent study of national adaptation to the budget deficit criteria of the Economic and Monetary Union (Hallerberg 2004a). Although not dealing with transposition per se, this work applies theoretical insights based on collective action theory to studying the Europeanization of public policy. Hallerberg argues that, although the EU provided inducements for member states to adjust their fiscal policies, it was the presence or absence of specific coordination mechanisms at the domestic level that determined the pattern of national convergence. The cabinets that delegated budgetary powers to finance ministers or coordinated policy through "fiscal contracts" were able to bring their budget deficits below 3 percent of GDP. In contrast, the cabinets that adopted a fiefdom form of internal governance—characterized by extensive ministerial autonomy—found it extremely difficult to maintain the required fiscal rectitude. Although Hallerberg does not use the concept of the core executive, it is interesting to note that delegation and fiscal contracts imply the reinforcement of the core executive rules through hierarchical and collectivity-based instruments. Furthermore, cabinets with a fiefdom structure presuppose a limited availability of central institutional levers for extending selective incentives and monitoring to line departments.

The above findings from the Western variant of the Europeanization literature show that, notwithstanding the reservations voiced earlier, the core executive variable may have a broader application in the study of EU compliance. Indeed, it is not difficult to see that it is compatible with—and may be used to improve the predictive power of—the two models that have recently come to dominate the literature on EU compliance. The first model relies on the predictive power of the veto player theory (Tsebelis 1995, 2002). Following Haverland (2000), Giuliani has analyzed the transposition patterns in the old 15 member states to find that a country's record is strongly related to the number of veto players (2003). This finding is compatible with the results of this study to the extent that ideologically incohesive cabinets with many supporting parties may find it difficult to develop and maintain a strong core executive. But difficult does not necessarily mean impossible. As shown in this research, administrative traditions, critical junctures, and external pressures may combine to facilitate the reinforcement of the core even where cabinets are characterized by many veto players and are ideologically incohesive. The Polish Buzek majority government in late 1999 is a case in point. A focus on the core executive may thus contribute to the explanatory power of the veto point approach.

The other model has been proposed in recent research by Falkner, Treib, Hartlapp, Leiber (Falkner, Hartlapp, et al. 2004; Falkner, Treib, et al. 2005; Falkner, Hartlapp, and Treib 2007). Inspired by insights from normative institutionalism, Falkner and her colleagues argue that variation in the transposition records may be explained with reference to a "domestic compliance culture in the field of EU law" (Falkner, Treib, et al. 2005). Accordingly, they categorize all of the old EU member states into three worlds of law observance, domestic politics, and neglect. A key differentiating factor is the political importance of compliance with EU law, which, in turn, is contingent on whether the society expects compliance and exerts relevant pressures on the political elites. In brief, transposition depends on the "political will" of the national government. An issue on which Falkner et al. are perhaps less specific is how political systems organize to give effect to political intentions. If the findings from the present study may be of any guidance, it is to show that national governments must organize internally before they achieve better levels of transposition. Hence, an explicit focus on the core executive may offer interesting insights about factors that determine the effectiveness of political determination in the area of EU compliance.

Finally, it is interesting to find that the core executive argument resonates well with the practical recommendations that the European Commission has laid down for member state governments on improving institutional capacity for legal compliance (2004b). The Commission recommends, for example, that a senior cabinet minister should be responsible for monitoring transposition of all directives; progress should be discussed regularly at committee and cabinet level; central guidelines should be issued on transposition technique; a central database should be maintained to store all relevant information; reminders should be sent to ministries before and after the deadline for transposition; and remedial measures should be taken if delays are found. It is difficult to overlook the parallels with the argument made in this book. The above inventory of institutional devices makes it clear that what the Commission advocates is a reinforcement of the core executive capacities for planning, monitoring, and—if need be—managing the transposition process.

Interestingly, the European Commission data demonstrate a correlation between the institutional capacity of core executives in the old member states and transposition compliance (2006b). Figure 7.2 below plots the relationship between core executive strength and transposition deficits. The core executive scores are calculated by assigning one point for complying with each of key nine institutional features.[1] The score can take a value from zero to nine. The transposition deficit is defined as the percentage of nonnotified directives. Figure 7.2 shows that there is a positive correlation between the core executives and transposition performance. The states with stronger cores tend to have lower transposition deficits and the states with weaker cores have a tendency for higher deficits. Of course this evidence should not be overinterpreted, not least because it is based on a bivariate correlation of 15 cases. If anything, it serves as a promising invitation for further research.

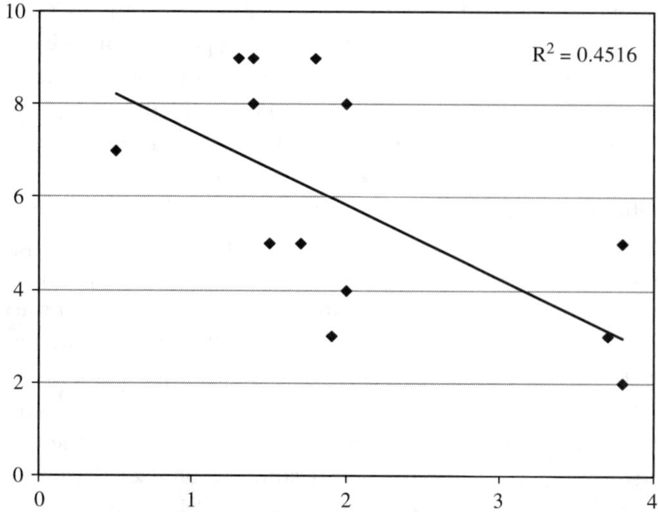

Source: Own compilation based on European Commission 2006b.

Figure 7.2 Relationship between core executive capacity and transposition deficit (the horizontal axis shows transposition deficit and the vertical axis shows core executive capacity)

Relevance beyond Europeanization Studies

This book also holds interesting lessons reaching beyond the Europeanization studies. It opens promising avenues for further research on core executives and their impact on state capacity to formulate and implement policies. From an empirical perspective, an attractive line of enquiry would be to develop a more sophisticated categorization of core executive rules that can be employed to extend incentives and monitoring to line ministries. The empirical findings in the present volume offer some preliminary ideas in the regard. For example, the authority rules may be further subdivided into rules that specify powers to act as agenda setters or arbiters, and the rules that specify powers to sanction and reward. A promising new category of "temporal rules" may be created to cover mechanisms such as the "set-aside" practice developed by some of the Central European cabinets for dealing with more contentious issues. The core executive mobilization may also take the shape of "restrictive rules" through which the prime minister and the cabinet may make it increasingly difficult to amend legislative drafts as they move through the governmental machinery. Better typologies of core executive rules should facilitate a more informed investigation of how such instruments vary across countries and time. They should also make it possible to measure the effects of institutional configurations with greater precision.

The findings of this research resonate well with the existing theoretical propositions in the literature on core executives. They lend support to a long-standing argument about a strong positive correlation between the success of policy reform and centralization of authority in the executive (cf. Hall 1983; Boston 1992; Geddes 1994; Brusis and Dimitrov 2001). Above all, this proposition stresses the importance of "change teams" located at the heart of the executive and operating with strong political backing but in relative isolation from bureaucratic and societal demands. Yet, at the same time, this study recognizes that the radical nature of the policy reforms required by the EU accession may have rendered the operation of the core executive variable more pronounced. The accession state in Central Europe had to transpose in a few years the legislation that the EU took over four decades to develop. It is thus possible that strong centers (core executives) tend to be necessary for implementing radical policy reforms, while gradual policy change could be undertaken without a major reinforcement of the center (cf. Stark and Bruszt 1998; Lindquist 1999).

The latter proposition ties in with arguments that the effectiveness of organizational designs depends on "selective centralization on a small number of functions and a good deal of decentralization on the rest" (Aucoin 1990, p. 130). Centralization within the executive is said to work best when it applies to a small number of issues that should be managed personally by the prime minister and the cabinet, whereas decentralization is a favorable solution when priorities are not sufficiently specific. Further research on core executives configurations and their impact on policy would thus benefit from a more contextualized approach. It would, for example, need to be sensitive not only to examples of undercentralization but also to cases in which governments tend to overcentralize by extending central coordination and control too widely. The risk of overcentralization may be particularly high in governments that have limited capacities at the ministerial level since core executive agencies may then have a natural proclivity for accumulating more tasks in order to address resource problems at lower levels.

The need to demonstrate selectivity in institutional design also raises the issue of the core executive capacity to "distinguish between pressing political problems and specific political priorities" (Aucoin 1990, p. 130).

Last but not least, besides empirical and theoretical considerations, the present study holds some interesting implications for the normative notion of "good government." It argues that a key problem with effective democratic governance is related to the resolution of the institutional tension between collective and sectoral rationalities within government. To achieve maximum democratic responsiveness, parliamentary and executive actors need to produce policies that bring diffuse benefits to many voter constituencies. But, individually, all have strong incentives to maximize the interests of narrow geographical, sectoral, or other voter constituencies. This is because the electoral mechanism increases the diversity of interests that government actors stand for. Democratic parliaments consist of hundreds of deputies, each of whom represents a distinct geographical or other voter constituency. The same applies to ministers who come under pressure to cater to the interests of sectoral or party clientele. To solve such tension between collective and sectoral rationalities, institutional mechanisms must be developed that mobilize individual actors toward achieving collective goals. This book has identified the existence of a strong core executive as a necessary precondition for the resolution of such collective action dilemmas and, consequently, for effective democratic governance.

Appendix: List of Interviewees

Interview number	Interviewee position	Organization	Transcript available
1	Advisor	Polish Parliament	No
2, 3	Minister	KPRM, Poland	No, Yes
4	Director	KPRM, Poland	Yes
5	Middle-ranking official	KPRM, Poland	No
6	Minister	KPRM, Poland	Yes
7	Middle-ranking official	KPRM, Poland	Yes
8	Director	UKIE, Poland	Yes
9	Director	UKIE, Poland	No
10, 11, 12	Director	UKIE, Poland	No, Yes, Yes
13	Director	UKIE, Poland	Yes
14	Minister	UKIE, Poland	Yes
15	Minister	UKIE, Poland	Yes
16	Minister	UKIE, Poland	Yes
17	Minister	UKIE, Poland	Yes
18	Director	Polish Parliament	Yes
19	Middle-ranking official	Polish Line Ministry	Yes
20	Minister	UKIE, Poland	No
21	Middle-ranking official	UKIE, Poland	No
22	Minister	Polish Line Ministry	Yes
23	Advisor	KPRM, Poland	Yes
24	Minister	Polish Line Ministry	Yes
25	Director	UKIE, Poland	Yes
26	Director	UKIE, Poland	Yes
27	Director	UKIE, Poland	Yes
28, 29	Minister	KPRM, Poland	Yes, Yes
30, 31	Director	UKIE, Poland	Yes, No
32	Middle-ranking official	UKIE, Poland	Yes

Interview number	Interviewee position	Organization	Transcript available
33	Middle-ranking official	UKIE, Poland	Yes
34	Director	UKIE, Poland	Yes
35	Advisor	KPRM, Poland	Yes
36	Minister	UKIE, Poland	Yes
37	Director	Foreign Ministry, Poland	Yes
38	Minister	Foreign Ministry, Poland	Yes
39	Director	UKIE, Poland	Yes
40	Director	UKIE, Poland	No
41	Director	Polish Line Ministry	Yes
42	Director	Polish Line Ministry	Yes
43	Director	Polish Line Ministry	Yes
44	Middle-ranking official	Polish Parliament	Yes
45	Middle-ranking official	UKIE, Poland	Yes
46	Director	UKIE, Poland	Yes
47	Director	KPRM, Poland	Yes
48	Director	KPRM, Poland	Yes
49	Minister	KPRM, Poland	Yes
50	Middle-ranking official	UKIE, Poland	Yes
51	Middle-ranking official	European Commission	No
52	Middle-ranking official	UKIE, Poland	Yes
53	Director	European Commission	No
54	Advisor	European Commission	No
55	Middle-ranking official	European Commission	No
56	Director	KPRM, Poland	Yes
57	Minister	KPRM, Poland	Yes
58	Director	UKIE, Poland	No
59	Director	KPRM, Poland	Yes
60	Advisor	UKIE, Poland	No
61	Minister	PMO, Hungary	Yes
62	Administrative state secretary	PMO, Hungary	Yes

Interview number	Interviewee position	Organization	Transcript available
63	Minister	Ministry, Hungary	No
64	Middle-ranking official	Justice Ministry, Hungary	Yes
65	Political state secretary	PMO, Hungary	Yes
66	Minister	Ministry, Hungary	Yes
67	Minister	Ministry, Hungary	Yes
68	Administrative state secretary	PMO, Hungary	Yes
69	Administrative state secretary	Ministry, Hungary	Yes
70	Administrative state secretary	Ministry, Hungary	Yes
71	Minister	Ministry, Hungary	Yes
72	Administrative state secretary	Ministry, Hungary	Yes
73	High-ranking official	Government Office (GO), Czech Republic	Yes
74	Minister	Ministry, Czech Republic	Yes
75	Minister	Ministry, Czech Republic	Yes
76	Deputy minister	Ministry, Czech Republic	Yes
77	High-ranking official	Ministry, Czech Republic	Yes
78	High-ranking official	Government Office (GO), Czech Republic	Yes
79	Minister	GO, Czech Republic	Yes
80	Minister	Ministry, Czech Republic	Yes
81	Minister	Ministry, Czech Republic	Yes
82	Deputy minister	Ministry, Czech Republic	Yes
83	High-ranking official	GO, Czech Republic	Yes
84	High-ranking official	Ministry, Czech Republic	Yes
85	Deputy minister	Ministry, Czech Republic	Yes

Interview number	Interviewee position	Organization	Transcript available
86	High-ranking official	Ministry, Czech Republic	Yes
87	Administrative state secretary	Ministry, Hungary	Yes
88	Administrative state secretary	Ministry, Hungary	Yes
89	Minister	Ministry, Hungary	Yes

Notes

Chapter 4

1. In Poland, cabinet ministers function formally as supreme bodies of state administration within their policy jurisdictions. The constitutional practice also allows the creation of collective committee-type supreme bodies of state administration whose formal status is analogous to that of a cabinet minister. Such collective administrative bodies are then represented on the cabinet by their chairs, who have the rank of constitutional cabinet ministers.

Chapter 7

1. The following are the nine features of core executive strength: (i) coordination of EU affairs by one senior member of government, (ii) regular report on transposition in cabinet or committee, (iii) responsibility for transposition to one ministry, (iv) guidelines on transposition, (v) a central national database, (vi) reminders before the deadline, (vii) reminders after the deadline, (viii) preparation of a planning schedule for transposition, and (ix) measures taken to remedy late transposition. These features correspond to practices 1.1, 1.2, 2.1, 2.3, 2.4, 2.5, 2.6, 3.1 and 5.1 in figure 17 in European Commission 2006b p. 25.

Bibliography

Primary Sources

Czech Government. 1999. Resolution of the Government of the Czech Republic of 15 November, No. 1212, on the methodological guidelines for approximating the law of the Czech Republic with that of the European Union.

European Commission. 2004a. Internal Market Scoreboard, Scoreboard No. 13, July. Brussels.

———. 2004b. Recommendation from the Commission on the Transposition into National Law of Directives Affecting the Internal Market. Brussels, 12.7.2004, SEC(2004) 918 final.

———. 2004c. Progress in Notification of National Measures Implementing Directives, Reference Date 15/11/2004. Brussels.

———. 2005. Internal Market Scoreboard, Scoreboard No. 14, July. Brussels.

———. 2006a. Internal Market Scoreboard, Scoreboard No. 14bis, February. Brussels.

———. 2006b. Internal Market Scoreboard, Scoreboard No. 15, July. Brussels.

———. 2007. Internal Market Scoreboard, Scoreboard No. 15bis, February. Brussels.

European Parliament. 2003. Harbour Report. Brussels, A5 0026/2003.

———. 2004. Miller Report. Brussels, A5 0116/2004.

Internal Memo 06/07/2000. 2000. "Notatka wewnętrzna z dnia 6 lipca 2000 r. od dyrektor DONA do ministra Jana Kułakowskiego w sprawie spotkania DONA z podsekretarzem stanu w UKIE Cezarym Banasińskim w dniu 5 lipca 2000."

Internal Memo DHPiST/141/99. 1999. "Notatka wewnętrzna z dnia 19 maja 1999 od dyrektora DHP do p.o. sekretarza KIE w sprawie udostępniania stanowisk negocjacyjnych."

Internal Memo DHPiST/173/98. 1998. "Notatka wewnętrzna z dnia 20 lipca 1998 od naczelnika W1 do dyrektora DHP w sprawie notatki ws poszerzonego kierownictwa UKIE."

Internal Memo DNA/355/99. 1999. "Notatka z dnia 25 marca 1999 od wicedyrektora DNA do ministra Pawła Sameckiego w sprawie porównania stanowisk negocjacyjnych z NPPC."

Internal Memo DNA/1632/98. 1998. "Notatka wewnętrzna z dnia 9 października 1998 r. od dyrektora DNA do ministra Jarosława Pietrasa."

Internal Memo DPI 12/10/1999. 1999. "Notatka wewnętrzna z dnia 12 października 1999 od pracownika DPI do podsekretarza stanu Jarosław Pietrasa w sprawie projektu ustawy o inspekcji transportu drogowego."

Internal Memo DPI/7/12/1999. 1999. "Notatka wewnętrzna z dnia 7 grudnia 1999 r od dyrektora DPI do dyrektora Sekretariatu Urzędu Komitetu Integracji Europejskiej w sprawie skróconego zapisu z KIE w dniu 6 grudnia 1999 w pkt IIIb - Lista ustaw, których uchwalenie jest niezbędne w związku z przystąpieniem Polski do Unii Europejskiej."

Internal Memo KIE 26/03/1997. 1997. "Notatka z dnia 26 marca 1997 r. dla Pana Włodzimierza Cimoszewicza, Prezesa Rady Ministrow, w sprawie punktu 4 porządku obrad KIE w dniu 3 kwietnia 1997 r. dot. projektu harmonogramu działan dostosowujących polski system prawny do zaleceń Białej Księgi Komisji Europejskiej w sprawie integracji z jednolitym rynkiem UE."

KIE Protocol 3/1997. 1997. "Protokół ustaleń Nr 3/97 posiedzenia Komitetu Integracji Europejskiej w dniu 3 kwietnia 1997 r."

KIE Protocol 3/1999. 1999. "Protokół ustaleń Nr 3/99 posiedzenia Komitetu Integracji Europejskiej w dniu 10 marca 1999 r."

KIE Protocol 4/1997. 1997. "Protokół ustaleń Nr 4/97 posiedzenia Komitetu Integracji Europejskiej w dniu 25 kwietnia 1997 r."

KIE Protocol 5/1997. 1997. "Protokół ustaleń Nr 5/97 posiedzenia Komitetu Integracji Europejskiej w dniu 4 czerwca 1997 r."

KIE Protocol 5/1999. 1999. "Protokół ustaleń Nr 5/99 posiedzenia Komitetu Integracji Europejskiej w dniu 24 maja 1999 r."

KIE Protocol 6/1999. 1999. "Protokół ustaleń Nr 6/99 posiedzenia Komitetu Integracji Europejskiej w dniu 31 maja 1999 r."

KIE Protocol 7/1999. 1999. "Protokół ustaleń Nr 7/99 posiedzenia Komitetu Integracji Europejskiej w dniu 14 czerwca 1999 r."

KIE Protocol 7/2000. 2000. "Protokół ustaleń nr 7/00 z posiedzenia Komitetu Integracji Europejskiej w dniu 10 kwietnia 2000 r."

KIE Protocol 8/1998. 1998. "Protokół ustaleń Nr 8/98 posiedzenia Komitetu Integracji Europejskiej w dniu 28 wrzesnia 1998 r."

KIE Protocol 16/2000. 2000. "Protokół ustaleń nr 16/00 z posiedzenia Komitetu Integracji Europejskiej w dniu 8 listopada 2000 r."

KIE Protocol 18/1999. 1999. "Protokół ustaleń nr 18/99 z posiedzenia Komitetu Integracji Europejskiej w dniu 6 grudnia 1999 r."

Komisja ds Ukladu Europejskiego. 1994. "Opinia nr 4 Komisji do Spraw Układu Europejskiego uchwalona na posiedzeniu w dniu 30 września 1994 roku do Prezesa Rady Ministrow." Warsaw: Sejm.

———. 1996. "Biuletyn nr 2666/II, stenogram posiedzenia Komisji ds Układu Europejskiego nr 62 w dniu 11 czerwca 1996 r."

KPRM. 1999. "Negocjacje członkowskie: Polska na drodze do Unii Europejskiej." Warsaw: Pełnomocnik Rządu ds Negocjacji o Członkostwo RP w UE.

KPRM Internal Document 17/12/1998. 1998. "Memorandum w sprawie działań Głównego Negocjatora i Zespołu Negocjacyjnego w pierwszym roku funkcjonowania (1998)."

KPRM Internal Document. 2000. "Sprawozdanie z działalnosci Pełnomocnika Rządu ds Negocjacji o Członkostwo RP w UE za okres 1 stycznia do 30 czerwca 2000 r."

KPRM Internal Document RM-20-1-00. 2000. "Plan pracy Rady Ministrów na rok 2000."

KPRM Internal Document SS/2/1/034. 1998. "Notatka z dnia 2 listopada 1998 r na posiedzenie Zespołu Negocjacyjnego w sprawie wniosków wynikających z dotychczasowego przebiegu screeningu."

Official Communication DWZ.V.078/88/99/PKM. 1999. "Pismo z dnia 15 września 1999 do podsekretarz stanu w Ministerstwie Pracy i Polityki Socjalnej, Ireny Boruty, do Pełnomocnika Rządu ds Negocjacji o Członkostwo RP w Unii Europejskiej w sprawie przekazania wypełnionego formularza dotyczącego weryfikacji zobowiazań przyjętych w stanowiskach negocjacyjnych."

Official Communication IE60/sjr/ask/725/99. 1999. "Pismo z dnia 22 września 1999 do sekretarza stanu w Ministerstwie Gospodarki do Pełnomocnika Rządu ds Negocjacji o Członkostwo w Unii Europejskiej w sprawie przekazania zestawienia zobowiązań implementacyjnych."

Official Communication IE/WHP/1383/EP/99. 1999. "Pismo z dnia 10 września 1999 r od dyrektora departamentu Integracji Europejskiej i Organizacji Międzynarodowych w Ministerstwie Gospodarki do podsekretarza stanu Jarosława Pietrasa w sprawie przekazania zestawienia zobowiązań implementacyjnych."

Official Communication MI-1/22.21/1139/KM/99. 1999. "Pismo z września 1999 r od podsekretarza stanu w Ministerstwie Finansów do Pełnomocnika

Rządu ds Negocjacji o Członkostwo w Unii Europejskiej w sprawieprzekazania zestawień zobowiązań implementacyjnych."

Official Communication MJP/859/99/TN. 1999. "Pismo z dnia 8 października 1999 r od podsekretarza stanu Jarosława Pietrasa do sekretarza stanu w KPRM Wojciecha Arkuszewskiego w sprawie zobowiązań implementacyjnych w latach 1999–2000."

Official Communication SEkrMinCB/336/2000/mk. 2000. "Pismo z dnia 29 listopada 2000 od podsekretarza stanu Cezarego Banasińskiego do Sekretarza Komitetu Integracji Europejskiej."

Official Communication SEkrMinDH/174/97/DHP. 1997. "Pismo z dnia 29 stycznia 1997 r. od sekretarza Komitetu Integracji Europejskiej do ministerstw i urzędów centralnych w sprawie materiału 'Harmonizacja prawa polskiego z prawem europejskim - zasady, organizacja i procedury.'"

Official Communication SekrMinDH/533/97/DK-jp. 1997. "Notatka z dnia 17 marca 1997 od sekretarza KIE do Prezesa Rady Ministrów, Przewodniczącego KIE w sprawie problemów i opóźnień w sferze harmonizacji prawa i pojawianie się na tym tle problemów spornych w stosunkach z Unią Europejską."

Official Communication SekrMinJP/355/w/98/DPI-ES. 1998. "Pismo z dnia 30 czerwca 1998 od podsekretarza stanu w Urzędzie Komitetu Integracji Europejskiej do dyrektorów komórek integracji europejskiej w ministerstwach i urzędach centralnych."

Official Communication SekrMinJSW/1797/2000. 2000. "Pismo z dnia 13 listopada 2000 r. od sekretarza Komitetu Integracji Europejskiej do p.o. sekretarza Rady Ministrów z wnioskiem o wniesienie pod obrady Rady Ministrów w dniu 14 listopada 2000 'Propozycji listy ustaw do przyjęcia przez Radę Ministrów w roku 2001.'"

Official Communication SekrMInJSW/5558/2000. 2000. "Pismo z dnia 12 października 2000 od ambasadora RP przy UE do sekretarza Komitetu Integracji Europejskiej."

Official Communication SekrMinJSW/7041/2000. 2000. "Pismo z dnia 14 grudnia 2000 od ambasadora RP przy UE do Sekretarza Komitetu Integracji Europejskiej."

Official Communication SekrMinMKF/644/98/os. 1998. "Pismo od p.o. sekretarza Komitetu Integracji Europejskiej do Głównego Negocjatora RP z dnia 9 października 1998 r."

Official Communication SekrMinPS/920/2000/TN. 2000. "Pismo z dnia 14 marca 2000 od p.o. sekretarza KIE do Prezesa Rady Ministrów w sprawie opoźnień w realizacji harmonogramu przekazywania do Sejmu RP projektów ustaw dostosowujących."

Official Communication SekrMinPS/1296/99. 1999. "Pismo p.o. sekretarza Komitetu Integracji Europejskiej do podsekretarza stanu w Ministerstwie Finansów."

Official Communication SekrMinPS/1497/99/DHP/ap. 1999. "Pismo z dnia 7 lipca 1999 r od p.o. sekretarza Komitetu Integracji Europejskiej do sekretarza do spraw parlamentarnych w Kancelarii Prezesa Rady Ministrów."

Official Communication SekrMinPS/1768/99/DPI-mk. 1999. "Pismo z dnia 30 lipca 1999 r od p.o. sekretarza Komitetu Integracji Europejskiej do p.o. szefa Kancelarii Prezesa Rady Ministrów zawierające 'Zestawienie decyzji Komitetu Integracji Europejskiej przyspieszających proces dostosowań do wymogów Układu Europejskiego i członkostwa w UE wraz z informacją na temat ich realizacji wymagających pilnego zakończenia' (materiał na KIE w dniu 2 sierpnia 1999)."

Official Communication SekrMinRCZ/2047/w/98/DPI-TBG. 1998. "Pismo z dnia 26 czerwca 1998 od przewodniczącego Komitetu Integracji Europejskiej do Sekretarza Rady Ministrów."

Official Communication SJK/7-37/98. 1998. "Pismo z dnia 16 czerwca 1998 r. od Pełnomocnika rządu ds negocjacji o członkostwo Polski w UE do ministra-przewodniczącego Komitetu Integracji Europejskiej."

Official Communication SJK/456-315(1)/mcm/99. 1999. "Pismo od Pełnomocnika Rządu do Spraw Negocjacji o Członkostwo RP w Unii Europejskiej do członkow Zespołu Negocjacyjnego o przygotowanie zestawień zobowiązań negocjacyjnych wynikających ze stanowisk negocjacyjnych w związku z przyjęciem przez KIE dokumentu pt 'Weryfikacja realizacji zobowiązań przyjętych w stanowiskach negocjacyjnych.'"

Official Communication SJK/456-406/99. 1999. "Pismo z dnia 13 października 1999 r od Ambasadora RP przy UE do Andrzeja Ananicza, Jana Kułakowskiego i Jarosława Pietrasa w sprawie wstępnego komentarza do Regular Report i Composite Paper."

Official Communication SJK/4561-5/99. 1999. "Pismo z dnia 6 stycznia 1999 r od Pełnomocnika Rządu ds Negocjacji o Członkostwo RP w Unii Europejskiej do przewodniczących podzespołów zadaniowych Miedzyresortowego Zespołu do spraw Przygotowania Negocjacji Akcesyjnych w sprawie opracowania wstępnego szacunku skutków budżetowych związanych z realizacją stanowisk negocjacyjnych."

Official Communication SJK/4561-9(1)/MDW/2000. 2000. "Pismo z dnia 10 stycznia 2000 od Pełnomocnika Rządu ds Negocjacji o Członkostwo RP w UE do podsekretarz stanu w Ministerstwie Fianansow w sprawie przygotowania zestawienia kosztow budzetowych dla stanowisk egocjacyjnych."

Official Communication SKJ/458-11/BZ/00. 2000. "Pismo z dnia 28 stycznia 2000 r od Jana Kułakowskiego Pełnomocnika Rządu ds Negocjacji o Członkostwo RP w UW do czlonkow Zespołu Negocjacyjnego w sprawie sposobu przygotowywania raportów o stanie przyjmowania i wdrażania *acquis communautaire.*"

Official Communication SWA-10-28/99. 1999. "Pismo z dnia 16 grudnia 1999 r od sekretarza stanu Wojciecha Arkuszewskiego do podsekretarza stanu Pawła Sameckiego w sprawie projektu harmonogramu prac rządu dotyczących ustaw związanych z integracją Polski z UE."

Official Communication SWA-20-1/2000. 2000. "Pismo z dnia 10 stycznia 2000 od Sekretarza Stanu Wojciecha Arkuszewskiego do Sekretarza Stanu, po. Szefa Kancelarii PRM, Jerzego Widzyka."

Official Communication SWA-45-39(3)/1999. 1999. "Pismo do sekretarza stanu Wojciecha Arkuszewskiego do Pawła Sameckiego, podsekretarza stanu w Urzędzie Komitetu Inetgracji Europejskiej w sprawie przekazania listy '67' ustaw przewidzianych do przyjęcia w pierwszej połowie 2000 r - ważnych ze względu na zobowiązania negocjacyjne."

Official Communication SWA-45-39/99. 1999. "Pismo z dnia 21 października 1999 r od Wojciecha Arkuszewskiego sekretarza stanu w Kancelarii Prezesa Rady Ministrów do Jerzego Buzka Prezesa Rady Ministrów."

Pakt. 2000. "Pakt na rzecz integracji - wspólna deklaracja Jerzego Buzka (AWSP), Macieja Płażynskiego (PO), Leszka Millera (SLD) i Bronisława Geremka (UW)." Warsaw.

Sejm RP. 1999. "Dezyderat nr 4 Komisji Integracji Europejskiej z dnia 3 listopada 1999 do Prezesa Rady Ministrów w sprawie najpilniejszych działań dostosowujących prawo polskie do prawa Unii Europejskiej."

————. 2000. "Uchwała Sejmu RP z dnia 18 lutego 2000 w sprawie przygotowań do członkostwa RP w Unii Europejskiej."

Senat RP. 2000. "Uchwała Komisji Spraw Zagranicznych i Integracji Europejskiej z dnia 31 marca 2000 w sprawie przygotowań do członkostwa RP w Unii Europejskiej." Warsaw.

Trojporozumienie. 2000. "Deklaracja Marszałka Sejmu RP, Marszałka Senatu RP oraz Prezesa Rady Ministrów RP: Trójporozumienie dla przyspieszenie procesu dostosowania prawa polskiego do prawa Unii Europejskiej." Warsaw.

UKIE. 1997. "Harmonogram dzialań dostosowujacych polski system prawny do zaleceń Białej Księgi Komisji Europejskiej ws Integracji z Jednolitym Rynkiem UE." Warsaw.

————. 1998. "Raport Rządu RP zawierający ocenę stopnia adaptacji prawa polskiego do prawa wspólnotowego." Warsaw: Urząd Komitetu Integracji

Europejskiej, in cooperation with Centrum Europejskie Uniwersytetu Warszawskiego.

———. 2000. "Informacja rządu RP dla Sejmu RP o najważniejszych działaniach dostosowawczychw Polsce do wymogów członkostwa w Unii Europejskiej w 1999 roku." Warsaw.

———. 2001. "Bilans otwarcia w sprawach integracji Polski z Unią Europejską." Warsaw.

———. 2002a. "Bilans przygotowań do członkostwa w Unii Europejskiej." Warsaw.

———. 2002b. "Harmonogram przyjmowania przez Radę Ministrów projektów ustaw dostosowujących prawo polskie do prawa Unii Europejskiej do końca 2002 roku." Warsaw.

———. 2003a. "Udział Polski w Jednolitym Rynku - Korzyści i koszty dla poszczególnych grup i wybranych sektorów." Warsaw.

———. 2003b. "Zapewnienie skuteczności prawu Unii Europejskiej w prawie polskim - wytyczne polityki legislacyjnej i techniki prawodawczej." Warsaw.

UKIE Internal Document 10/12/1997. 1997. "Informacja Przewodniczącego Komitetu Integracji Europejskiej w sprawie przygotowania dokumentu Narodowy Program Przyjmowania Acquis (Materiał na KIE w dniu 10 grudnia 1997)."

UKIE Internal Document 12/07/1999. 1999. "Weryfikacja realizacji zobowiązań przyjętych w stanowiskach negocjacyjnych (materiał przyjęty przez zespół negocjacyjny przedstawiony na KIE w dniu 26 lipca 1999)."

UKIE Internal Document 16/06/1999. 1999. "Informacja nt przyspieszenia procesu dostosowań do wymogów Układu Europejskiego i członkostwa w UE (materiał na konferencję miedzyrzadową 22 czerwca 1999 r)."

UKIE Internal Document 28/06/1999. 1999. "Informacja nt decyzji Komitetu Integracji Europejskiej przyspieszających proces dostosowań do wymogów Układu Europejskiego i członkostwa w UE oraz ich realizacji (stan na dzień 28 czerwca 1999) - materiał UKIE na posiedzenie KIE w dniu 5 lipca 1999 r."

UKIE Internal Document. 1998a. "Protokoły z posiedzeń Zespołu Negocjacyjnego w latach 1998–2000."

———. 1998b. "Protokoły z posiedzeń Komitetu Integracji Europejskiej w latach 1996–2002."

———. 2000a. "Uchwała Komitetu Integracji Europejskiej nr 3 z dnia 24 lipca 2000 r. w sprawie trybu postępowania z rządowymi projektami ustaw dostosowującymi prawo polskie do prawa Unii Europejskiej." Dziennik Urzędowy Komitetu Integracji Europejskiej 2(02).

————. 2000b. "Uchwała Komitetu Integracji Europejskiej nr 2 z dnia 10 maja 2000 r. w sprawie zatwierdzenia wykazu działań legislacyjnych, których realizacja powinna zostać zakończona do czerwca i września 2000 r., w sposób umożliwiający odnotowanie postępu w Regularnym Raporcie Komisji Europejskiej na rok 2000." Dziennik Urzędowy Komitetu Integracji Europejskiej 2 (02).

UKIE Internal Document DPI 16/06/1999. 1999. "Informacja nt decyzji Komitetu Integracji Europejskiej przyspieszających proces dostosowań do wymogów Układu Europejskiego i Członkostwa w Unii Europejskiej (projekt materiału na KIE w dniu 21 czerwca 1999) - stan na 16 czerwca 1999."

UKIE Internal Document June 1999. 1999. "Główne wnioski i propozycje działań wynikające z VII posiedzenia Komitetu Stowarzyszenia RP-UE."

UKIE Internal Document March 1997. 1997. "Informacja o procesie dostosowania prawa polskiego do prawa europejskiego: materiał informacyjny." Warsaw.

UKIE Internal Document SS/2/1/009. 1998. "Materiał do punktu IIIb na posiedzeniu KIE w dniu 28 września 1998 r."

URM. 1995a. "Biała Księga. Polska - Unia Europejska. Opracowania i Analizy. Prawo." Warsaw.

URM. 1995b. "Założenia reformy Centrum Gospodarczego Rządu." Warsaw.

Secondary Sources

Ágh, A. 1999. "Europeanization of Policy-Making in East Central Europe: The Hungarian Approach to EU Accession." *Journal of European Public Policy* 6, no. 5:839–854.

————. 2001a. "Early Consolidation and Performance Crisis: The Majoritarian-Consensus Democracy Debate in Hungary." *West European Politics* 24, no. 3:89–112.

————. 2001b. "Early Democratic Consolidation in Hungary and the Europeanization of the Hungarian Polity." In *Prospects for Democratic Consolidation in East-Central Europe*, edited by G. Pridham and A. Ágh. Manchester: Manchester University Press.

Ágh, A., and A. Rozsas. 2003. "Managing Europe from Home: The Europeanization of the Hungarian Core Executive." Occasional Paper 5.1-09.03, Dublin European Institute.

Andeweg, R. 1997. "Collegiality and Collectivity: Cabinets, Cabinet Committees and Cabinet Ministers." In *The Hollow Crown: Countervailing*

Trends in Core Executives, edited by P. Weller, H. Bakvis, and R. A. W. Rhodes. London: Macmillan.

———. 2000. "Ministers as Double Agents? The Delegation Process between Cabinet and Ministers." *European Journal of Political Research* 37:377–395.

Apanowicz, P. 1999. "Konieczne przyspieszenie prac." *Rzeczpospolita* (Warsaw), May 26.

Apanowicz, P., and J. Bielecki. 1999. "Nie dotrzymane obietnice ministra: możemy wypaść z grona faworytów." *Rzeczpospolita* (Warsaw), September 27.

Argyris, C., and D. Schön. 1996. *Organizational Learning II: Theory, Method and Practice.* Reading, MA: Addison-Wesley.

Aucoin, P. 1986. "Organizational Change in the Machinery of Canadian Government: From Rational Management to Brokerage Politics." *Canadian Journal of Political Science* 19, no. 1:3–27.

———. (1990). "Administrative Reform in Public Management: Paradigms, Principles, Paradoxes and Pendulums." *Governance* 3, no. 2:115–137.

———. 1994. "Prime Ministerial Leadership: Position, Power and Politics." In *Leaders and Leadership in Canada*, edited by M. Mancuso, R. G. Price, and R. Wagenberg. Toronto: Oxford University Press.

Bakvis, H. 1997. "Advising the Executive: Think Tanks, Consultants, Political Staff and Kitchen Cabinets." In *The Hollow Crown: Countervailing Trends in Core Executives*, edited by P. Weller, H. Bakvis, and R. A. W. Rhodes. London: Macmillan.

Barker, A., and B. G. Peters, eds. 1993. *The Politics of Expert Advice: Creating, Using and Manipulating Scientific Knowledge for Public Policy.* Edinburgh: Edinburgh University Press.

Baylis, T. A. 1989. *Governing by Committee: Collegial Leadership in Advanced Societies.* New York: State University of New York Press.

Bielecki, J. 1998. "Zatrzeć wspomnienie błędów." *Rzeczpospolita* (Warsaw), September 19.

Bilčík, Vladimír. 2004. "Inštitucionálna adaptácia pri vstupe SR do EÚ." In *EÚ Monitoring 2003: Prístupový proces Slovenska a implikácie pre politické inštitúcie, právny štát a regionálnu politiku,* edited by Vladimír Bilčík, pp. 3–24. Bratislava, Slovakia: Slovenská spoločnosť pre zahraničnú politiku a FES.

Blondel, J., and M. Cotta, eds. 1996. *Party and Government: An Inquiry into the Relationship between Governments and Supporting Parties in Liberal Democracies.* Basingstoke, UK: Macmillan.

———. 2000. *The Nature of Party Government.* Basingstoke, UK. Palgrave Macmillan.

Blondel, J., and N. Manning. 2002. "Do Ministers Do What They Say? Ministerial Unreliability, Collegial and Hierarchical Governments." *Political Studies* 50:455–476.

Börzel, T. A. 2001. "Pace-Setting, Foot-Dragging, and Fence-Sitting. Member State Responses to Europeanization." Queen's Papers on Europeanisation No. 4/2001, University of Belfast.

Boston, J. 1992. "The Problems of Policy Coordination: The New Zealand Experience." *Governance: An International Journal of Policy and Administration* 5, no. 1:88–103.

Bovens, M., and K. Yesilkagit. 2004. "The Impact of European Legislation on National Legislation: Some Preliminary Findings for the Netherlands." Paper presented at the EGPA 2004 Annual Conference "Four Months After Administering the New Europe," Ljubljana, Slovenia, September 1–4.

Brusis, M. 2004. "Europeanization, Party Government or Legacies? Explaining Executive Governance in Bulgaria, the Czech Republic and Hungary." *Comparative European Politics* no. 2:163–184.

———. 2006 "Hungary: A Core Supreme." In *Governing after Communism: Institutions and Policy,* edited by V. T. Dimitrov, K. H. Goetz, and H. Wollmann. Lanham, MD: Rowman and Littlefield.

Brusis, M., and V. T. Dimitrov. 2001. "Executive Configurations and Fiscal Performance in Post-Communist Central and Eastern Europe." *Journal of European Public Policy* 8, no. 6:888–910.

Buchanan, J. M., and G. Tullock. 1962. *The Calculus of Consent: Logical Foundations of Constitutional Democracy.* Ann Arbor: University of Michigan Press.

Bulmer, S., and M. Burch. 2001. "The Europeanization of Central Government: The UK and Germany in Historical Institutionalist Perspective." In *The Rules of Integration: Institutionalist Approaches to the Study of Europe,* edited by G. Schneider and M. Aspinwall. Manchester: Manchester University Press.

Campbell, C. 1988. "The Search for Coordination and Control: When and How Are Central Agencies the Answer?" In *Organizing Governance: Governing Organizations,* edited by C. Campbell and B. G. Peters. Pittsburgh, PA: University of Pittsburgh Press.

Caporaso, J. A., M. G. Cowles, et al., eds. 2001. *Transforming Europe: Europeanization and Domestic Change.* Ithaca, NY: Cornell University Press.

Cox, G. W., and M. D. McCubbins. 1993. *Legislative Leviathan. Party Government in the House.* Berkeley: University of California Press.

Craig, P., and G. De Burca. 1998. *EU Law: Text, Cases, and Materials.* Oxford: Oxford University Press.

Daintith, T., and A. Page. 1998. *The Executive in the Constitution: Structure, Autonomy, and Internal Control.* Oxford: Oxford University Press.

Dimitrakopoulos, D. 2001. "Learning and Steering: Changing Implementation Patterns and the Greek Central Government." *Journal of European Public Policy* 8, no. 4:604–622.

Dimitrov, V. T., K. H. Goetz, and H. Wollmann. 2006. *Governing after Communism: Institutions and Policy.* Lanham, MD: Rowman and Littlefield.

Dimitrov, V. T., and R. Zubek. 2006. "The Czech Republic: A Core Neglected." In *Governing after Communism: Institutions and Policy*, edited by V. T. Dimitrov, K. H. Goetz, and H. Wollmann. Lanham, MD: Rowman and Littlefield.

Dimitrova, A., ed. 2004. *Driven to Change: The European Union's Enlargement Viewed from the East.* Manchester: Manchester University Press.

Dimitrova, A., and K. Maniokas. 2004. "Linking Co-ordination of European Affairs and European Policy: New Member States in the Decision-Making Process of the EU." Paper presented at the 12th NISPACee conference on "Central and Eastern European Countries Inside and Outside the European Union: Avoiding a New Divide," Vilnius, Lithuania, May 13–15.

Döring, H., ed. 1995. *Parliaments and Majority Rule in Western Europe.* Mannheim, Germany: Mannheim Centre for European Social Research.

Döring, H., and M. Hallerberg, eds. 2004. *Patterns of Parliamentary Behaviour: Passage of Legislation across Western Europe.* Aldershot, UK: Ashgate.

Downs, A. 1957. *An Economic Theory of Democracy.* New York: Harper and Row.

Drabczyk, S. 1998. "Instrumenty Wspomagania w Sferze Prawnej Procesu Integracji Polski z Unią Europejską." *Zeszyty Naukowe, Kolegium Nauk Społecznych i Administracji PW,* no. 11:9–48.

Dunleavy, P. 1991. *Democracy, Bureaucracy and Public Choice.* Hemel Hampstead, UK: Harvester Wheatsheaf.

Dunleavy, P., and R. A. W. Rhodes. 1990. "Core Executive Studies in Britain." *Public Administration* 68:3–28.

Elgie, R. 1997. "Models of Executive Politics: A Framework for the Study of Executives Power Relations in Parliamentary and Semi-Presidential Regimes." *Political Studies* 45:217–231.

EuroPap. 2001. "Udało sie zrobić prawie wszystko - wywiad z Cezarym Banasińskim, byłym wiceministrem w UKIE." Warsaw.

Evans, G., and N. Manning. 2000. "A Practical Approach to Assessing Central Government Policy-Making Institutions in Cabinet Government: Learning Lessons from Recent World Bank Institutional Analyses." Unpublished manuscript, World Bank.

Fabbrini, S., and A. Dona. 2002. "Europeanization of the Governmental System as Strengthening of Domestic Executive Power: The Italian Experience and the Case of the 'Legge Communitaria.'" Paper presented at the ECPR Joint Session workshop on "Europeanization and National Political Institutions," University of Turin, April 22–27.

Falkner, G., M. Hartlapp, et al. 2004. "Non-Compliance with EU Directives in the Member States: Opposition through the Backdoor?" *West European Politics* 27, no. 3:452–473.

Falkner, G., M. Hartlapp, and O. Treib. 2007. "Worlds of Compliance: Why Leading Approaches to European Union Implementation Are Only 'Sometimes-True Theories.'" *European Journal of Political Research* 46:395–416.

Falkner, G., O. Treib, et al. 2005. *Complying with Europe? The Impact of EU Minimum Harmonisation and Soft Law in the Member States.* Cambridge: Cambridge University Press.

Featherstone, K., and C. M. Radaelli, eds. 2003. *The Politics of Europeanization.* Oxford: Oxford University Press.

Fink-Hafner, D., and D. Lajh. 2003. *Managing Europe From Home: The Europeanization of the Slovenian Core Executive.* Ljubljana, Slovenia: Faculty of Social Sciences.

Fiorina, M. P., and K. A. Shepsle. 1989. "Formal Theories of Leadership: Agents, Agenda-Setters and Entrepreneurs." In *Leadership and Politics: New Perspectives in Political Science,* edited by B. D. Jones. Kansas: University Press of Kansas.

Frohlich, N., and J. A. Oppenheimer. 1970. "I Get by with a Little Help from My Friends." *World Politics* 23, no. 1:104–120.

Frohlich, N., J. A. Oppenheimer, et al. 1971. *Political Leadership and Collective Goods.* Princeton, NJ: Princeton University Press.

Gazeta Wyborcza. 1999. "Początek nowego początku: koalicja szuka klucza do lepszego rządzenia." *Gazeta Wyborcza* (Warsaw), September 29.

Geddes, B. 1994. *Politician's Dilemma: Building State Capacity in Latin America.* Berkeley: University of California Press.

George, A. L., and A. Bennett. 2004. *Case Studies and Theory Development in the Social Sciences.* Cambridge: MIT Press.

Giuliani, M. 2003. "Europeanization in Comparative Perspective: Institutional Fit and National Adaptation." In *The Politics of Europeanization,* edited by K. Featherstone and C. M. Radaelli. Oxford: Oxford University Press.

Goetz, K. H. 2003. "Living with Europe: Power, Constraint, and Contestation." In *Germany, Europe, and the Politics of Constraint,* edited by K. H. F. Dyson and K. H. Goetz. Oxford: Oxford University Press.

Goetz, K. H., and S. Hix, eds. 2000. "Special Issue: Europeanized Politics? European Integration and National Political Systems." *West European Politics* 23, no. 4.

Goetz, K. H., and H. Wollmann. 2001. "Governmentalizing Central Executives in Post-Communist Europe: A Four-Country Comparison." *Journal of European Public Policy* 8, no. 6:864–887.

Goetz, K. H., and R. Zubek. 2007. "Government, Parliament and Lawmaking in Poland." *Journal of Legislative Studies* 13, no. 4.

Górka, M. 1997. "Realizacja Białej Księgi Komisji Europejskiej w porządku prawnym Rzeczypospolitej Polskiej jako element procesu dostosowania prawa polskiego do standardów Unii Europejskiej." In *Polska w Unii Europejskiej: Perspektywy, Warunki, Szanse i Zagrożenia,* edited by C. Mik. Torun, Poland: TNOiK.

Górniak, J., and J. Jerschina. 1995. "From Corporatism to . . . Corporatism: The Transformation of Interest Representation in Poland." In *Strategic Choice and Path-Dependency in Post-Socialism: Institutional Dynamics in the Transformation Process,* edited by J. Hausner, B. Jessop, and K. Nielsen. Cheltenham, UK: Edward Elgar.

Grabbe, H. 2001. "How does Europeanization Affect CEE Governance? Conditionality, Diffusion and Diversity." *Journal of European Public Policy* 8, no. 6:1013–1031.

———. 2002. "European Union Conditionality and the *Acquis Communautaire.*" *International Political Science Review* 23, no. 3:249–268.

———. 2003. "Europeanization Goes East: Power and Uncertainty in the EU Accession Process." In *The Politics of Europeanization,* edited by K. Featherstone and C. M. Radaelli. Oxford: Oxford University Press.

———. 2006. *The EU's Transformative Power: Europeanization Through Conditionality in Central and Eastern Europe.* Basingstoke, UK: Palgrave Macmillan.

Groblewski, K. 1998. "Urząd nie spełnionych nadziei." *Rzeczpospolita* (Warsaw), June 9.

Guyomarch, A. 1993. "The European Effect: Improving French Policy Co-ordination." *Staatswissenschaften und Staatspraxis* 3, no. 4:455–478.

Hall, P. 1983. "Policy Innovation and the Structures of the State: The Politics-Administration Nexus in France and Britain." *Annals AAPSS* 466:43–59.

Hallerberg, M. 2000. *The Importance of Domestic Political Institutions: Why and How Belgium and Italy Qualified for EMU.* Bonn: Centre for European Integration Studies.

———. 2004a. *Domestic Budgets in a United Europe: Fiscal Governance from the End of Bretton Woods to EMU.* Ithaca and London: Cornell University Press.

———. 2004b. "Electoral Law, Government and Law Production." In *Patterns of Parliamentary Behaviour: Passage of Legislation Across Western Europe*, edited by H. Döring and M. Hallerberg. Aldershot, UK: Ashgate.

Hardin, R. 1982. *Collective Action*. Washington: The Johns Hopkins University Press.

Hausner, J., M. Marody, et al., eds. 2000. *The Quality of Governance: Poland Closer to the European Union?* Warsaw: Friedrich Ebert Foundation.

Haverland, M. 2000. "National Adaptation to European Integration: The Importance of Institutional Veto Points." *Journal of Public Policy* 20, no. 1:83–103.

Hayward, J., and V. Wright. 2002. *Governing from the Centre: Core Executive Coordination in France*. Oxford: Oxford University Press.

Heinrich, H. G. 1999. *The Hierarchy of Legal Norms in CEE Constitutional Systems. Brussels*. Brussels: TAIEX.

Héritier, A., D. Kerwer, et al., eds. 2001. *Differential Europe: New Opportunities and Constraints for National Policy-Making*. Lanham, MD: Rowman and Littlefield.

Herrnfeld, H. H. 1996. *European by Law: Legal Reform and Approximation of Law in the Visegrad Countries*. Germany: Bertelsmann Foundation Publishers.

Hood, C. 1983. *Tools of Government*. London: Macmillan.

Hughes, J., G. Sasse, et al. 2004. "Conditionality and Compliance in the EU's Eastward Enlargement: Regional Policy and the Reform of Sub-National Government." *Journal of Common Market Studies* 42, no. 3:523–551.

Ibanez, A. J. G. 1999. *The Administrative Supervision and Enforcement of EC Law: Powers, Procedures and Limits*. Oxford-Portland, OR: Hart Publishing.

Jaskiernia, J. 1999. "Badania zgodności projektów ustaw z prawem Unii Europejskiej w sejmowym postępowaniu ustawodawczym." *Państwo i Prawo* 54, no. 7:19–33.

Kabele, J., and L. Linek. 2004. "Decision-Making of the Czech Cabinet, EU Accession and Legislative Planning between 1998 and 2004." Paper presented at the ECPR Joint Sessions, Workshop No. 10 on the Process of Decision-Making in Cabinets in Central-Eastern and Southern Europe, Uppsala, Sweden, April 13–18.

Kassim, H., G. Peters, et al., eds. 2000. *The National Co-ordination of EU Policy: the Domestic Level*. Oxford: Oxford University Press.

Knill, C. 2001. *The Europeanization of National Administrations: Patterns of Institutional Change and Persistence*. Cambridge: Cambridge University Press.

Kublik, A. 1999. "Początek rekonstrukcji rządu: odchudzanie Kancelarii." *Gazeta Wyborcza* (Warsaw), March 3.

Laffan, B. 1981. "Ireland and Denmark in the EU: Political and Administrative Aspects." *Administration* 29, no. 1:43–62.

———. 2003. "Managing Europe from Home: Impact of the EU on Executive Government: A Comparative Analysis." Occasional Paper 0.1-09.03, Dublin European Institute.

Lane, J.-E., and S. Ersson. 2000. *The New Institutional Politics: Performance and Outcomes.* London and New York: Routledge.

Lindquist, E. A. 1999. "Reconceiving the Centre: Leadership, Strategic Reform, and Coherence in Public Sector Reform." Paper presented at "Government of the Future: Getting from Here to There," an OECD/SIGMA symposium held in Paris, September 14–15.

Lippert, B. and G. Umbach. 2005. *The Pressure of Europeanisation: From Post-Communist State Administrations to Normal Players in the EU System.* Baden-Baden, Germany: Nomos Verlagsgesellschaft.

Lippert, B., G. Umbach, et al. 2001. "Europeanization of CEE Executives: EU Membership Negotiations as a Shaping Power." *Journal of European Public Policy* 8, no. 6.

Manning, N., N. Barma, et al. 1999. *Strategic Decisionmaking in Cabinet Government: Institutional Underpinnings and Obstacles.* Washington, D.C.: World Bank.

Mastenbroek, E. 2005. "EU Compliance: Still a 'Black Hole'?" *Journal of European Public Policy* 12, no. 6:1103–1120.

Mattli, W., and T. Plümper. 2004. "The Internal Value of External Options: How the EU Shapes the Scope of Regulatory Reforms in Transition Countries." *European Union Politics* 5, no. 3:307–330.

Meny, Y., P. Müller, et al., eds. 1996. *Adjusting to Europe: The Impact of the EU on National Institutions and Policy.* London: Routledge.

Metcalfe, L. 1994. "International Policy Co-ordination and Public Management Reform." *International Review of Administrative Sciences* 60, no. 2:271–2909.

Monge, P. R. 1995. "Theoretical and Analytical Issues in Studying Organizational Processes." In *Longitudinal Field Research Methods: Studying Processes of Organizational Change,* edited by G. P. Huber and A. H. Van den Ven. Thousand Oaks, CA: Sage.

Mueller, D. 2003. *Public Choice III.* Cambridge: Cambridge University Press.

Müller, W. C., W. Philipp, et al. 1993. "Prime Ministers and Cabinet Decision-Making Processes." In *Governing Together: The Extent and Limits of Joint Decision-Making in Western European Cabinets,* edited by J. Blondel and F. Müller-Rommel. New York: St. Martin's Press.

Müller, W. C., and K. Strøm, eds. 2000. *Coalition Governments in Western Europe.* Oxford: Oxford University Press.

Müller-Rommel, F. 1993. "Ministers and the Role of the Prime Ministerial Staff." In *Governing Together: The Extent and Limits of Joint Decision-Making in Western European Cabinets*, edited J. Blondel and F. Müller-Rommel. New York, St. Martin's Press.

Nakrosis, V. 2003. "Assessing Governmental Capabilities to Manage European Affairs: The Case of Lithuania." In *The Road to the European Union: Estonia, Latvia, Lithuania*, edited by V. Pettai and J. Zielonka. Vol. 2. Manchester and New York: Manchester University Press.

Németh, A. 2000. "Kis magyar jogharmonizációs tükör." *Európai tükör* 6: 16–26.

Nicolaides, P. 1999. *Enlargement of the EU and Effective Implementation of Community Rules: An Integration-Based Approach. Maastricht.* Maastricht: EIPA.

———. 2002. *From Graphite to Diamond: The Importance of Institutional Structure in Establishing Capacity for Effective and Credible Application of EU Rules.* Maastricht: EIPA.

NIK. 1996. *Informacja o wynikach kontroli systemu koordynowania i finansowania realizacji postanowień Układu Europejskiego.* Warsaw: Najwyższa Izba Kontroli.

North, D. C. 1990. *Institutions, Institutional Change and Economic Performance.* Cambridge: Cambridge University Press.

Nowak-Far, A. 2004. *Krajowa administracja w unijnym procesie podejmowania decyzji.* Warsaw: ISP.

Nowina-Konopka, P. 1996. Address in Parliament. 2nd Parliament, Session 75, Day 1 (March 13), Agenda Item 2 and 3. Warsaw.

Nunberg, B. 2000. *Ready for Europe: Public Administration Reform and European Union Accession in Central and Eastern Europe.* Washington: World Bank.

Olson, M. 1965. *The Logic of Collective Action. Public Goods and the Theory of Goods.* Cambridge, MA: Harvard University Press.

Olson, D. M., and P. Norton. 2007. "Post-Communist and Post-Soviet Legislatures: Beyond Transition." *Journal of Legislative Studies, Special Issue* 13, no. 1.

Ostrom, E. 1990. *Governing the Commons: The Evolution of Institutions for Collective Action.* Cambridge: Cambridge University Press.

———. 1998. "A Behavioural Approach to the Rational Choice Theory of Collective Action." *American Political Science Review* 92, no. 1:1–22.

———. 2003a. "How Types of Goods and Property Rights Jointly Affect Collective Action." *Journal of Theoretical Politics* 15, no. 3:239–270.

———. (2003b). "Understanding Institutional Diversity." Manuscript available at http://www.indiana.edu/~workshop/ui/.

Page, E. C. 1998. "The Impact of European Legislation on British Public Policy Making: A Research Note." *Public Administration* 76 (Winter): 803–809.

Paradowska, J. 1999a. "Korkociąg: nieznośna niemożność rządzenia." *Polityka* 41.

———. 1999b. "Styl to człowiek - rozmowa 'Polityki' z Jerzym Buzkiem, prezesem Rady Ministrów." *Polityka* 43.

Paradowska, J., and W. Wladyka. 2002. "Więcej Rządu w Rządzie - Wywiad z Leszkiem Millerem, premierem RP." *Polityka* 38.

Pavlik, P. 2002. "Europeanisation and Transformation of Public Administration: The Case of the Czech Republic." EIP Working Paper, EIP, Berlin.

Pedersen, K., and R. Zubek. 2004. "Executive Capacity in Poland: Key Findings from a Survey of Former Cabinet Ministers." DEMSTAR Research Report No. 17, Department of Political Science, Aarhus University, Denmark.

Peters, B. G., and A. Barker, eds. 1993. *Advising West European Governments: Inquiries, Expertise and Public Policy.* Edinburgh: Edinburgh University Press.

Peters, B. G., R. A. W. Rhodes, et al., eds. 2000. *Administering the Summit: Administration of the Core Executive in Developed Countries.* Basingstoke, UK: Macmillan.

Plümper, T., and C. W. Martin. 2003. "Democracy, Government Spending, and Economic Growth: A Political-Economic Explanation of the Barro Effect." *Public Choice* 117:27–50.

Pol, M. 1996a. Address in Parliament. The Sejm Extraordinary Committee for the COG Reform, Session No. 5, April 17.

———. 1996b. Address in Parliament. The Sejm Extraordinary Committee for the COG Reform, Session No. 3, March 28.

———. 1996c. Address in Parliament. The Sejm Extraordinary Committee for the COG Reform, Session No. 3, March 28.

Pszczółkowska, D. 2001. "Upomnienie, nie dymisja: sąd nad Saryuszem-Wolskim." *Gazeta Wyborcza* (Warsaw), May 25.

Rada Legislacyjna. 1994. "Stanowisko Rady Legislacyjnej w sprawie dostosowania prawa polskiego do systemu prawa Unii Europejskiej." *Biuletyn Rady Legislacyjnej*, no. 1:87–97.

Rada Ministrów. 2000. *Raport w sprawie korzyści i kosztów integracji RP z Unią Europejską.* Warsaw: KPRM.

Ramsey, L. E. 1996. "The Copy Out Technique: More of a 'Cop Out' than a Solution?" *Statute Law Review* 17, no. 3:218–228.

Rhodes, R. A. W. 1995. *From Prime Ministerial Power to Core Executive.* In *Prime Minister, Cabinet and Core Executive*, edited by R. A. W. Rhodes and P. Dunleavy. New York: St. Martin's Press.

————, ed. 2000. *Transforming British Government: Vol. 1 and Vol. 2.* Basingstoke, UK: Macmillan.

Rhodes, R. A. W., and P. Dunleavy, eds. 1995. *Prime Minister, Cabinet and Core Executive.* New York: St. Martin's Press.

Runge, C. F. 1984. "Institutions and the Free Rider: The Assurance Problem in Collective Action." *The Journal of Politics* 46, no. 1:154–181.

Rupp, M. A. 1999. The Pre-Accession Strategy and the Governmental Structure of the Visegrad Countries. In *Back to Europe: Central and Eastern Europe and the European Union,* edited by K. Henderson. London: UCL Press.

Rydlewski, G. 2000. *Rządzenie Koalicyjne w Polsce.* Warsaw: Elipsa.

————. 2002. *Rządowy system decyzyjny w Polsce: studium politologiczne okresu transformacji.* Warsaw: Elipsa.

Rzeczpospolita. 1998. "Zapowiedź zmian w KIE." July 21, Warsaw.

Samuels, A. 1998. "Incorporating, Translating or Implementing European Union Law into UK Law." *Statute Law Review* 19, no. 2:80–92.

Sarjusz-Wolski, M. 1999. "To nieszczeście, kiedy sprawy pilne nie zostawiają miejsca dla ważnych." *Unia & Polska* (Warsaw), no. 17 (July).

Savoie, D. J. 1999. *Governing from the Centre: The Concentration of Power in Canadian Politics.* Toronto; Buffalo, New York; London: University of Toronto Press.

Scarpetta, S., and T. Tressel. 2002. "Productivity and Convergence in a Panel of OECD Industries: Do Regulations and Institutions Matter?" Economics Department Working Paper No. 342, OECD, Paris.

Scharpf, F. 2000. "Institutions in Comparative Policy Research." Working Paper No. 3/00, Max-Planck Institute for the Study of Societies, Germany.

Scharpf, F. W. 1997. *Games Real Actors Play: Actor-Centred Institutionalism in Policy Research.* Boulder, CO: Westview.

Schiemann, J. W. 2004. "Hungary: The Emergence of Chancellor Democracy." *The Journal of Legislative Studies* 10, no. 2/3:128–141.

Schimmelfennig, F., S. Engert, et al. 2003. "Costs, Commitment and Compliance: The Impact of EU Democratic Conditionality on Latvia, Slovakia and Turkey." *Journal of Common Market Studies,* 41, no. 3:495–518.

Schimmelfennig, F., and U. Sedelmeier. 2004 "Governance by Conditionality: EU Rule Transfer to the Candidate Countries of Central and Eastern Europe." *Journal of European Public Policy* 11, no. 4:661–679.

————, eds. 2005. *Europeanization of Central and Eastern Europe.* Ithaca and London: Cornell University Press.

Scootla, G., and E. Scootla. 2004. "National Coordination of EU Policy-Making: The Impact of Institutional Context vs. Smallness." Paper presented at the EGPA 2004 Annual Conference "Four Months After: Administering the New Europe," Ljubljana, Slovenia, September 1–4.

Scott, W. R. 2001. *Institutions and Organizations.* Thousand Oaks, CA: Sage.

Sedelmeier, U. 2007. "After Conditionality: Post-Accession Compliance in the New EU Member States from East Central Europe." Paper prepared for the workshop "Beyond Conditionality: International Institutions in Postcommunist Europe after Enlargement," London School of Economics and Political Science, UK, May 31–June 2.

Shepsle, K. A., and B. R. Weingast. 1994. "Positive Theories of Congressional Institutions." *Legislative Studies Quarterly* 19, no. 2:149–179.

Siedentopf, H., and J. Ziller, eds. 1988. *Making European Policies Work: The Implementation of Community Legislation in the Member States.* London: Sage.

Šmejkal, V. 1998 "European Policy-Making in the Czech Republic—Institutional and Political Framework." In *Towards EU Membership: Transformation and Integration in Poland and the Czech Republic,* edited by B. Lippert and P. Becker. Bonn: Europa Union Verlag.

Sołtysiński, S. 1996. "Dostosowanie prawa polskiego do wymagań Układu Europejskiego." *Państwo i Prawo* 51, no. 4–5:31–43.

Staniszkis, J. 1999. *Post-Communism: The Emerging Enigma.* Warsaw: Instytut Studiów Politycznych PAN.

———. 2000. "The Post-Communist State: In Search of a Paradigm." *Polish Sociological Review,* no. 2:193–214.

Stark, D., and L. Bruszt. 1998. *Postsocialist Pathways: Transforming Politics and Property in East-Central Europe.* Cambridge: Cambridge University Press.

Steunenberg, B. 2007. "A Policy Solution to the European Union's Transposition Puzzle: Interaction of Interests in Different Domestic Arenas." *West European Politics* 30, no. 1:23–49.

Steunenberg, B., and A. Dimitrova. 2007. "Compliance in the EU Enlargement Process: The Limits of Conditionality." European Integration Online Papers, Vol. 11.

Subotić, M. 1998. "Kłótnia ministrów: Nowina-Konopka i Czarnecki." *Rzeczpospolita* (Warsaw), July 8.

———. 1999a. "Jest ale go nie ma: UKIE 4 miesiące nie ma szefa." *Rzeczpospolita* (Warsaw), April 16.

———. 1999b. "UKIE: od czterech miesięcy nie ma szefa." *Rzeczpospolita* (Warsaw), April 21.

———. 2000. "Specjalne ustawy europejskie." *Rzeczpospolita* (Warsaw), June 17.

Sverdrup, U. 2004. "Compliance and Conflict Management in the European Union: Nordic Exceptionalism." *Scandinavian Political Studies* 27, no. 1:23–43.

Thiebault, J.-L. 1993. "The Organizational Structure of Western European Cabinets and its Impact on Decision Making." In *Governing Together: The Extent and Limits of Joint Decision-Making in Western European Cabinets*, edited by J. Blondel and F. Müller-Rommel. New York: St. Martin's Press.

Thies, M. F. 2001. "Keeping Tabs on Partners: The Logic of Delegation in Coalition Governments." *American Journal of Political Science* 45, no. 3:580–598.

Tsebelis, G. 1995. "Decision Making in Political Systems: Veto Players in Presidentialism, Parliamentalism, Multicameralism and Multipartyism." *British Journal of Political Science* 25:289–325.

———. 2002. *Veto Players: How Political Institutions Work*. Princeton, NJ: University Press/Russell Sage Foundation.

Vachudova, M. 2005 *Europe Undivided: Democracy, Leverage and Integration After Communism*. Oxford: Oxford University Press.

Vida, K. 2002. "The Management of Accession to the European Union: EU-Related Decision and Policy-Making in Hungary." In *The Management of Accession to the European Union in Poland and Hungary*, edited by D. Pyszna and K. Vida. Budapest: Institute for World Economics.

Von Hagen, J. 2003. "Budgeting Institutions and Public Spending." In *Ensuring Accountability When There Is No Bottom Line, Vol. 1 of Handbook of Public Sector Performance Reviews*, edited by A. Shah. Washington, D.C.: World Bank.

Von Hagen, J., and I. J. Harden. 1994. "National Budgets and Fiscal Performance." *European Economy. Reports and Studies* 3:311–418.

Weingast, B. R. 1998. "Political Institutions: Rational Choice Perspectives." In *A New Handbook of Political Science*, edited by R. E. Goodin and H.-D. Klingemann. Oxford: Oxford University Press.

Weller, P. 1985. *First Among Equals: Prime Ministers in Westminster Systems*. Sydney: Allen & Unwin.

———. 1991. "Support for Prime Ministers: A Comparative Perspective." In *Executive Leadership in Anglo-American Systems*, edited by C. Campbell and M. J. Wyszomirski. Pittsburgh, PA: University of Pittsburgh Press.

Weller, P., H. Bakvis, et al., eds. 1997. *The Hollow Crown: Countervailing Trends in Core Executive*. London: Macmillan.

Wielowieyska, D. 1999. "Osiatyński nie chce być zastępcą: rozmowa z Jerzym Osiatyńskim." *Gazeta Wyborcza* (Warsaw), April 21.

————. 2000. "Powódź ustaw: długa kolejka projektów do rozpatrzenia." *Gazeta Wyborcza* (Warsaw), January 21.

Wojciechowski, J. A. 1996. "Dostosowanie prawa polskiego do prawa europejskiego - proces bez końca." *Przegląd prawa europejskiego,* no. 1:7–10.

————. 1998. "Stan przygotowania Polski do implementacji prawa wspólnotowego." In *Implementacja dyrektyw wspólnotowych w państwach członkowskich Unii Europejskiej,* edited by M. Gorka. Łódź, Poland: Instytut Europejski.

Wright, V. 1996. "The National Co-ordination of European Policy Making: Negotiating the Quagmire." In *European Union: Power and Policy-Making,* edited by J. Richardson, pp. 148–169. London: Routledge.

Zubek, R. 2001. "A Core in Check: The Transformation of the Polish Core Executive." *Journal of European Public Policy* 8, no. 6:1–22.

————. 2005. "Complying with Transposition Commitments in Poland: Collective Dilemmas, Core Executive and Legislative Outcomes." *West European Politics* 28, no. 3:592–619.

————. 2006. "Poland: A Core Ascendant?" In *Governing after Communism: Institutions and Policy,* edited by V. T. Dimitrov, K. H. Goetz, and H. Wollmann. Lanham, MD: Rowman and Littlefield.

————. 2007. "Legislative Time, Executive Rules and Government Lawmaking." Paper prepared for ECPR Joint Sessions Helsinki 2007 Workshop 12, "Political Power in Parliamentary Executives," May 7–12.

Index